ENGLISH
FOR EVERYONE

ENGLISH GRAMMAR GUIDE

Consultant, British English

Diane Hall has been working in English language teaching for over 30 years, as a teacher, trainer, editor, publisher, and writer. She has published several books, both general courses and grammar books, for major English-language publishers. She has an MA in Applied Linguistics, and is currently also an Associate Lecturer in English grammar and functional linguistics at the Open University.

Consultant, American English

Professor Susan Barduhn is an experienced English-language teacher, teacher trainer, and author, who has contributed to numerous publications. In addition to directing English-language courses in at least four different continents, she has been President of the International Association of Teachers of English as a Foreign Language, and an adviser to the British Council and the US State Department. She is currently a Professor at the School for International Training in Vermont, USA.

ENGLISH
FOR EVERYONE

ENGLISH GRAMMAR GUIDE

US Editors Jenny Siklos, Allison Singer
Project Editor Ben Ffrancon Davies
Art Editors Dominic Clifford, Paul Drislane,
Sunita Gahir, Clare Shedden
Editorial Assistants Sarah Edwards, Helen Leech
Illustrators Edwood Burn, Michael Parkin
Jacket Designers Suhita Dharamjit, Ira Sharma
Jacket Editor Claire Gell
Jacket Design Development Manager
Sophia MTT
Producer, Pre-Production Andy Hilliard
Producer Mary Slater
Managing Editor Daniel Mills
Managing Art Editor Anna Hall
Publisher Andrew Macintyre
Art Director Karen Self
Publishing Director Jonathan Metcalf

DK India
Senior Managing Art Editor Arunesh Talapatra
Senior Art Editor Chhaya Sajwan
Art Editor Meenal Goel
Assistant Art Editor Rohit Dev Bhardwaj

First American Edition, 2016
Published in the United States by DK Publishing
345 Hudson Street, New York, New York 10014

Copyright © 2016 Dorling Kindersley Limited
DK, a Division of Penguin Random House LLC
17 18 19 20 10 9 8 7 6 5 4 3
013–289769–Dec/2016

A catalog record for this book
is available from the Library of Congress.
ISBN 978-1-4654-5269-6

DK books are available at special discounts when purchased
in bulk for sales promotions, premiums, fund-raising, or educational
use. For details, contact: DK Publishing Special Markets, 345 Hudson
Street, New York, New York 10014
SpecialSales@dk.com

Printed and bound in China

All images © Dorling Kindersley Limited
For further information see: www.dkimages.com

A WORLD OF IDEAS:
SEE ALL THERE IS TO KNOW

www.dk.com

Contents

01 The present simple

The present simple is used to make simple statements of fact, to talk about things that happen repeatedly, and to describe things that are always true.

See also:
Present continuous **4**   Present for future events **19**   Adverbs of frequency **102**

1.1 THE PRESENT SIMPLE

To make the present simple of most verbs, use the base form (the infinitive without "to").

I eat lunch at noon every day.

The base form of the verb "to eat."

Adverbs of frequency are often used with the present simple.

She eats lunch at 2pm every day.

With "he," "she," and "it," add "-s" to the base form.

FURTHER EXAMPLES

We drink coffee every morning.

We start work at 9am.

They leave work at 5pm.

She drinks coffee every morning.

He starts work at 11am.

Rob leaves work at 7pm.

HOW TO FORM

The base form of the verb.

SUBJECT	VERB	REST OF SENTENCE
I / You / We / They	eat	lunch at 2pm every day.
He / She / It	eats	

With "he," "she," and "it," "-s" is added.

1.2 "-S" AND "-ES" ENDINGS

With some verbs, "-es" is added for "he," "she," and "it."
These include verbs ending with "-sh," "-ch," "-o," "-ss," "-x," and "-z."

I go to bed.

He goes to bed.

"-es" is added to verbs ending with "-o."

I finish work.

He finishes work.

"-es" is added to verbs ending with "-sh."

I watch TV.

She watches TV.

"-es" is added to verbs ending with "-ch."

I cross the road.

She crosses the road.

"-es" is added to verbs ending with "-ss."

I fix cars.

She fixes cars.

"-es" is added to verbs ending with "-x."

Their phones buzz all day.

His phone buzzes all day.

"-es" is added to verbs ending with "-z."

FURTHER EXAMPLES

Tom does the dishes every evening.

She teaches English to six students.

He washes the windows on Fridays.

He blushes when he's embarrassed.

⚠ COMMON MISTAKES FORMING THE PRESENT SIMPLE

When the present simple is used with "he," "she," "it," or one person's name, it always ends in "-s" or "-es."

An "s" is added to the base form "start."

He starts work at 11am. ✔

He start work at 11am. ✘

"Start" without an "s" is only used for "I," "you," "we," and "they."

There is no need to add the auxiliary verb "do" when forming the present simple. It is only used to form questions and negatives.

I eat lunch at noon every day. ✔

I do eat lunch at noon every day. ✘

"Do" is only used as an auxiliary verb when forming negatives or questions.

"BE" IN THE PRESENT SIMPLE

"Be" is an important verb with an irregular present simple form.

I am 25 years old.

You are a chef.

"Are" also follows "we" and "they."

He is happy.

"Is" also follows "she" and "it."

HOW TO FORM

SUBJECT	"BE"	REST OF SENTENCE
I	am	
You	are	
He / She / It	is	happy.
We / They	are	

FURTHER EXAMPLES

I am **a doctor.**

They are **students.**

My grandma is **92 years old.**

Contractions can also be used.

We're **late for work.**

He's **American.**

Ruby's **seven years old.**

1.4 "HAVE" IN THE PRESENT SIMPLE

"Have" is an irregular verb. The third person singular form is "has" not "haves."

I have a garage.

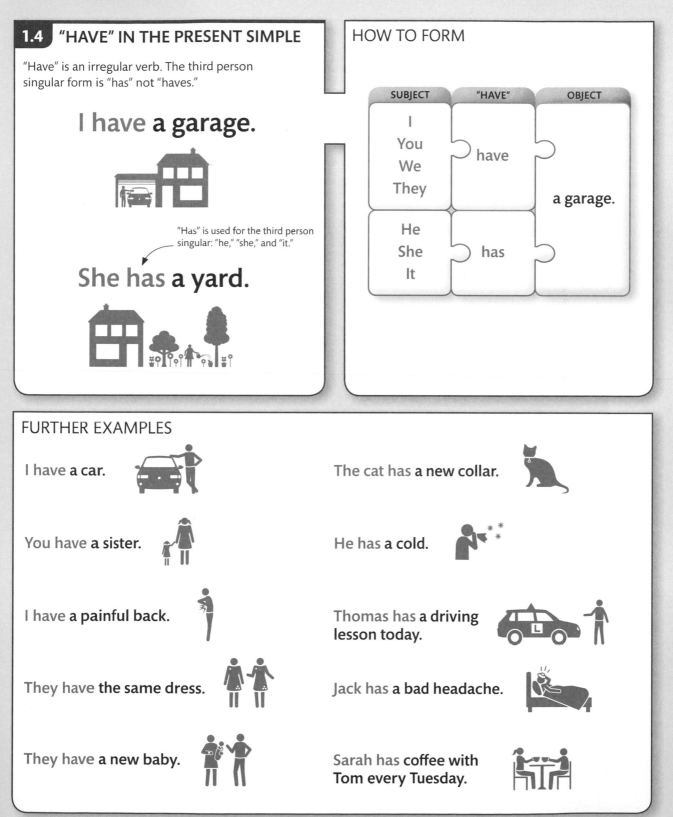

"Has" is used for the third person singular: "he," "she," and "it."

She has a yard.

HOW TO FORM

SUBJECT	"HAVE"	OBJECT
I You We They	have	a garage.
He She It	has	

FURTHER EXAMPLES

I have a car.

You have a sister.

I have a painful back.

They have the same dress.

They have a new baby.

The cat has a new collar.

He has a cold.

Thomas has a driving lesson today.

Jack has a bad headache.

Sarah has coffee with Tom every Tuesday.

02 The present simple negative

To make negative sentences using "be" in the present simple, "not" is added after the verb. For other verbs, the auxiliary verb "do not" or "does not" is used.

See also:
Present simple **1**   Present overview **5**
Types of verbs **49**

2.1 NEGATIVES WITH THE VERB "BE"

The verb "be" takes the same form in positive and negative sentences. The only difference is adding "not."

I am a farmer. I am not a doctor.

HOW TO FORM

SUBJECT + "BE"	"NOT"	REST OF SENTENCE
I am		a doctor.
She is	not	
We are		doctors.

2.2 NEGATIVE CONTRACTIONS

"Is not" and "are not" can be contracted in two ways. The subject and verb can be contracted, or the verb and "not." They mean the same thing.

You are not a doctor.

"You are" becomes "you're."

You're not
You aren't } **a doctor.**

"Are not" becomes "aren't."

FURTHER EXAMPLES

I'm not a teacher.

"I amn't" is incorrect.

He's not
He isn't } **a farmer.**

They're not
They aren't } **American.**

2.3 NEGATIVES WITH OTHER VERBS IN THE PRESENT SIMPLE

For verbs other than "be," "do not" or "does not" goes before the verb to make the negative.

I work outside.

⬇

I do not work outside.

He works inside.

⬇

He does not work inside.

Verb in base form.

HOW TO FORM

SUBJECT	"DO / DOES" + "NOT"	BASE FORM	REST OF SENTENCE
I / You / We / They	do not	work	outside.
He / She / It	does not		

The base form is used no matter what the subject is.

FURTHER EXAMPLES

You do not have a computer.

He does not live in Los Angeles.

We don't start work at 8am.

He doesn't have a car.

This is the contracted form of "does not."

⚠ COMMON MISTAKES FORMING NEGATIVE SENTENCES

The main verb in a negative sentence always stays in its base form, even if the subject is "he," she," or "it."

He does not work outside. ✔

He does not works outside. ✖

13

03 Present simple questions

Questions in the present simple with "be" are formed by swapping the verb and subject. For other verbs, the auxiliary verb "do" or "does" must be added before the subject.

See also:
Present simple **1** Forming questions **34**
Question words **35** Open questions **36**

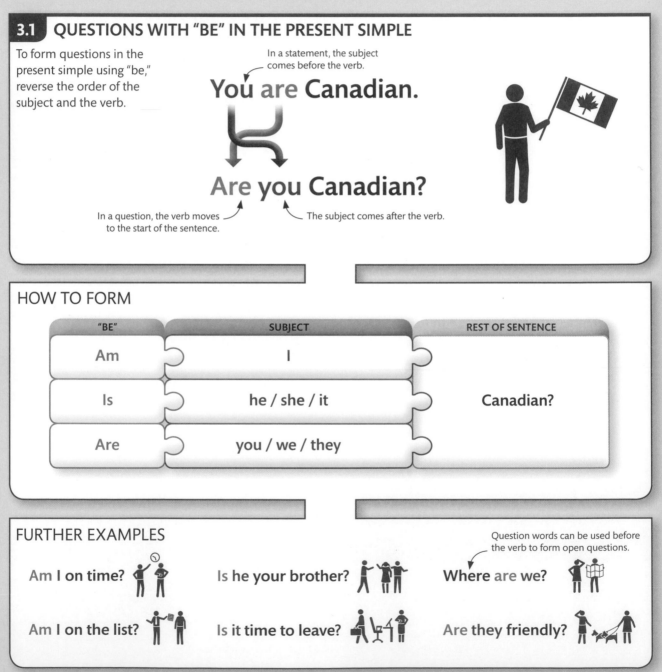

3.1 QUESTIONS WITH "BE" IN THE PRESENT SIMPLE

To form questions in the present simple using "be," reverse the order of the subject and the verb.

In a statement, the subject comes before the verb.

You are Canadian.

Are you Canadian?

In a question, the verb moves to the start of the sentence.

The subject comes after the verb.

HOW TO FORM

"BE"	SUBJECT	REST OF SENTENCE
Am	I	
Is	he / she / it	Canadian?
Are	you / we / they	

FURTHER EXAMPLES

Question words can be used before the verb to form open questions.

Am I on time?

Is he your brother?

Where are we?

Am I on the list?

Is it time to leave?

Are they friendly?

14

3.2 QUESTIONS WITH "DO" AND "DOES"

For questions with verbs other than "be," start the question with "do" or "does." Don't swap the subject and the main verb.

You work in an office.

↓

Do you work in an office?

Add "do" to questions with "I," "you," "we," and "they."

She works in a school.

↓

Does she work in a school?

Add "does" to questions with "he," "she," and "it."

The main verb goes in its base form.

HOW TO FORM

"DO / DOES"	SUBJECT	BASE FORM OF VERB	REST OF SENTENCE
Do	I / you / we / they	work	in an office?
Does	he / she / it		

The verb never takes an "-s" or "-es" when you ask a question.

FURTHER EXAMPLES

Do they live in Paris?

Do you usually finish work at 4pm?

Does Tom get up at 6am?

When does the party start?

Question words can be used before "do" or "does" to form open questions.

⚠ COMMON MISTAKES FORMING PRESENT SIMPLE QUESTIONS

Never add "-s" or "-es" to the base form of the verb when asking a question, even in the third person singular ("he," "she," or "it").

Does he finish work on time? ✓

The main verb always goes in its base form in questions.

Does he finishes work on time? ✗

Do not add "-s" or "-es" to the main verb when asking a question.

04 The present continuous

The present continuous is used to talk about continued actions that are happening in the present moment. It is formed with "be" and a present participle.

See also:
Present simple **1**   Action and state verbs **50**
Infinitives and participles **51**

4.1 THE PRESENT CONTINUOUS

The present continuous is used to describe a current, continued action.

This is the present simple. It describes a repeated action or situation.

Julie usually wears jeans, but today she is wearing a dress.

The present continuous uses the verb "be."

This is the present continuous. It describes what is happening right now.

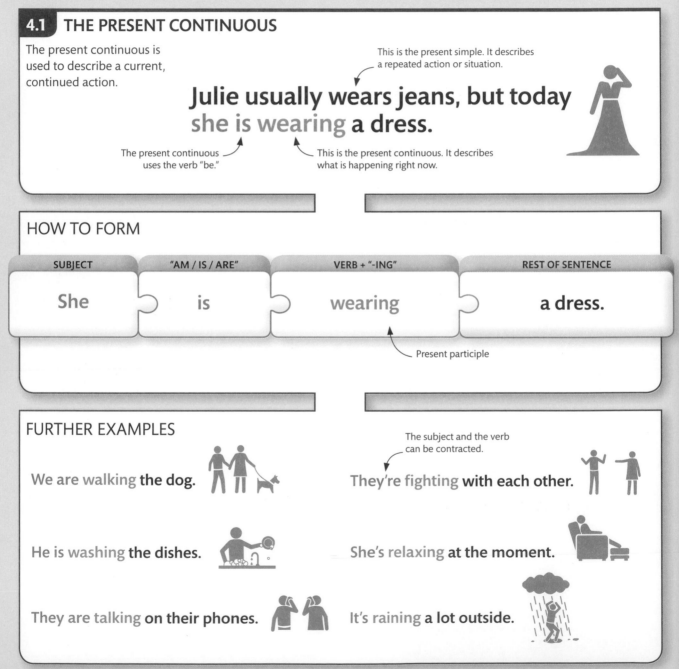

HOW TO FORM

SUBJECT	"AM / IS / ARE"	VERB + "-ING"	REST OF SENTENCE
She	is	wearing	a dress.

Present participle

FURTHER EXAMPLES

We are walking **the dog.**

He is washing **the dishes.**

They are talking **on their phones.**

The subject and the verb can be contracted.

They're fighting **with each other.**

She's relaxing **at the moment.**

It's raining **a lot outside.**

4.2 PRESENT PARTICIPLE SPELLING RULES

The present participle is formed by adding "-ing" to the base form
of the verb. Some participles have slightly different spelling rules.

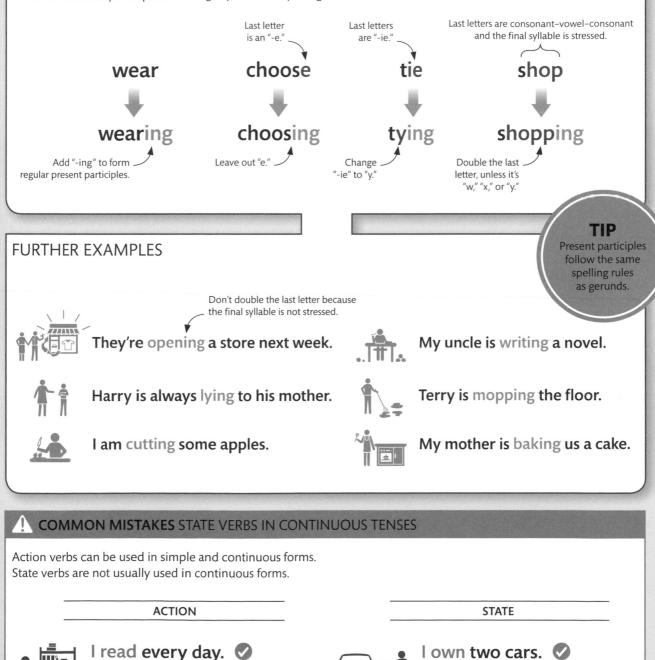

Last letter
is an "-e."

Last letters
are "-ie."

Last letters are consonant–vowel–consonant
and the final syllable is stressed.

wear   **choose**   **tie**   **shop**

wearing   **choos**ing   **ty**ing   **shopp**ing

Add "-ing" to form
regular present participles.

Leave out "e."

Change
"-ie" to "y."

Double the last
letter, unless it's
"w," "x," or "y."

FURTHER EXAMPLES

Don't double the last letter because
the final syllable is not stressed.

They're opening a store next week.

My uncle is writing a novel.

Harry is always lying to his mother.

Terry is mopping the floor.

I am cutting some apples.

My mother is baking us a cake.

TIP
Present participles
follow the same
spelling rules
as gerunds.

⚠ COMMON MISTAKES STATE VERBS IN CONTINUOUS TENSES

Action verbs can be used in simple and continuous forms.
State verbs are not usually used in continuous forms.

ACTION	STATE
I read every day. ✓	I own two cars. ✓
I am reading right now. ✓	I am owning two cars. ✗

4.3 QUESTIONS IN THE PRESENT CONTINUOUS

To ask questions in the present continuous, swap the subject and the form of "be."

"He" is the subject.

He is playing tennis.

Is he playing tennis?

In a question, the verb moves to the start of the sentence.

This action is happening right now.

HOW TO FORM

"AM / IS / ARE"	SUBJECT	VERB + "-ING"	REST OF SENTENCE
Is	he	playing	tennis?

FURTHER EXAMPLES

Are they going **to the park?**

Question words such as "what," "where," and "how" can be used before the verb to form open questions.

Where are we going **today?**

Is he cycling **to work?**

Are you coming **to the party?**

Is she eating **pizza?**

What are you eating **for dinner?**

Are they working **late?**

Is it raining **outside?**

4.4 THE PRESENT CONTINUOUS NEGATIVE

To make the negative of the present continuous, add "not" after "be."

He is wearing **a tie, but** he $\left\{\begin{array}{c} \text{is not} \\ \text{isn't} \end{array}\right\}$ wearing **a hat.**

Add "not" after "be" to make the negative. Contractions are also possible.

The present participle stays the same when you make the negative.

HOW TO FORM

SUBJECT	"AM / IS / ARE" + "NOT"	VERB + "-ING"	REST OF SENTENCE
He	is not	wearing	a hat.

The present participle doesn't change.

FURTHER EXAMPLES

He **isn't** walking **the dog.**

We **aren't** taking **the bus today.**

They **aren't** singing **well today.**

You **aren't** doing **your job!**

She **isn't** cleaning **up her bedroom.**

James **isn't** reading **his book.**

They **aren't** looking **where they're going.**

We **aren't** eating **out this week.**

He **isn't** playing **football today.**

You **aren't** doing **well at school this year.**

05 Present tenses overview

5.1 THE PRESENT SIMPLE AND THE PRESENT CONTINUOUS

The present simple is used to talk about permanent situations, regular occurrences, things that are always true, repeated actions, and ongoing states.

This is always true.

The sun rises in the East.

The present continuous is used to refer to temporary situations, repeated actions around the present moment, and ongoing actions in the present moment.

This is a temporary situation.

It is raining in San Francisco right now.

5.2 PRESENT TENSE QUESTIONS

Present simple questions with "be" are formed differently from other verbs.

Are **you** **English?**

The form of "be" comes before the subject.

Do **you** **speak** **English?**

"Do" or "does" is added before the subject.

Present continuous questions are always formed in the same way.

Is **it** **raining?**

The form of "be" comes before the subject.

⚠ COMMON MISTAKES USING "S" IN THE PRESENT SIMPLE

"-s" is never added to the base form of the verb when asking a **question** or making a **negative** sentence, even in the third person singular ("he," "she," or "it").

AFFIRMATIVE

An "-s" is added to the base form in affirmative sentences.

He starts work at 7am. ✓

He start work at 7am. ✗

The base form without an "-s" is only used for "I," "you," "we," and "they."

The present simple and present continuous are used in different situations. There are different ways to form questions and negatives with these tenses.

See also:
Present simple **1**   Present continuous **4**
Forming questions **34**   Infinitives and participles **51**

This is a repeated action.

Giorgio plays golf every weekend.

Robert lives in London.

This is a continuing state.

This is a repeated action happening around the present moment.

Julia is playing lots of golf these days.

At the moment, Robert is watching TV.

This is an ongoing action in the present moment.

5.3 PRESENT TENSE NEGATIVES

Present simple negatives with "be" are formed differently from other verbs.

I am not French.

"Not" is added after the form of "be."

I do not speak French.

"Do not" or "does not" is added between the subject and main verb.

Present continuous negatives are always formed in the same way.

It is not raining.

"Not" is added after the form of "be."

QUESTION

The verb always goes in its base form in questions.

Does he finish work on time? ✓

Does he finishes work on time? ✗

"-s" or "-es" are not added to the main verb when asking a question.

NEGATIVE

The base form is used in the negative.

He does not work weekends. ✓

He does not works weekends. ✗

"-s" or "-es" are not added to the main verb in negative sentences.

06 Imperatives

Imperatives are used to give commands or to make requests. They can also be used to give warnings or directions.

See also:
Types of verbs **49**   Suggestions and advice **59**
Indefinite pronouns **79**

6.1   IMPERATIVES

Imperatives are formed using the base form of the verb (the infinitive without "to").

An exclamation mark is used if the imperative is urgent.

Stop!

The base form of the verb "to stop."

FURTHER EXAMPLES

Get up.

Be careful!

Give that to me.

Eat your breakfast.

Help!

Read this book.

6.2   NEGATIVE IMPERATIVES

"Do not" or "don't" can be added before the verb to make an imperative negative.

Do not
Don't } turn right.

FURTHER EXAMPLES

Don't eat that cake.

I've just painted that door.
Don't touch it.

Don't rush. I'm not in a hurry.

Don't sit there. That chair is broken.

6.3 SUBJECTS WITH IMPERATIVES

An imperative sentence does not usually have a subject, but sometimes a noun or a pronoun is used to make it clear who is being talked to.

Everybody sit down.

FURTHER EXAMPLES

Phillip, **come here.**

You **stay there.**

For emphasis "you" can be used in an imperative clause.

Someone **open the window.**

Have fun, Anne.

The subject can also be placed at the end.

6.4 POLITE REQUESTS

Imperatives in English can be considered rude. Words can be added to make them more polite.

Please **close the door.**

"Please" can be placed before the imperative verb to make a request more polite.

Just **give me a minute,** please.

"Just" can go before the imperative.

"Please" can also be placed at the end of the sentence.

Do **come in.**

"Do" can go before the imperative verb to make a request more formal.

6.5 MAKING SUGGESTIONS WITH "LET'S"

"Let's" can be used to make a suggestion for an activity that includes the speaker.

It's sunny today. Let's go out.

Base form.

It's cold. Let's not go out.

"Not" goes after "let's" to form the negative.

23

07 The past simple

The past simple is used to talk about completed actions that happened at a fixed time in the past. It is the most commonly used past tense in English.

See also:
Past simple negative **8**   Past simple questions **9**
Present perfect simple **11**

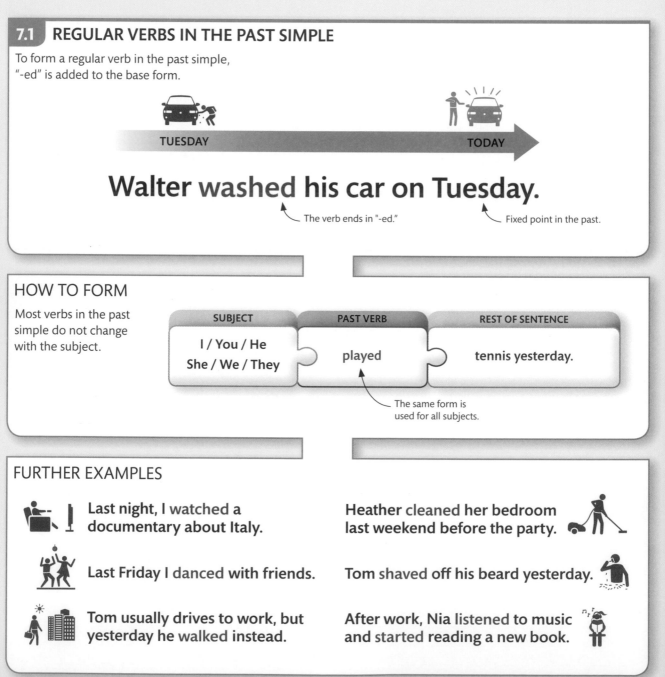

7.1 REGULAR VERBS IN THE PAST SIMPLE

To form a regular verb in the past simple,
"-ed" is added to the base form.

TUESDAY

TODAY

Walter washed his car on Tuesday.

The verb ends in "-ed."

Fixed point in the past.

HOW TO FORM

Most verbs in the past simple do not change with the subject.

SUBJECT	PAST VERB	REST OF SENTENCE
I / You / He She / We / They	played	tennis yesterday.

The same form is used for all subjects.

FURTHER EXAMPLES

Last night, I watched a documentary about Italy.

Heather cleaned her bedroom last weekend before the party.

Last Friday I danced with friends.

Tom shaved off his beard yesterday.

Tom usually drives to work, but yesterday he walked instead.

After work, Nia listened to music and started reading a new book.

SPELLING RULES FOR THE PAST SIMPLE

The past simple of all regular verbs ends in "-ed," but for
some verbs, there are some spelling changes, too.

wash

→

washed

For many regular
verbs, "-ed"
is added.

Last letter is "-e."

dance

→

danced

Just a "-d"
is added.

Last letters are a
consonant and a "-y."

try

→

tried

The "-y" is removed
and "-ied" is
added instead.

A stressed final syllable ending
consonant-vowel-consonant.

stop

→

stopped

The last consonant
is doubled and
"-ed" is added.

FURTHER EXAMPLES

jump
↓
jumped

arrive
↓
arrived

carry
↓
carried

drop
↓
dropped

work
↓
worked

save
↓
saved

cry
↓
cried

hop
↓
hopped

play
↓
played

decide
↓
decided

hurry
↓
hurried

step
↓
stepped

7.3 IRREGULAR VERBS IN THE PAST SIMPLE

Some verbs do not take "-ed" to form the past simple. There are no specific rules about how to form irregular verbs in the past simple.

"Went" is the past simple of "go."

I went swimming yesterday.

YESTERDAY   TODAY

COMMON IRREGULAR VERBS IN THE PAST SIMPLE

go	have	do	put	come	see
↓	↓	↓	↓	↓	↓
went	had	did	put	came	saw

FURTHER EXAMPLES

I swam in the 500m race.

Sam ate two pizzas.

I came to the US in 1980.

We went to the zoo last week.

We saw some rare birds.

They drank all the lemonade.

I did really well in school.

They had a great vacation.

Steve put his cup on the table.

Sheila drove to the park.

7.4 "BE" IN THE PAST SIMPLE

The past simple of "be" is completely irregular. It is the only verb in the past simple which changes depending on the subject.

The traffic was bad, so we were late for school.

PAST

NOW

HOW TO FORM

The past simple of "be" changes with the subject.

SUBJECT	"BE"	REST OF SENTENCE
I	was	
You	were	late for school.
He / She	was	
We / They	were	

FURTHER EXAMPLES

He was a doctor for 40 years.

We were at the library yesterday.

She was a Broadway star in the 1960s.

There were lots of people at the party.

There was a party last night.

They were at the movies last week.

08 The past simple negative

The past simple negative is used to talk about things that did not happen in the past. It is always formed the same way, unless the main verb is "be."

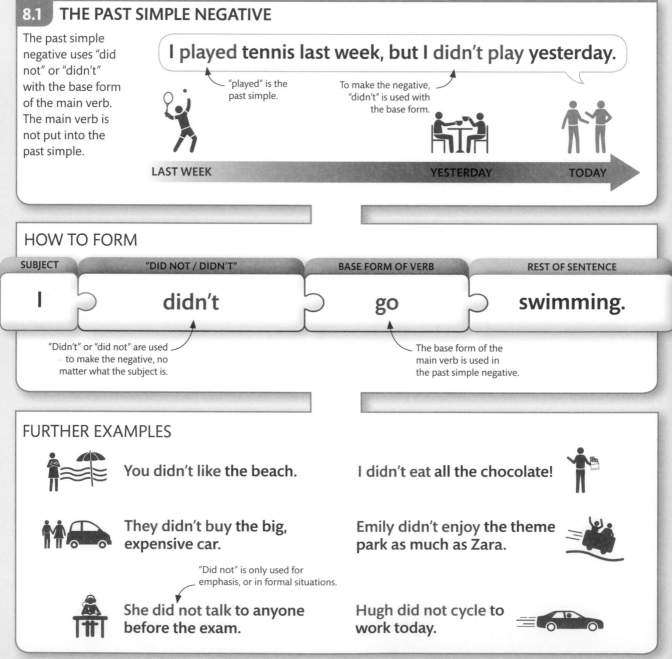

See also:
Past simple **7**   Present simple negative **2**
Types of verbs **49**

8.1 THE PAST SIMPLE NEGATIVE

The past simple negative uses "did not" or "didn't" with the base form of the main verb. The main verb is not put into the past simple.

I played **tennis last week, but I** didn't play **yesterday.**

"played" is the past simple.

To make the negative, "didn't" is used with the base form.

LAST WEEK   YESTERDAY   TODAY

HOW TO FORM

SUBJECT	"DID NOT / DIDN'T"	BASE FORM OF VERB	REST OF SENTENCE
I	**didn't**	**go**	**swimming.**

"Didn't" or "did not" are used to make the negative, no matter what the subject is.

The base form of the main verb is used in the past simple negative.

FURTHER EXAMPLES

You didn't like **the beach.**

I didn't eat **all the chocolate!**

They didn't buy **the big, expensive car.**

Emily didn't enjoy **the theme park as much as Zara.**

"Did not" is only used for emphasis, or in formal situations.

She did not talk **to anyone before the exam.**

Hugh did not cycle to **work today.**

28

⚠ COMMON MISTAKES BASE FORMS IN THE PAST SIMPLE NEGATIVE

When using the negative form of the past simple, "didn't" plus the main verb in the base form is used. The main verb is never in the past simple.

"Play" should be in the base form.

I didn't **play tennis last night.** ✓

The main verb should only go into the past simple if it's a positive statement.

I didn't **played tennis last night.** ✗

8.2 THE PAST SIMPLE NEGATIVE OF "BE"

To form the past simple negative of "be," "not" is added after "was" or "were."

The book was interesting, but the movie was not.

The books were great, but the movies were not.

HOW TO FORM

SUBJECT	"WAS / WERE"	"NOT"	REST OF SENTENCE
The movie	was	not	interesting.
The movies	were	not	interesting.

FURTHER EXAMPLES

Kate was **not feeling well.**

My parents were **not pleased.**

The cat wasn't **in the house.**

"Was not" is often shortened to "wasn't."

The computers weren't **working.**

"Were not" is often shortened to "weren't."

29

09 Past simple questions

Questions in the past simple are formed using "did." For past simple questions with "be," the subject and the verb "was" or "were" are swapped around.

See also:
Past simple **7**   Forming questions **34**
Types of verbs **49**

9.1 QUESTIONS IN THE PAST SIMPLE

Use "did" plus the base form of the verb to ask a question in the past simple.

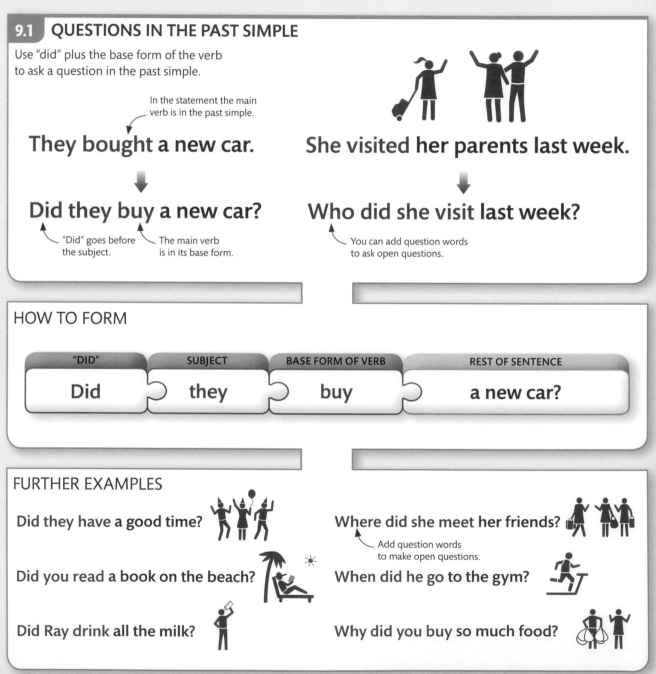

In the statement the main verb is in the past simple.

They bought a new car.

Did they buy a new car?

"Did" goes before the subject.   The main verb is in its base form.

She visited her parents last week.

Who did she visit last week?

You can add question words to ask open questions.

HOW TO FORM

"DID"	SUBJECT	BASE FORM OF VERB	REST OF SENTENCE
Did	**they**	**buy**	**a new car?**

FURTHER EXAMPLES

Did they have a good time?

Did you read a book on the beach?

Did Ray drink all the milk?

Where did she meet her friends?

Add question words to make open questions.

When did he go to the gym?

Why did you buy so much food?

9.2 QUESTIONS IN THE PAST SIMPLE WITH "BE"

To make a question using the verb "be" in the past simple, swap the order of the subject and "was" or "were."

In a statement, the subject comes before the verb.

She **was** excited.

Was she excited?

In a question, the verb and the subject swap places.

You **were** excited.

Were you excited?

The subject comes after the verb.

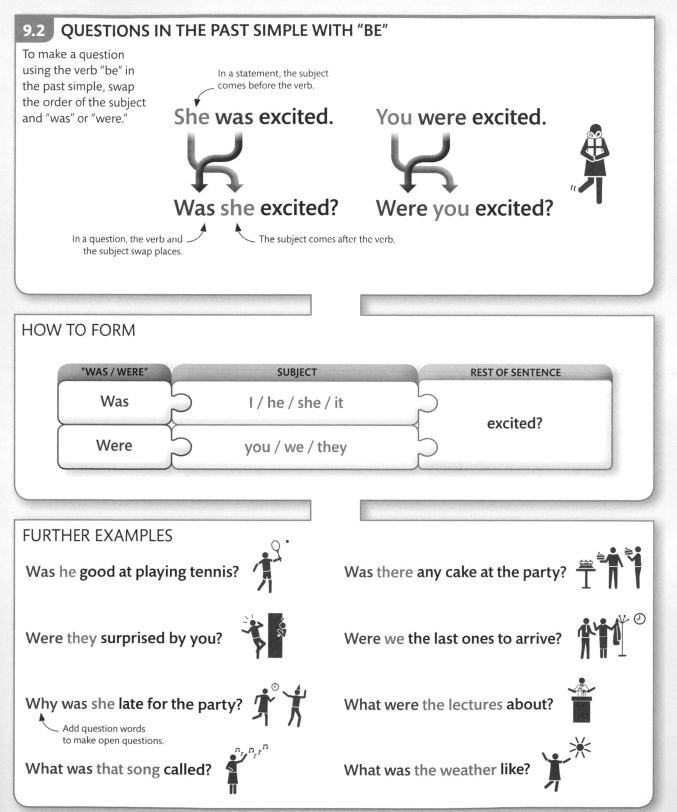

HOW TO FORM

"WAS / WERE"	SUBJECT	REST OF SENTENCE
Was	I / he / she / it	excited?
Were	you / we / they	

FURTHER EXAMPLES

Was he **good at playing tennis?**

Were they **surprised by you?**

Why was she **late for the party?**

Add question words to make open questions.

What was that song **called?**

Was there **any cake at the party?**

Were we **the last ones to arrive?**

What were the lectures **about?**

What was the weather **like?**

10 The past continuous

The past continuous is used in English to talk about actions or events that were in progress at some time in the past. It is formed with "was" or "were" and a present participle.

See also:
Past simple **7**
Infinitives and participles **51**

10.1 THE PAST CONTINUOUS

English uses the past continuous to talk about ongoing actions that were in progress at a certain time in the past.

The past continuous shows the action went on for some time, but is now finished.

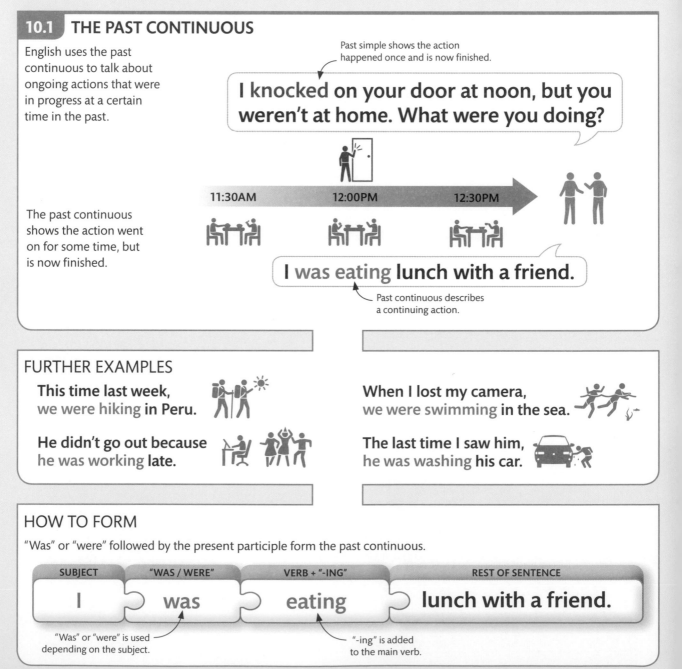

Past simple shows the action happened once and is now finished.

I knocked on your door at noon, but you weren't at home. What were you doing?

11:30AM 12:00PM 12:30PM

I was eating lunch with a friend.

Past continuous describes a continuing action.

FURTHER EXAMPLES

This time last week, we were hiking in Peru.

He didn't go out because he was working late.

When I lost my camera, we were swimming in the sea.

The last time I saw him, he was washing his car.

HOW TO FORM

"Was" or "were" followed by the present participle form the past continuous.

SUBJECT	"WAS / WERE"	VERB + "-ING"	REST OF SENTENCE
I	was	eating	lunch with a friend.

"Was" or "were" is used depending on the subject.

"-ing" is added to the main verb.

10.2 THE PAST CONTINUOUS FOR SCENE-SETTING

The past continuous is often used in storytelling
to set a scene or describe a situation.

It was a beautiful day.
The sun was shining and the birds were singing.
Children were laughing and playing in the street.

10.3 THE PAST CONTINUOUS AND THE PAST SIMPLE

When English uses the past continuous and past simple together, the
past continuous describes a longer, background action, and the past
simple describes a shorter action that interrupts the background action.

CONTINUING BACKGROUND ACTION   INTERRUPTING MAIN ACTION

I was taking a photo when a monkey grabbed my camera.

FURTHER EXAMPLES

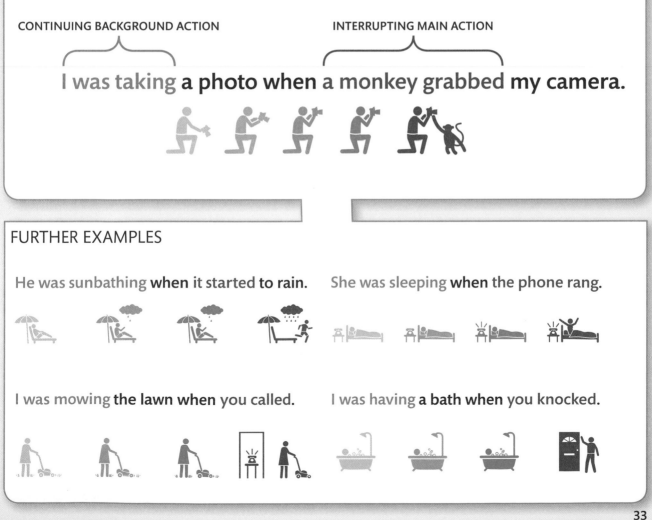

He was sunbathing when it started to rain.   She was sleeping when the phone rang.

I was mowing the lawn when you called.   I was having a bath when you knocked.

11 The present perfect simple

The present perfect simple is used to talk about events in the recent past that still have an effect on the present moment. It is formed with "have" and a past participle.

See also:
Past simple **7**   Present perfect continuous **12**
Infinitives and participles **51**

11.1 PRESENT PERFECT

The present perfect can be used to talk about the past in a number of different ways:

To give new information or news.

Hi! I have arrived in London! My plane landed five minutes ago.

To talk about a repeated action that continues to happen over a period of time.

I have visited California every summer since I was 18.

To talk about an event that started in the past and is still happening now.

Olivia has gone on a trip to Egypt.

FURTHER EXAMPLES THE PRESENT PERFECT

Look! I've cooked dinner for us.

You haven't cleared the table. It's a mess!

John has just washed the dishes.

Have you cleaned up your bedroom?

HOW TO FORM

SUBJECT	"HAVE / HAS"	PAST PARTICIPLE	REST OF SENTENCE
I	have	arrived	in London.

"Has" is used for "he," "she," and "it."

11.2 REGULAR PAST PARTICIPLES

Regular past participles are formed
by adding "-ed" to the base form.

ask ➡ asked

call ➡ called

help ➡ helped

need ➡ needed

play ➡ played

talk ➡ talked

walk ➡ walked

want ➡ wanted

watch ➡ watched

work ➡ worked

11.3 IRREGULAR PAST PARTICIPLES

English has a lot of irregular past participles, which
sometimes look very different from the base form.

be ➡ been

buy ➡ bought

come ➡ come

do ➡ done

have ➡ had

give ➡ given

go ➡ gone

make ➡ made

say ➡ said

see ➡ seen

⚠ COMMON MISTAKES PAST SIMPLE FORMS AND PAST PARTICIPLES

It is important not
to mix up past
simple forms with
past participles.

This is the past participle of "see."

I have seen lots of great things here. ✔

I have saw lots of great things here. ✘

This is the past simple form of "see,"
and shouldn't be used in perfect tenses.

11.4 "GONE / BEEN"

"Be" and "go" are both used in the present perfect to talk about going somewhere, but they have different meanings.

I haven't seen Joan recently. Where is she?

She's gone to Florida.

She is still in Florida.

Hi, Joan. You're looking well.

Yes, I've been to Florida.

She went to Florida, but now she is back home.

FURTHER EXAMPLES

Where's Ben?

He's gone to the mall.

You look relaxed.

Yes, we've been in Bermuda. We had a great time.

Where's Ariana?

She's gone windsurfing.

Your hair looks great!

Thanks! I've just been to the hair salon.

Where are Julie and Jack?

They've gone to see a play.

Where have you been?

We've been to visit Joan in the hospital. She's not very well.

11.5 THE PRESENT PERFECT SIMPLE AND THE PAST SIMPLE

The past simple is used to talk about something that happened at a definite time. The present perfect is used when a particular time is not specified.

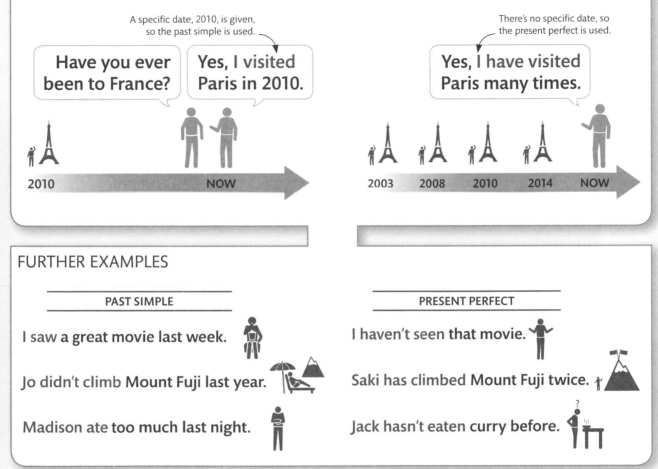

A specific date, 2010, is given, so the past simple is used.

Have you ever been to France?

Yes, I visited Paris in 2010.

2010 NOW

There's no specific date, so the present perfect is used.

Yes, I have visited Paris many times.

2003 2008 2010 2014 NOW

FURTHER EXAMPLES

_____ PAST SIMPLE _____

I saw a great movie last week.

Jo didn't climb Mount Fuji last year.

Madison ate too much last night.

_____ PRESENT PERFECT _____

I haven't seen that movie.

Saki has climbed Mount Fuji twice.

Jack hasn't eaten curry before.

11.6 THE PRESENT PERFECT IN US ENGLISH

US English often uses the past simple when UK English would use the present perfect.

No dessert for me! I ate too much. (US)
No dessert for me! I've eaten too much. (UK)

I can't find my passport. Did you see it? (US)
I can't find my passport. Have you seen it? (UK)

12 The present perfect continuous

The present perfect continuous is used to talk about a continuing activity in the past that still has an effect on the present moment. It usually refers to the recent past.

See also:
Past simple **7**   Present perfect simple **11**
Infinitives and participles **51**

12.1   THE PRESENT PERFECT CONTINUOUS

The present perfect continuous describes an activity that took place over a period of time in the recent past. The activity might just have stopped or might still be happening.

PRESENT PERFECT CONTINUOUS

The past activity often affects the present moment.

I have been painting the house all day. I'm exhausted!

FURTHER EXAMPLES

"I have" can be shortened to "I've."

I've been cooking this evening. Now I have to do the dishes.

"He has" can be shortened to "He's."

He's been waiting for the bus for an hour. He is going to be late for work.

HOW TO FORM

SUBJECT	"HAS / HAVE"	"BEEN"	VERB + "-ING"	OBJECT
I	have	been	painting	the house.

Use "have" or "has," depending on the subject.

"Been" stays the same for all subjects.

"-ing" is added to the main verb.

The present perfect continuous is used to show that an activity in the past was in progress. It is possible that the activity is still taking place.

PRESENT PERFECT CONTINUOUS

I've been fixing my car. I'm covered in oil.

The present perfect simple is used to show that an activity in the past is finished.

PRESENT PERFECT SIMPLE

I've fixed my car. Now I can drive to work again.

FURTHER EXAMPLES

I've been cooking dinner. It will be ready soon.

I've cooked dinner. It's ready now.

Vicky has been running today. Now she's really tired!

Vicky has just run a race. Now she's receiving a medal.

I've been eating too much cake. I must eat less!

I've eaten all the cake. The plate is empty.

We've been looking at houses. We want to move.

We've bought a new house. We're moving in June.

13 The past perfect simple

English uses the past perfect simple with the past simple
to talk about two or more events that happened
at different times in the past.

See also:
Past simple **7**   Present perfect simple **11**
Past perfect continuous **14**   Participles **51**

13.1 THE PAST PERFECT SIMPLE

When talking about two events that happened at different times in the
past, the past simple describes the event that is closest to the time of
speaking. The past perfect describes an event further back in the past.

PAST PERFECT SIMPLE   PAST SIMPLE

The train had left before we arrived at the station.

8:10PM   8:20PM   NOW

Pablo had gone to work when I knocked on his door.

7:00AM   7:30AM   NOW

HOW TO FORM

Use "had" followed by the past participle to form the past perfect.

SUBJECT	"HAD"	PAST PARTICIPLE	REST OF SENTENCE
The train	had	left	before we arrived at the station.

"Had" does not change
with the subject.

The past participle expresses
the action in the past.

FURTHER EXAMPLES

He **had cooked dinner before**
Sally **got back from work.**

She **had already read the play**
by the time she **went to see it.**

Even if the past simple action is first in
the sentence, it still happened later.

The traffic **was bad because**
a car **had broken down on the road.**

When we **arrived at the stadium,**
the game **had already started.**

13.2 THE PRESENT PERFECT AND PAST PERFECT

PRESENT PERFECT SIMPLE

The present perfect is used to talk about
an action that took place in the recent past
and is still relevant to the present moment.

I'm so excited.
I have just passed
my driving test.

ONE HOUR AGO   NOW

PAST PERFECT SIMPLE

The past perfect is used to talk
about an action that took place
before another moment in the past.

I was so excited.
I had just passed
my driving test.

ONE HOUR BEFORE   PAST   NOW

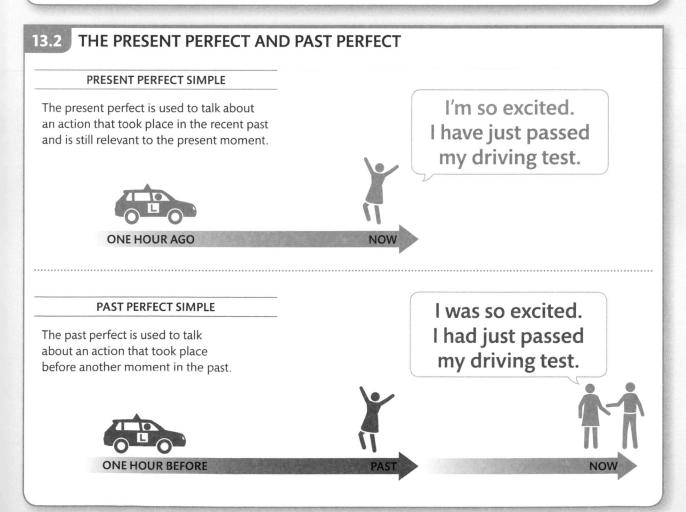

14 The past perfect continuous

English uses the past perfect continuous with the past simple to talk about an activity that was in progress before another action or event happened.

See also:
Past simple **7**   Present perfect continuous **12**
Infinitives and participles **51**

14.1 THE PAST PERFECT CONTINUOUS

The past simple refers to a specific completed event in the past. The past perfect continuous describes a repeated action or continuing activity that was taking place before that completed event.

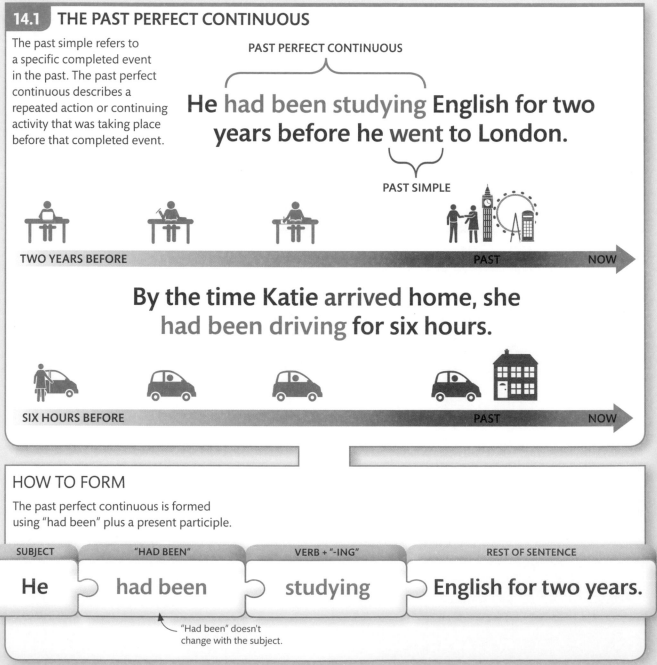

PAST PERFECT CONTINUOUS

He had been studying English for two years before he went to London.

PAST SIMPLE

TWO YEARS BEFORE   PAST   NOW

By the time Katie arrived home, she had been driving for six hours.

SIX HOURS BEFORE   PAST   NOW

HOW TO FORM

The past perfect continuous is formed using "had been" plus a present participle.

SUBJECT	"HAD BEEN"	VERB + "-ING"	REST OF SENTENCE
He	**had been**	**studying**	**English for two years.**

"Had been" doesn't change with the subject.

FURTHER EXAMPLES

She decided to buy a new car because her old one hadn't been working for weeks.

I went to see the doctor after I'd been feeling unwell for a few days.

The band had been rehearsing every day, so they won the competition.

I had been training to be a dancer until I broke my leg.

14.2 THE PRESENT PERFECT CONTINUOUS AND PAST PERFECT CONTINUOUS

PRESENT PERFECT CONTINUOUS

The present perfect continuous is used to talk about an action in progress or repeated activity that was taking place until the present moment.

I'm really thirsty. I have been cycling for two hours.

TWO HOURS AGO   NOW

PAST PERFECT CONTINUOUS

The past perfect continuous is used to talk about an ongoing action or repeated activity that was taking place until another specified moment in the past.

I was really thirsty. I had been cycling for two hours.

TWO HOURS BEFORE   PAST   NOW

43

15 "Used to" and "would"

When talking about habits or states in the past, "used to" or "would" are often used. English often uses these forms to contrast the past with the present.

See also:
Present simple **1**   Past simple **7**
Past continuous **10**   Adverbs of frequency **102**

15.1 "USED TO"

"Used to" can be used with the base form of a verb to talk about past habits.

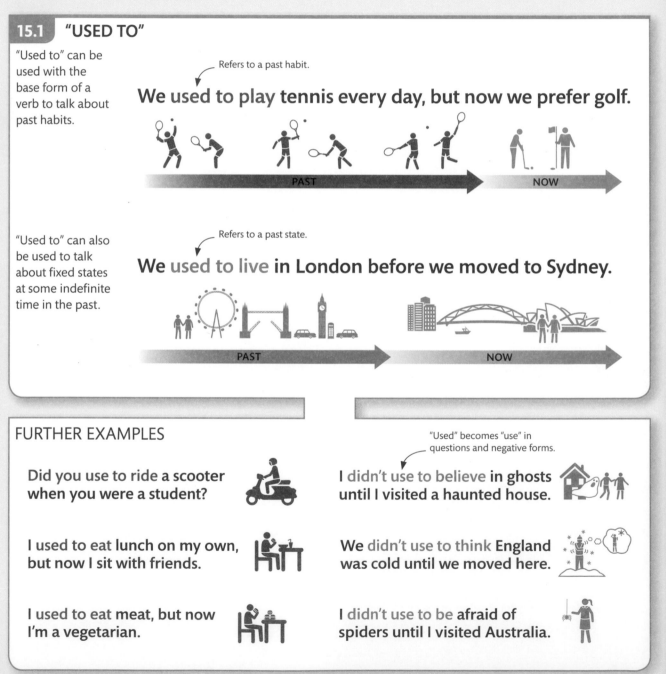

Refers to a past habit.

We used to play tennis every day, but now we prefer golf.

PAST   NOW

"Used to" can also be used to talk about fixed states at some indefinite time in the past.

Refers to a past state.

We used to live in London before we moved to Sydney.

PAST   NOW

FURTHER EXAMPLES

"Used" becomes "use" in questions and negative forms.

Did you use to ride a scooter when you were a student?

I didn't use to believe in ghosts until I visited a haunted house.

I used to eat lunch on my own, but now I sit with friends.

We didn't use to think England was cold until we moved here.

I used to eat meat, but now I'm a vegetarian.

I didn't use to be afraid of spiders until I visited Australia.

When talking about habits in the past, "used to" should be used. It is incorrect to use the past continuous in this context.

We used to play lots of board games when we were younger. ✓

We were playing lots of board games when we were younger. ✗

The past continuous shouldn't be used to talk about past habits.

15.2 ANOTHER WAY TO SAY "USED TO" WITH HABITS

"Used to" can be replaced by "would" in writing and formal speech, but only to talk about past habits. These statements often include a reference to time to describe when, or how often something happened.

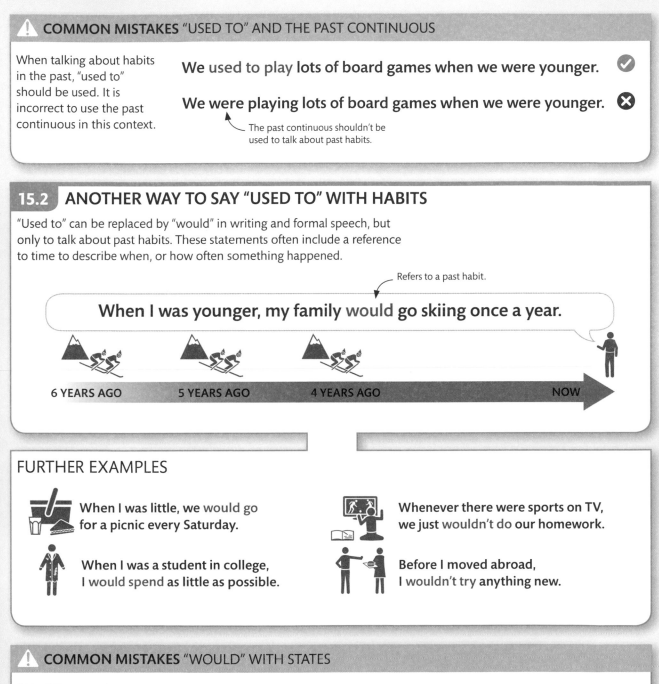

Refers to a past habit.

When I was younger, my family would go skiing once a year.

6 YEARS AGO   5 YEARS AGO   4 YEARS AGO   NOW

FURTHER EXAMPLES

When I was little, we would go for a picnic every Saturday.

When I was a student in college, I would spend as little as possible.

Whenever there were sports on TV, we just wouldn't do our homework.

Before I moved abroad, I wouldn't try anything new.

⚠ **COMMON MISTAKES** "WOULD" WITH STATES

"Would" cannot be used to talk about states in the past. "Used to" must be used instead.

We used to live in London before we moved to Sydney. ✓

We would live in London before we moved to Sydney. ✗

"Would" cannot be used in this way with state verbs.

16 Past tenses overview

16.1 PAST TENSES

The past simple refers to a single, completed action in the past.

Phil washed his car on Tuesday.

This is a completed action in the past that is now over.

The past continuous refers to a continuing action in the past.

The last time I saw Phil, he was washing his car.

At that moment, he was in the process of washing his car.

The present perfect simple refers to an unfinished action or series of actions that started in the past, or past actions that still have a consequence in the present moment.

Eve has arrived in London.

Eve is still in London, so it is still relevant to the present moment.

The present perfect continuous refers to a continuing activity in the past that still has a consequence in the present moment.

I have been painting the house all day. I'm exhausted!

This is a consequence in the present moment.

16.2 PAST SIMPLE AND PRESENT PERFECT SIMPLE

The past simple is used to refer to single, completed actions or events in the past. These no longer have a consequence in the present moment.

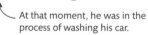

The essay is finished, so the past simple is used.

I wrote my essay about Ancient Greece.

This is no longer relevant to the present moment, because the keys were found.

I lost my keys, but I found them on my desk.

The present perfect simple is used to refer to actions or events in the past that are unfinished, or still have consequences in the present moment.

The essay is unfinished, so the present perfect simple is used.

I have written half of my essay, but I need to finish it.

The keys are still lost in the present moment, so the present perfect simple is used.

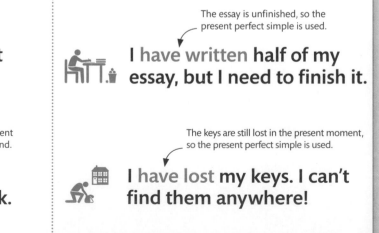

I have lost my keys. I can't find them anywhere!

There are eight different ways to talk about the past in English. The differences between the past simple and the present perfect simple are particularly important.

See also:
Past simple **7** Present perfect simple **11**
Infinitives and participles **51**

The **past perfect simple** refers to an action or event that took place before another action or event in the past.

The game had started when I arrived at the stadium.

The **past perfect continuous** refers to a continuing action or event that was taking place before another action or event that happened in the past.

I had been feeling unwell for days, so I went to the doctor.

"**Used to**" and "**Would**" are used to talk about repeated actions in the past that no longer happen.

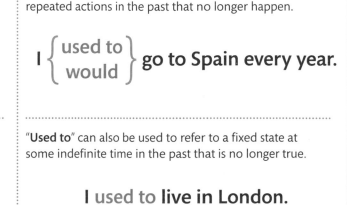

The **past perfect continuous** refers to a continuing action or event that was taking place before another action or event that happened in the past.

"**Used to**" can also be used to refer to a fixed state at some indefinite time in the past that is no longer true.

I used to live in London.

"Live" is a state, so "would" can't be used.

16.3 KEY LANGUAGE NARRATIVE TENSES

Narrative tenses are types of past tense that are used when telling a story.
The past continuous is used to set the scene. **The past simple** describes actions in the story.
The past perfect is used to talk about things that happened before the beginning of the story.

A crowd of people were celebrating the New Year when one of the young men kneeled down in front of his girlfriend and asked her to marry him. He had planned everything beforehand.

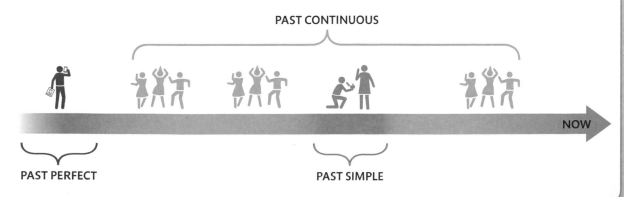

PAST CONTINUOUS

NOW

PAST PERFECT

PAST SIMPLE

17 The future with "going to"

Future forms in English are formed using auxiliary verbs. One of the most commonly used constructions is "going to" plus the base form of the main verb.

See also:
The future with "will" **18**
Future continuous **20**   Future in the past **22**

17.1   HOW TO FORM THE FUTURE WITH "GOING TO"

SUBJECT	"BE"	"GOING TO"	BASE FORM OF VERB	REST OF SENTENCE
He	is	going to	buy	a new car.

17.2   "GOING TO" FOR FUTURE PLANS

"Going to" is used to talk about future events that have been planned in advance, rather than decided upon at the time of speaking.

Base form of verb.

I'm going to **buy a new car.**

We are going to **cook dinner tonight.**

"Be" matches the subject of the sentence.

"Going to" doesn't change with the subject.

FURTHER EXAMPLES

I'm going to **start reading this book soon.**

Sam's going to **get fit before his next birthday.**

"Not" is added after the verb "be" to make the negative.

I'm not going to **eat any chocolate this month.**

We're going to **cycle from Boston to Cape Cod next weekend.**

17.3 "GOING TO" FOR PREDICTIONS

"Going to" is also used to make predictions when there is evidence in the present moment.

"Going to" gives the prediction.

Look at those clouds. It's going to rain soon.

Evidence in the present moment means that you can make a prediction.

FURTHER EXAMPLES

Oh no! She's going to slip and fall over.

Look! The waiter is going to drop those plates.

That hill is too steep. Jon is going to crash!

He's wearing a raincoat, so he's not going to get wet.

They're going to break a window if they're not careful.

Oh dear, I think she's going to fall off that ladder!

17.4 QUESTIONS WITH "GOING TO"

Questions with "going to" are formed by swapping the subject and "be."

Michelle is going to be at the meeting.

Is Michelle going to be at the meeting?

FURTHER EXAMPLES

Is Rhian going to come to work tomorrow?

Question words can be added to the start of the question.

What are you going to wear to the party?

Is Tim going to be at the party?

When is he going to get here?

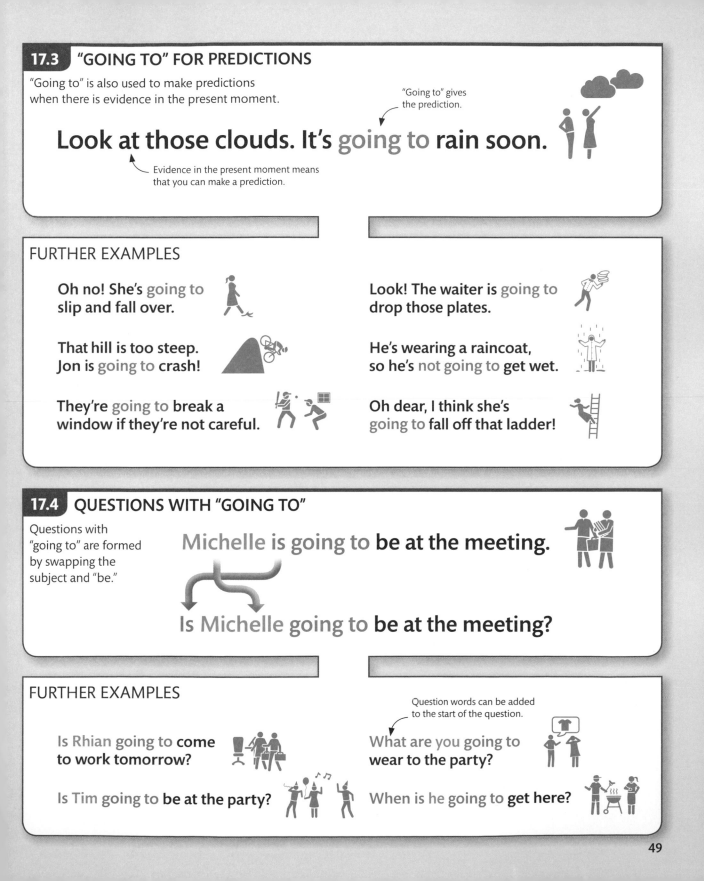

18 The future with "will"

"Will" is used to form some future tenses in English. It can be used in several different ways, which are all different from the future with "going to."

See also:
The future with "going to" **17**
Infinitive and participles **51**

18.1 HOW TO FORM THE FUTURE WITH "WILL"

SUBJECT	"WILL"	BASE FORM OF VERB	REST OF SENTENCE
She	will	love	the new movie.

"Will" doesn't change with the subject.

18.2 THE FUTURE USING "WILL"

English uses "will" when talking about the future in four main ways:

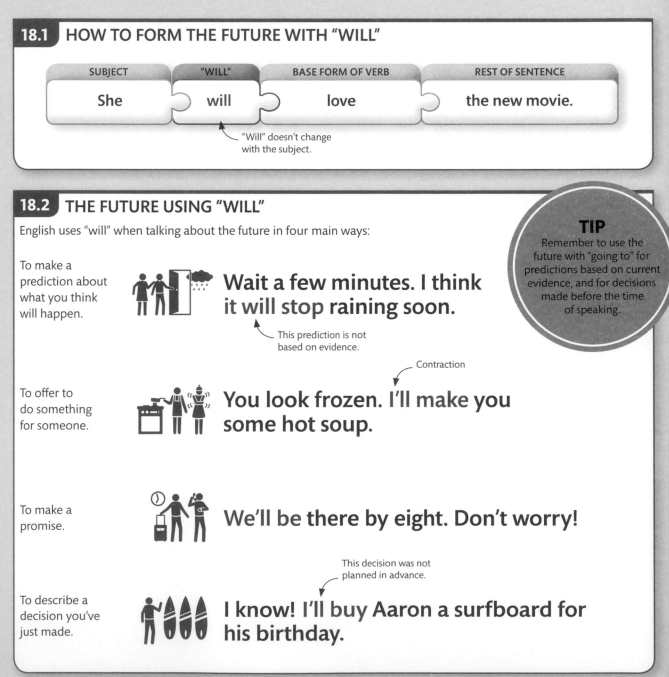

To make a prediction about what you think will happen.

Wait a few minutes. I think it will stop raining soon.

This prediction is not based on evidence.

To offer to do something for someone.

Contraction

You look frozen. I'll make you some hot soup.

To make a promise.

We'll be there by eight. Don't worry!

This decision was not planned in advance.

To describe a decision you've just made.

I know! I'll buy Aaron a surfboard for his birthday.

TIP
Remember to use the future with "going to" for predictions based on current evidence, and for decisions made before the time of speaking.

18.3 "WILL" FOR PREDICTIONS

"Will" is used to talk about predictions about the future when there is no firm evidence for that prediction.

This movie is great. You will love it.

There is no firm evidence that the person will like the movie.

FURTHER EXAMPLES

The mall will be so busy this afternoon.

They'll enjoy their trip to Venice.

"Probably" means something is likely, but not definite.

Jane will probably like the new house. It's really nice.

She'll be really angry when she finds out.

18.4 "WILL" FOR QUICK DECISIONS

"Will" is used to describe quick decisions that someone has made at the time of speaking. They are often a solution to an unexpected problem.

"Will" shows you have just made the decision.

Oh, it's raining! I'll take my umbrella.

FURTHER EXAMPLES

"Will not" or "won't" is the negative form of "will."

It's midnight. I won't walk home through the park.

This apple is delicious. I'll have another one.

"So" is often used to join a situation to a quick decision.

There's no juice, so I'll have some water instead.

The car has broken down, so I'll have to walk to work.

18.5 "WILL" FOR MAKING OFFERS

"Will" is also used to offer to do something for someone.

You seem busy. I'll pick the kids up from school today.

FURTHER EXAMPLES

I'll go to the post office for you if you want.

You must be starving! I'll make you a sandwich.

Sit down and relax, I'll make you a cup of tea.

Since you cooked, I'll do the dishes.

18.6 "WILL" FOR MAKING PROMISES

"Will" can be used when making a promise.

Don't worry, I'll be careful.

FURTHER EXAMPLES

We'll let you know as soon as your car's ready.

I'll feed the cat when I get home.

If you bring the food, we'll take care of the drinks.

I'll take care of everything while you're away.

Ben said he'll call us as soon as he gets home.

Don't worry, I'll lock the front door when I leave.

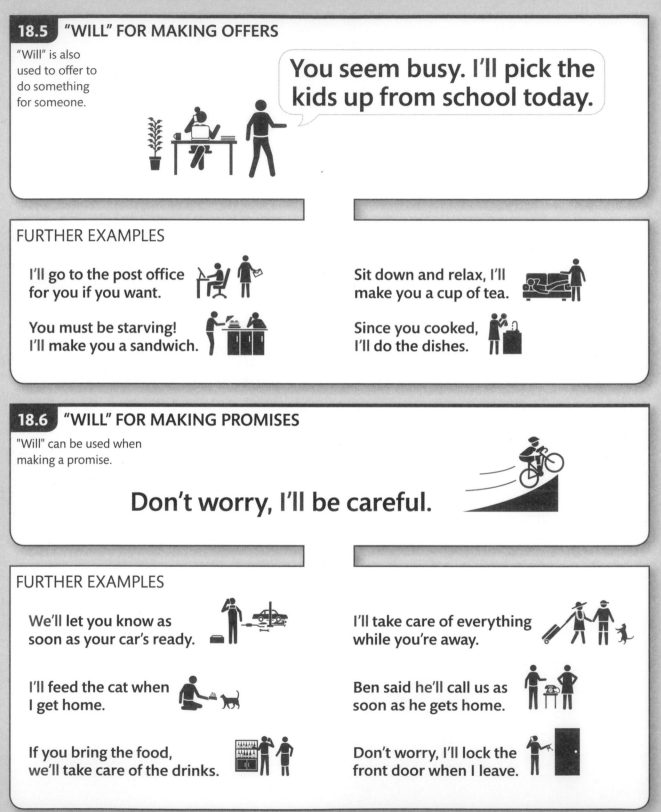

18.7 "THINK" WITH "WILL"

"Think" can be used with "will" to show that a prediction is just an opinion, or a decision is not final.

"That" is used after "think," but it can be left out.

This is an uncertain prediction.

I think that we'll have enough food for the party.

I'm tired. I think I'll go to bed.

This decision is still being considered.

FURTHER EXAMPLES

It's cold outside, but we don't think it'll snow today.

"Think" is made negative, rather than "will."

If we hurry, I think we'll get to the airport on time.

I think I'll cook chicken for dinner this evening.

I think I'll take the children ice-skating tomorrow.

18.8 FUTURE WITH "SHALL"

"Shall" is used instead of "will" when asking for a decision, or making offers or suggestions. In these cases, it is only used with "I" or "we." It is rarely used in US English.

Shall I pick you up or shall we meet at the restaurant?

"Shall" is being used to make an offer.

"Shall" is being used to make a suggestion.

FURTHER EXAMPLES

Shall I cook chicken or beef tonight?

It's so hot in here. Shall I open a window?

I'm bored, shall we go out for a walk?

Shall we try to finish the gardening today?

19 The present for future events

The present simple and present continuous can be used to talk about future events that are already planned. They are usually used with a future time word or time phrase.

See also:
Present simple **1**   Present continuous **4**
Prepositions of time **107**

19.1 THE PRESENT SIMPLE FOR FUTURE EVENTS

The present simple can be used to talk about events that are scheduled to take place in the future.

Present simple.

This refers to a point in the future.

The train arrives at 10pm tonight.

NOW   10PM

HOW TO FORM

SUBJECT	PRESENT SIMPLE	FUTURE TIME PHRASE
The train	arrives	at 10pm tonight.

FURTHER EXAMPLES

Don't forget we have an early meeting tomorrow morning.

The next flight to New York departs at 6 this evening.

The concert is next Wednesday. I hope we're ready by then!

The bank opens late tomorrow because it's the weekend.

19.2 THE PRESENT CONTINUOUS FOR FUTURE EVENTS

The present continuous can be used to talk about pre-arranged future events. Time markers usually show whether the event is in the present or future.

"At the moment" shows the action refers to the present.

Present continuous refers to Dave's present activity.

At the moment Dave is working, but tomorrow he is playing golf.

Time clause "tomorrow" shows the action refers to the future.

Present continuous refers to a future event that is planned.

NOW   TOMORROW

HOW TO FORM

SUBJECT	PRESENT CONTINUOUS	FUTURE TIME PHRASE
Dave	**is playing golf**	**tomorrow.**

FURTHER EXAMPLES

Jack's playing **soccer tomorrow.**

I'm seeing **a movie later.**

Sue is studying **this evening.**

Lisa is playing **golf tomorrow.**

I'm having **dinner with Mike next weekend.**

Jay is meeting **some friends tomorrow evening.**

Tom and Samantha are getting **married tomorrow.**

I'm running **a race for charity this weekend.**

20 The future continuous

The future continuous can be formed using "will" or "going to." It describes an event or situation that will be in progress at some point in the future.

See also:
Present continuous **4**   "Will" **18**
Infinitives and participles **51**

20.1 THE FUTURE CONTINUOUS WITH "WILL"

The future continuous describes an event that will be in progress at a given time in the future which is often stated. The event will start before the stated time and may continue after it.

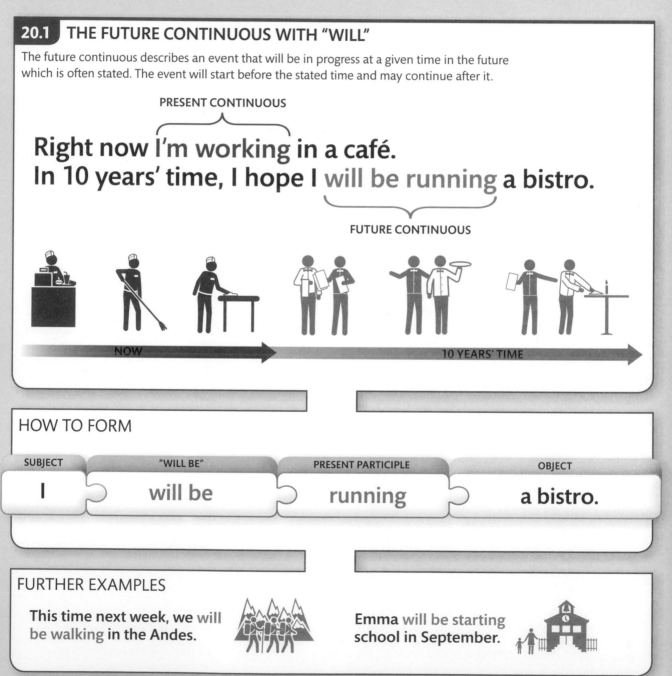

PRESENT CONTINUOUS

Right now I'm working in a café.
In 10 years' time, I hope I will be running a bistro.

FUTURE CONTINUOUS

NOW

10 YEARS' TIME

HOW TO FORM

SUBJECT	"WILL BE"	PRESENT PARTICIPLE	OBJECT
I	will be	running	a bistro.

FURTHER EXAMPLES

This time next week, we will be walking **in the Andes.**

Emma will be starting school **in September.**

20.2 THE FUTURE CONTINUOUS WITH "ANYWAY"

The future continuous can also be used to talk about events that are going to happen as a matter of course or "anyway."

Oh no, I've run out of milk.

I can get some for you later.

No, please don't worry!

It's okay, I'll be driving past the store anyway.

FURTHER EXAMPLES

You can send the parcel here. I'll be waiting in the house anyway.

I can give that to Freda for you. I'll be seeing her for lunch.

"Anyway" is implied here.

20.3 NEUTRAL QUESTIONS

The future continuous is also used to ask neutral questions: questions asked for information, not to make a request.

NEUTRAL QUESTION

Future continuous.

Will you be coming into work tomorrow?

Yes, I will.

OK, let's talk about the report then.

REQUEST

Future simple.

Will you come into work tomorrow please?

Sure, no problem.

FURTHER EXAMPLES

Will you be driving past the post office later?

Will you be attending the meeting this afternoon?

20.4 THE FUTURE CONTINUOUS TO TALK ABOUT THE PRESENT

You can also use the future continuous to speculate about what is happening at the present moment.

Have you noticed that Andrew isn't at work today?

He'll be working on his presentation at home.

It's more likely that he'll be watching the golf on TV!

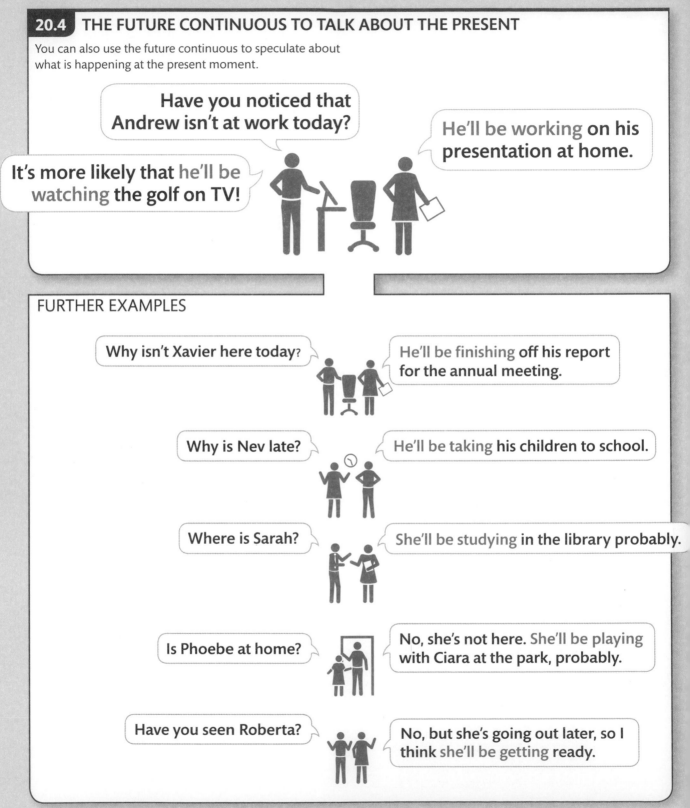

FURTHER EXAMPLES

Why isn't Xavier here today?

He'll be finishing off his report for the annual meeting.

Why is Nev late?

He'll be taking his children to school.

Where is Sarah?

She'll be studying in the library probably.

Is Phoebe at home?

No, she's not here. She'll be playing with Ciara at the park, probably.

Have you seen Roberta?

No, but she's going out later, so I think she'll be getting ready.

THE FUTURE CONTINUOUS WITH "GOING TO"

The future continuous can sometimes be formed with "going to" instead of "will," but this is less common. It can be used in most future continuous constructions except to speculate about the present.

I can't come out this evening.
I'm going to be studying all night.

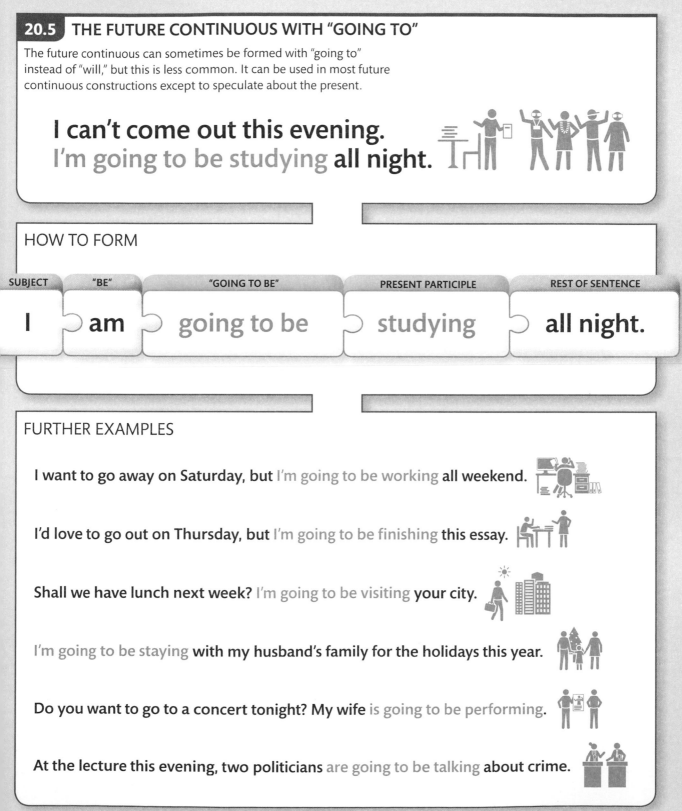

HOW TO FORM

SUBJECT	"BE"	"GOING TO BE"	PRESENT PARTICIPLE	REST OF SENTENCE
I	am	going to be	studying	all night.

FURTHER EXAMPLES

I want to go away on Saturday, but I'm going to be working all weekend.

I'd love to go out on Thursday, but I'm going to be finishing this essay.

Shall we have lunch next week? I'm going to be visiting your city.

I'm going to be staying with my husband's family for the holidays this year.

Do you want to go to a concert tonight? My wife is going to be performing.

At the lecture this evening, two politicians are going to be talking about crime.

21 The future perfect

The future perfect is used to talk about an event that will overlap with, or finish before, another event in the future. It can be used in simple or continuous forms.

See also:
Infinitives and participles **51**
Prepositions of time **107**

21.1 THE FUTURE PERFECT

The future perfect is used to describe an action or event that will be finished before a certain future time.

"By" has a similar meaning to "before."

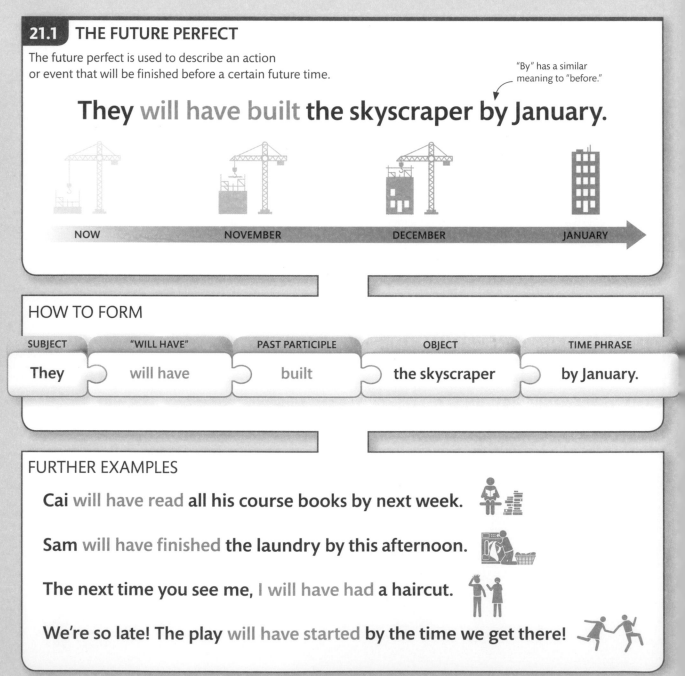

They will have built the skyscraper by January.

NOW   NOVEMBER   DECEMBER   JANUARY

HOW TO FORM

SUBJECT	"WILL HAVE"	PAST PARTICIPLE	OBJECT	TIME PHRASE
They	will have	built	the skyscraper	by January.

FURTHER EXAMPLES

Cai will have read all his course books by next week.

Sam will have finished the laundry by this afternoon.

The next time you see me, I will have had a haircut.

We're so late! The play will have started by the time we get there!

THE FUTURE PERFECT CONTINUOUS

The future perfect continuous can be used to predict the length of an activity.
This tense looks back from the imagined finishing time in the future.

By July, I will have been working here for a year.

LAST JULY   NOW   JULY

HOW TO FORM

TIME PHRASE	SUBJECT	"WILL HAVE BEEN"	PRESENT PARTICIPLE	REST OF SENTENCE
By July,	I	will have been	working	here for a year.

FURTHER EXAMPLES

By the time this is all ready, Andy will have been cooking all day!

By the time I arrive home, I will have been driving for six hours.

By this time next month, I will have been studying English for a year!

He will have been waiting for two hours by the time she arrives.

This case will have been going on for over a year before it is settled.

22 The future in the past

There are a number of constructions in English that can be used to describe thoughts about the future that someone had at some point in the past.

> **See also:**
> Past continuous **10**
> Infinitives and participles **51**

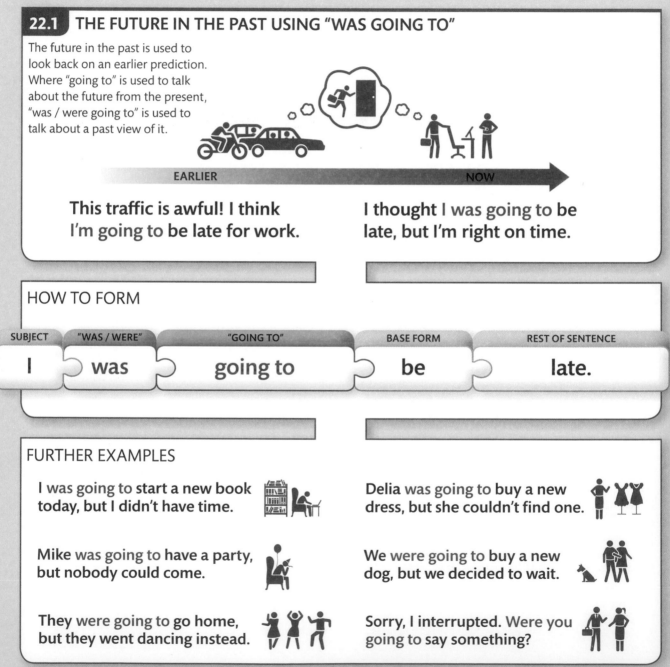

22.1 THE FUTURE IN THE PAST USING "WAS GOING TO"

The future in the past is used to look back on an earlier prediction. Where "going to" is used to talk about the future from the present, "was / were going to" is used to talk about a past view of it.

EARLIER   NOW

This traffic is awful! I think I'm going to be late for work.

I thought I was going to be late, but I'm right on time.

HOW TO FORM

SUBJECT	"WAS / WERE"	"GOING TO"	BASE FORM	REST OF SENTENCE
I	was	going to	be	late.

FURTHER EXAMPLES

I was going to start a new book today, but I didn't have time.

Delia was going to buy a new dress, but she couldn't find one.

Mike was going to have a party, but nobody could come.

We were going to buy a new dog, but we decided to wait.

They were going to go home, but they went dancing instead.

Sorry, I interrupted. Were you going to say something?

22.2 THE FUTURE IN THE PAST USING "WOULD"

Where "will" is used to talk about a future event from the present, "would" is used to talk about a past view of it.

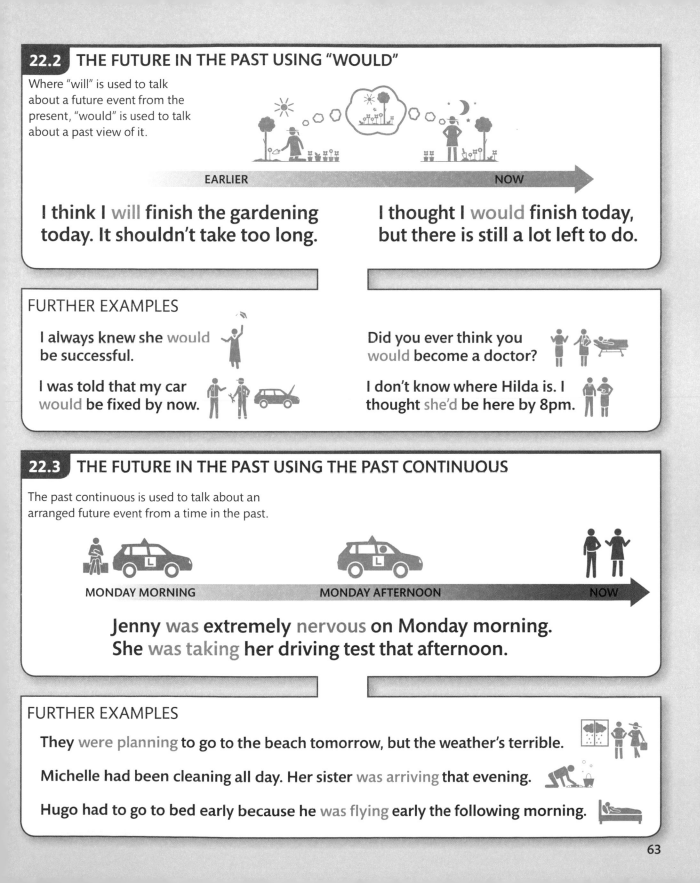

EARLIER   NOW

I think I will finish the gardening today. It shouldn't take too long.

I thought I would finish today, but there is still a lot left to do.

FURTHER EXAMPLES

I always knew she would be successful.

I was told that my car would be fixed by now.

Did you ever think you would become a doctor?

I don't know where Hilda is. I thought she'd be here by 8pm.

22.3 THE FUTURE IN THE PAST USING THE PAST CONTINUOUS

The past continuous is used to talk about an arranged future event from a time in the past.

MONDAY MORNING   MONDAY AFTERNOON   NOW

Jenny was extremely nervous on Monday morning.
She was taking her driving test that afternoon.

FURTHER EXAMPLES

They were planning to go to the beach tomorrow, but the weather's terrible.

Michelle had been cleaning all day. Her sister was arriving that evening.

Hugo had to go to bed early because he was flying early the following morning.

23 Future overview

23.1 THE FUTURE

The present simple can be used to talk about events that are timetabled or scheduled to take place in the future.

The train arrives at 10pm.

The present continuous can be used to talk about future arrangements and plans.

I'm traveling to Paris by train later this evening.

The simple future is the most common form used to refer to an event in the future.

$$\text{It} \left\{ \begin{array}{l} \text{will} \\ \text{is going to} \end{array} \right\} \text{rain tomorrow.}$$

The future continuous describes an event that will be in progress at a given time in the future. The event will start before the stated time and may continue after it.

$$\text{It} \left\{ \begin{array}{l} \text{will} \\ \text{is going to} \end{array} \right\} \text{be raining all weekend.}$$

23.2 "GOING TO" AND "WILL"

English uses both "going to" and "will" to talk about the future. They can sometimes have a very similar meaning, but there are certain situations where they mean different things.

"Will" is used to make predictions that aren't based on present evidence.

This is a prediction without firm evidence.

I think Number 2 will win.

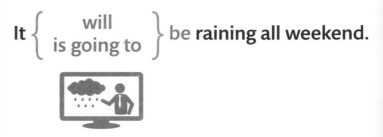

"Going to" is used when there is evidence in the present moment to support a prediction.

Look, Number 2 is going to win.

English uses different constructions to talk about the future. These are mostly formed with the auxiliary verb "will" or a form of "be" with "going to."

See also:
The future with "going to" 17
The future with "will" 18

The future perfect is used to predict when an action or event will be finished. This tense looks back from an imagined time in the future.

They will have built the skyscraper by next year.

The future perfect continuous is used to predict the eventual duration of an activity. This tense looks back from the endpoint of the action.

By July, they will have been working on it for a year.

The future in the past describes thoughts about the future that someone had at some point in the past. There are three ways to form this construction.

The traffic was terrible, so I knew I was going to be late.

"Am going to" becomes "was going to."

"Will" becomes "would."

I thought I would finish the gardening by the end of the day.

I was nervous on Sunday night. I was starting a new job the next day.

"Am starting" becomes "was starting."

"**Will**" is used when a decision is made at the time of speaking.

This decision was not planned in advance.

I know! I'll buy Jo a surfboard for her birthday.

"**Going to**" is used when talking about a decision that has already been made.

This decision has already been planned.

I'm going to buy her a surfboard that I saw last week.

24 The passive

In most sentences, the subject carries out an action and the object receives it, or the result of it. In passive sentences, this is reversed: the subject receives the action.

> **See also:**
> Present simple **1**   Present continuous **4**
> Infinitives and participles **51**

24.1 THE PRESENT SIMPLE PASSIVE

Passive sentences take emphasis away from the agent (the person or thing doing the action), and put it on the action itself, or the person or thing receiving the action. In the present simple passive, the present simple verb becomes a past participle.

The focus is on "many people."

Many people study **this book.**

The subject of the active sentence is "many people."

This book is studied **by many people.**

The focus is on "this book," which is the subject of the passive sentence.

"Study" changes to "is studied."

FURTHER EXAMPLES

The passive is used when the agent is obvious, unknown, or unimportant. It is also useful when describing a process where the result of the action is important.

The speaker doesn't mention the agent because the verb obviously refers to the police.

Criminals are arrested **every day in this town.**

The agent is not mentioned because the process is more important.

Are the posters printed **on quality paper?**

"Be" and the subject swap places to form questions.

HOW TO FORM

All passives use a form of "be" with a past participle. The agent (the thing doing the action) can be introduced with "by," but the sentence would still make sense without it.

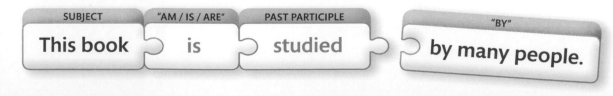

SUBJECT	"AM / IS / ARE"	PAST PARTICIPLE	"BY"
This book	**is**	**studied**	**by many people.**

THE PRESENT CONTINUOUS PASSIVE

The present continuous passive
is used to refer to ongoing actions.

PRESENT CONTINUOUS

Developers are building lots of new houses in the area.

Lots of new houses are being built in the area.

PRESENT CONTINUOUS PASSIVE

FURTHER EXAMPLES

You can't use the pool today
because it is being cleaned.

The robbery is being
investigated by the police.

We're living in a trailer while
our house is being rebuilt.

The course is being taught
by a well-known scientist.

I am being interviewed by
a news channel tomorrow.

Don't worry, the food is
being cooked as we speak.

Posters for the concert are
being put up all over town.

I have to walk to work while
my car is being repaired.

HOW TO FORM

SUBJECT	"AM / IS / ARE"	"BEING"	PAST PARTICIPLE	REST OF SENTENCE
New houses	**are**	**being**	**built**	**in the area.**

The thing that
receives the action.

Present simple
of "be."

The past participle describes
what happens to the subject.

25 The passive in the past

English uses the passive voice in the past to stress the effect of an action that happened in the past, rather than the cause of that action.

See also:
Past simple **7**   Past continuous **10**
Present perfect **11**   Past perfect **13**

25.1 THE PAST SIMPLE PASSIVE

The past simple passive is used when referring to a single completed action in the past, focusing on the effect rather than the cause.

PAST SIMPLE

The fire destroyed the buildings.

PAST SIMPLE PASSIVE

The buildings were destroyed by the fire.

FURTHER EXAMPLES

The trees were cut down **last year.**

The rail road was damaged **during the storm.**

Two people were injured **in the accident.**

HOW TO FORM

SUBJECT	"WAS / WERE"	PAST PARTICIPLE	REST OF SENTENCE
The buildings	**were**	**destroyed**	**in a fire.**

The thing that receives the action.

"Was" is for singular subjects, and "were" is for plural subjects.

The main verb is a past participle.

25.2 THE PAST CONTINUOUS PASSIVE

The past continuous can also be used in the passive voice. It is used to refer to ongoing actions in the past.

PAST CONTINUOUS

Secret agents were watching him.

PAST CONTINUOUS PASSIVE

He was being watched by secret agents.

FURTHER EXAMPLES

The students were being taught how to write good essays.

By the time I got back to my car, it was being taken away.

I went for lunch while my car was being fixed.

The new secretary was being shown how to use the computer.

We bought our house while it was being built.

HOW TO FORM

SUBJECT	"WAS / WERE"	"BEING"	PAST PARTICIPLE	"BY" + AGENT
He	**was**	**being**	**watched**	**by secret agents.**

The thing that receives the action.

"Was" is for singular subjects, and "were" is for plural subjects.

The main verb is expressed as a past participle.

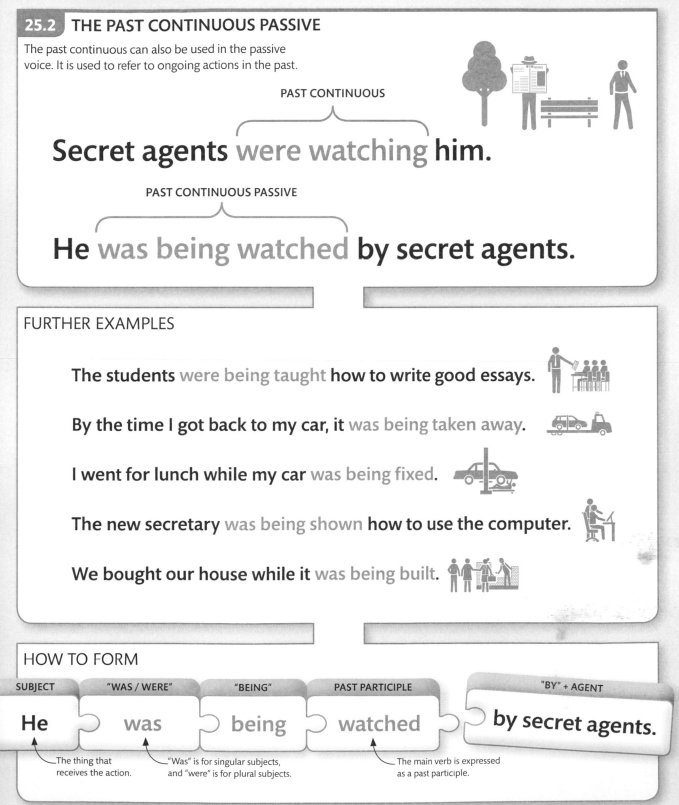

The present perfect passive is used to talk about events in the past that still have an effect on the present moment.

PRESENT PERFECT

Don't worry, I have fed the cats.

PRESENT PERFECT PASSIVE

Don't worry, the cats have been fed.

FURTHER EXAMPLES

This door has been painted beautifully.

Do you know if all the lights have been turned off?

Has your computer been fixed yet? It broke months ago!

The subject and verb swap places to form questions.

The new parts haven't been delivered yet, so you'll have to wait.

All of the smoke detectors have been replaced.

HOW TO FORM

SUBJECT	"HAS / HAVE"	"BEEN"	PAST PARTICIPLE
The cats	have	been	fed.

The thing that receives the action.

"Been" stays the same no matter what the subject is.

The main verb is expressed as a past participle.

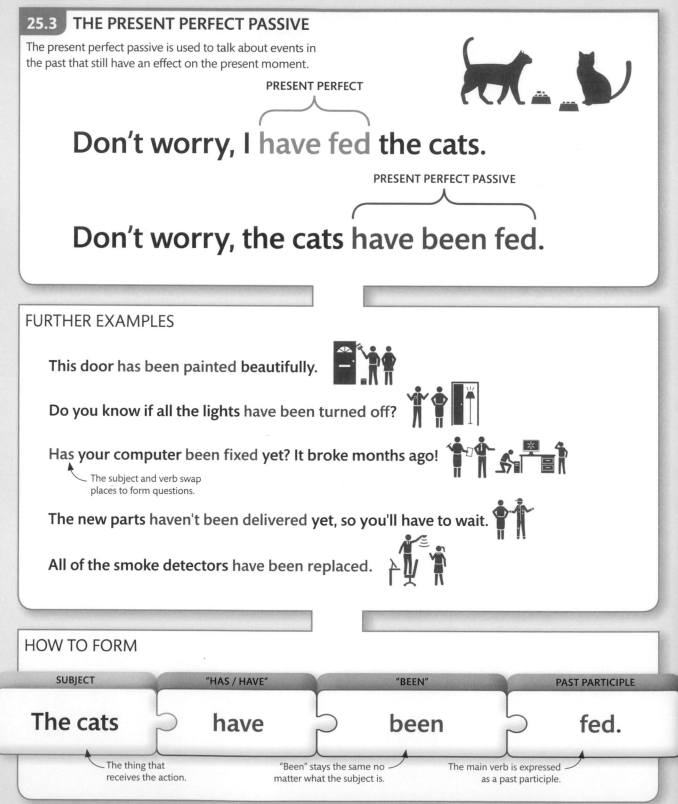

25.4 THE PAST PERFECT PASSIVE

The past perfect passive is used to refer to events that happened before another event in the past.

Unfortunately, the organizer had canceled the party.

PAST PERFECT

PAST PERFECT PASSIVE

Unfortunately, the party had been canceled.

FURTHER EXAMPLES

This part of the Arctic had never been explored before.

The class hadn't been told that the lecture had been canceled.

Sue didn't realize that the floor had just been polished.

We were about to sing *Happy Birthday*, but the cake had been eaten!

Anna was so happy that her cat had been found.

HOW TO FORM

SUBJECT	"HAD BEEN"	PAST PARTICIPLE
The party	had been	canceled.
The thing that receives the action.	"Had been" stays the same with any subject.	The main verb is expressed as a past participle.

26 The passive in the future

English uses the passive voice in the future to stress the effect of an action that will happen in the future, rather than the cause of that action.

See also:
Future with "will" 18   Future perfect 21
Infinitives and participles 51

26.1 THE FUTURE SIMPLE PASSIVE

The future simple passive is usually formed with "will" rather than "going to."

FUTURE SIMPLE

Hopefully, the police **will catch** the thief very soon.

FUTURE SIMPLE PASSIVE

Hopefully, the thief **will be caught** very soon.

It is not known or important who will catch the thief.

FURTHER EXAMPLES

Don't worry, the house **will be finished** very soon.

An email **will be sent** to you all next week with more details.

Sorry, but the power **will be turned off** between 2pm and 5pm.

HOW TO FORM

SUBJECT	"WILL BE"	PAST PARTICIPLE	REST OF SENTENCE
The thief	**will be**	**caught**	**very soon.**

The thing that receives the action.

"Will be" doesn't change with any subject.

The main verb is a past participle.

THE FUTURE PERFECT PASSIVE

The future perfect passive is used to talk about events that will be finished at some point in the future.

FUTURE PERFECT

The mechanic will have fixed the car by 5pm.

FUTURE PERFECT PASSIVE

The car will have been fixed by 5pm.

FURTHER EXAMPLES

We think every ticket will have been bought **before the end of the day.**

Hurry up or all the good seats will have been taken **already.**

You should call early, otherwise all the tables will have been booked.

Come back tomorrow. The park will have been cleaned **by then.**

Will **those letters** have been sent **out before lunchtime tomorrow?**

HOW TO FORM

SUBJECT	"WILL HAVE BEEN"	PAST PARTICIPLE
The car	will have been	fixed.
The thing that receives the action.	"Will have been" stays the same with any subject.	The main verb is a past participle.

27 The passive with modals

Modal verbs in English can be used in passive forms.
As with other passive constructions, the emphasis
changes to the object that receives the action.

See also:
Present perfect simple **11**   Passive **24**
Modal verbs **56**

27.1 MODALS IN THE PRESENT PASSIVE

Modals in passive forms don't change. The sentence starts with
the modal, then the verb "be" plus the past participle.

PRESENT WITH MODAL

You should tell Barbara the exciting news!

PRESENT PASSIVE WITH MODAL

Barbara should be told the exciting news!

FURTHER EXAMPLES

Should **the package** be delivered **to your house or your office?**

The treasure chest can only be opened **with a special key.**

All new employees must be shown **what to do if there's a fire.**

HOW TO FORM

SUBJECT	MODAL VERB	"BE"	PAST PARTICIPLE	REST OF SENTENCE
Barbara	**should**	**be**	**told**	**the news.**

The thing that receives the action.

Other modal verbs can go here.

"Be" stays the same no matter what the subject is.

The main verb is a past participle form.

MODALS IN THE PERFECT PASSIVE

Modals in perfect tenses can become passive
by replacing "have" with "have been."

PERFECT WITH MODAL

The managers should have given Daniel more time.

PERFECT PASSIVE WITH MODAL

Daniel should have been given more time.

FURTHER EXAMPLES

We should have been told that the concert was canceled!

The robber would have been arrested if he hadn't been so quick.

The leaking pipe might have been fixed now. Should we ask?

Lots of people think that the fire could have been prevented.

HOW TO FORM

SUBJECT	MODAL VERB	"HAVE BEEN"	PAST PARTICIPLE	REST OF SENTENCE
He	**should**	**have been**	**given**	**more time.**

The thing that receives the action.

Other modal verbs can go here.

"Have been" stays the same with any subject.

The main verb is a past participle form.

28 Other passive constructions

Many idioms in English use passive forms. Some idioms use standard rules for passive forms, while others are slightly different.

See also:
Passive voice **45**   Reporting verbs **24**
Defining relative clauses **81**

28.1 REPORTING WITH PASSIVES

Some passive constructions are used to distance the writer or speaker from the facts. They are often used in academic writing or news reports.

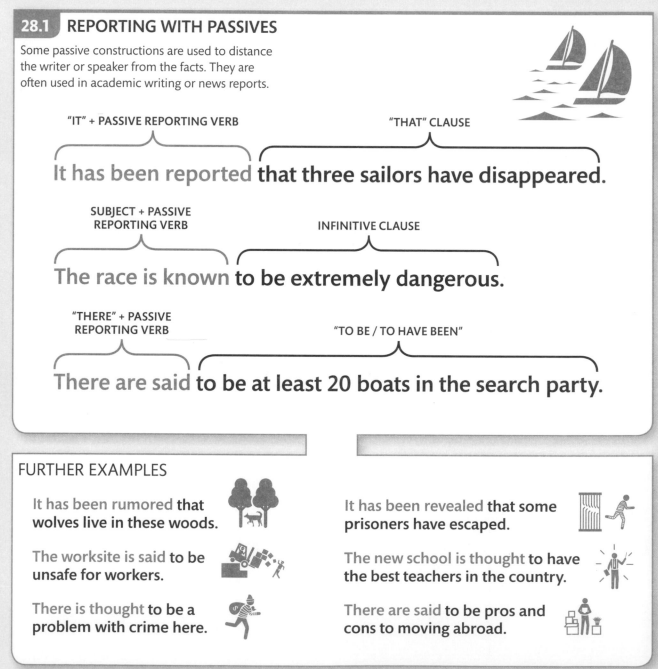

"IT" + PASSIVE REPORTING VERB

"THAT" CLAUSE

It has been reported that three sailors have disappeared.

SUBJECT + PASSIVE REPORTING VERB

INFINITIVE CLAUSE

The race is known to be extremely dangerous.

"THERE" + PASSIVE REPORTING VERB

"TO BE / TO HAVE BEEN"

There are said to be at least 20 boats in the search party.

FURTHER EXAMPLES

It has been rumored that wolves live in these woods.

The worksite is said to be unsafe for workers.

There is thought to be a problem with crime here.

It has been revealed that some prisoners have escaped.

The new school is thought to have the best teachers in the country.

There are said to be pros and cons to moving abroad.

USING "GET" IN PASSIVE CONSTRUCTIONS

"Get" can sometimes replace "be" in passive sentences.
This form is more informal than the passive with "be."

PRESENT SIMPLE PASSIVE

Bikes get stolen in this town every day.

My friend's bike got stolen yesterday.

PAST SIMPLE PASSIVE

FURTHER EXAMPLES

The windows get washed once a month.

My laptop gets updated every week by the IT team.

More and more items are getting recycled these days.

This package got delivered today. I wonder what it is.

I hope the air conditioning will get fixed soon.

Did you know that the company was getting sold?

HOW TO FORM

SUBJECT	"GET / GOT"	PAST PARTICIPLE	REST OF SENTENCE
His bike	**got**	**stolen**	**yesterday.**

The thing that receives the action.

A form of "get" is used instead of "be."

The past participle describes what happens to the subject.

29 Conditional sentences

Conditional sentences are used to describe real or hypothetical results of real or hypothetical situations. They can use many different verb forms.

See also:
Present simple **1**   Imperatives **6**
Past simple **7**   Future with "will" **18**

29.1 THE ZERO CONDITIONAL

The zero conditional, also called the "real" conditional, refers to things that are always true. It is used to describe the direct result of an action.

ACTION   RESULT

If / **When** } **you heat water, it boils.**

"If" and "when" mean the same thing in the zero conditional.

FURTHER EXAMPLES

If you heat ice, it melts.

When you put a rock in water, it sinks.

The result clause can go to the beginning of the sentence. The comma is removed in this case.

If you drop an apple, it falls.

Oil floats when you pour it onto water.

HOW TO FORM

"IF / WHEN"	ACTION (PRESENT SIMPLE)	COMMA	RESULT (PRESENT SIMPLE)
If / **When**	**you heat water**	**,**	**it boils.**

Present simple describes the action.

Comma goes at the end of the "if" or "when" clause.

Result is described using present simple.

CONDITIONALS WITH IMPERATIVES

Imperatives can be used in conditional sentences. The "if" clause describes a hypothetical situation and the imperative clause describes what someone should do if that hypothetical situation actually happens.

SITUATION   SUGGESTED ACTION

If you're cold, put on a coat.

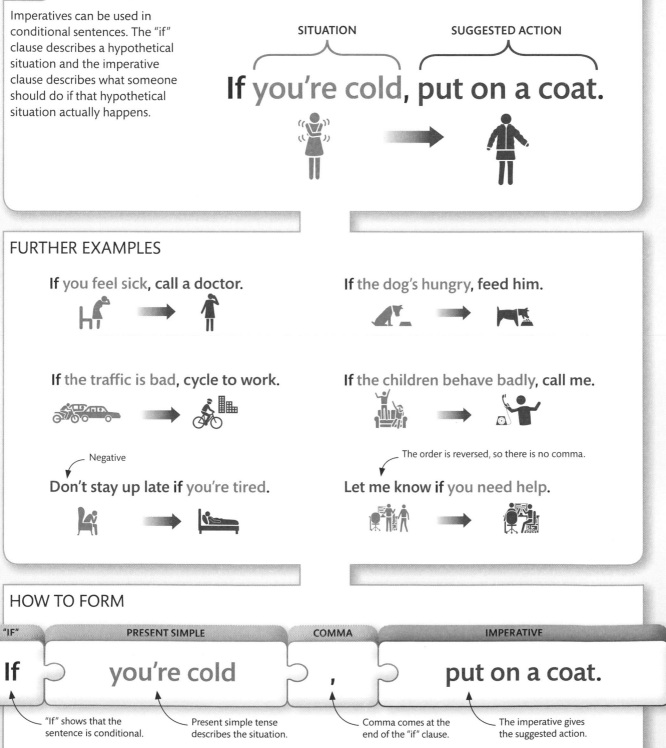

FURTHER EXAMPLES

If you feel sick, **call a doctor.**

If the dog's hungry, **feed him.**

If the traffic is bad, **cycle to work.**

If the children behave badly, **call me.**

Negative

Don't stay up late if you're tired.

The order is reversed, so there is no comma.

Let me know if you need help.

HOW TO FORM

"IF"	PRESENT SIMPLE	COMMA	IMPERATIVE
If	**you're cold**	**,**	**put on a coat.**

"If" shows that the sentence is conditional.

Present simple tense describes the situation.

Comma comes at the end of the "if" clause.

The imperative gives the suggested action.

29.3 THE FIRST CONDITIONAL

The first conditional, also called the "future real" conditional, uses "if" to describe a realistic action that might lead to a future result.

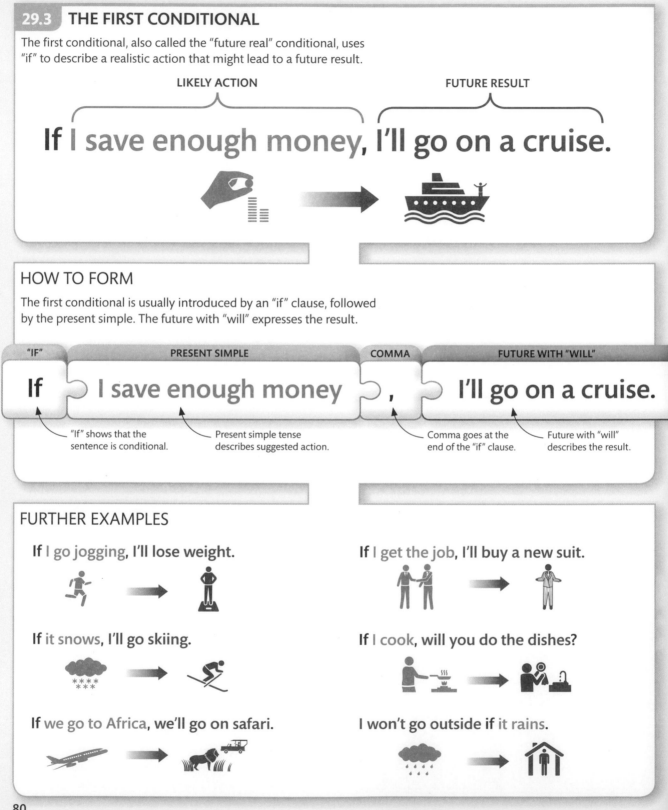

LIKELY ACTION   FUTURE RESULT

If I save enough money, I'll go on a cruise.

HOW TO FORM

The first conditional is usually introduced by an "if" clause, followed by the present simple. The future with "will" expresses the result.

"IF"	PRESENT SIMPLE	COMMA	FUTURE WITH "WILL"
If	**I save enough money**	**,**	**I'll go on a cruise.**

"If" shows that the sentence is conditional.

Present simple tense describes suggested action.

Comma goes at the end of the "if" clause.

Future with "will" describes the result.

FURTHER EXAMPLES

If I go jogging, I'll lose weight.

If it snows, I'll go skiing.

If we go to Africa, we'll go on safari.

If I get the job, I'll buy a new suit.

If I cook, will you do the dishes?

I won't go outside if it rains.

THE SECOND CONDITIONAL

The second conditional, also called the "unreal" conditional, uses "if" to describe an unlikely or unreal action or event. The described result is also very unlikely.

UNLIKELY EVENT   UNLIKELY RESULT

If I won the lottery, I would leave my job.

HOW TO FORM

The second conditional is usually introduced by an "if" clause with a past simple verb.
"Would" or "could" plus the base form of the main verb expresses the result.

"IF"	PAST SIMPLE	COMMA	"WOULD / COULD" + BASE FORM
If	**I won the lottery**	**,**	**I would leave my job.**

"If" shows that the sentence is conditional.

Past simple tense describes the action.

Comma goes at the end of the "if" clause.

Result is described using "would" + verb.

FURTHER EXAMPLES

If he wasn't so busy, **he'd take a break.**

I'd call her if I knew her number.

If I moved to Scotland, **I'd live in a cottage.**

If I saw a ghost, **I would be terrified.**

If I had more time, **I could take up karate.**

If I learned English, **I could visit London.**

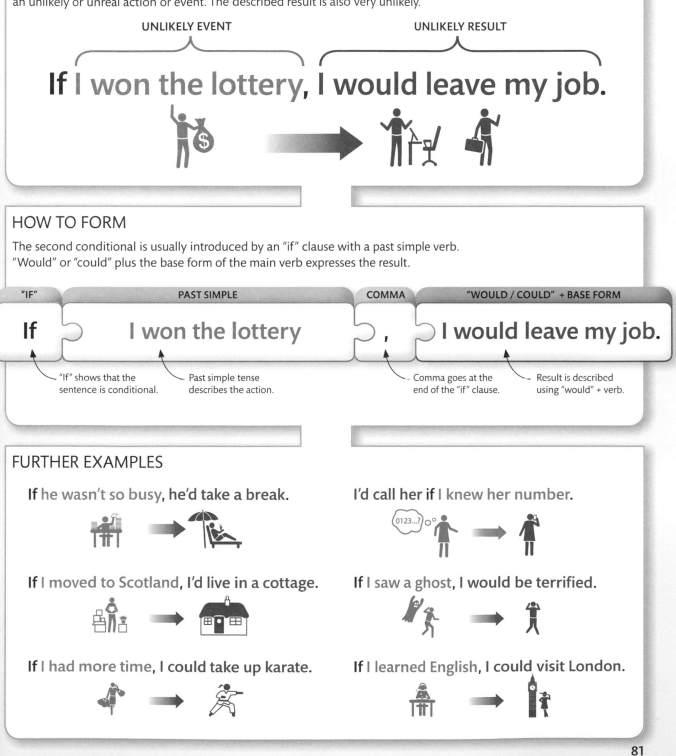

29.5 THE THIRD CONDITIONAL

The third conditional, also called the "past unreal" conditional, is used to describe unreal situations in the past. It is often used to express regret about the past because the hypothetical situation that it describes is now impossible as a consequence of another past action.

UNREAL PAST SITUATION   UNREAL PAST RESULT

If we had left earlier, we would have caught the train.

This didn't happen.

So this didn't happen either.

FURTHER EXAMPLES

If I had woken up on time,
I would have done my hair.

If you had been wearing a coat,
you might have stayed warm.

"Might" means this possibly would have happened.

If I had studied harder,
I could have been a doctor.

"Could" means this possibly would have happened.

If I had known it was your birthday,
I would have bought you a present.

HOW TO FORM

"IF"	"HAD" + PAST PARTICIPLE		"WOULD / COULD / MIGHT"	"HAVE" + PAST PARTICIPLE
If	**we had left earlier**	**,**	**we would**	**have caught the train.**

The "if" clause is the unreal past condition.

Using different modals changes the certainty of the imagined result.

The conditional clause is the unreal result.

29.6 THE MIXED CONDITIONAL

SECOND CONDITIONAL

The second conditional is used to talk about hypothetical situations in the present.

PAST SIMPLE

If I didn't believe in astrology, I wouldn't read my horoscope.

"WOULD" + INFINITIVE

THIRD CONDITIONAL

The third conditional is used to talk about hypothetical situations in the past.

PAST PERFECT

If I had known he was an Aquarius, I would not have gone out with him.

"WOULD" + "HAVE" + PAST PARTICIPLE

MIXED CONDITIONAL

Mixed conditionals are usually used to talk about hypothetical present reults of unreal past situations.

Unreal past.

If you had been born a month earlier, you would be a Virgo like me.

Unreal present.

FURTHER EXAMPLES

If you hadn't forgotten to bring the keys, **we wouldn't be locked out of the house.**

Mixed conditionals refer to future situations when used with future time markers.

You would be starting at a new school tomorrow if you hadn't failed your exams.

Mixed conditionals are often used to express regret.

If I had finished my assignment sooner, **I could be out with my friends today.**

We would be on a beach in Greece by now if we hadn't missed our flight.

30 Other conditional sentences

English allows for some variations in conditional sentence structures. These give more information about the context of the conditional.

See also:
Future with "will" **18**
Modal verbs **56**

30.1 CONDITIONAL SENTENCES WITH MODAL VERBS

First, second, and third conditional sentences can use different modal verbs in their "result" clauses. These can be used to express uncertainty, possibility, or obligation, amongst other things.

FIRST CONDITIONAL

In the first conditional, "will" can be replaced by a variety of modal verbs to talk about different ideas.

If I save enough money, I **will** buy a new car.

If I save enough money, I **can** buy a new car.

Different modal verbs can go here.

SECOND CONDITIONAL

In the second conditional, "would" can be replaced by "could" or "might" to express ability, possibility, or uncertainty.

If I saved enough money, I **would** buy a new car.

If I saved enough money, I { **could** / **might** } buy a new car.

THIRD CONDITIONAL

In the third conditional, "would" can be replaced by "could" or "might" to express ability, possibility, or uncertainty.

If I had saved enough money, I **would have** bought a new car.

If I had saved enough money, I { **could** / **might** } have bought a new car.

30.2 FIRST CONDITIONAL WITH "UNLESS"

"Unless" can be used instead of "if" in conditional sentences. "Unless" means "if… not," so the future result depends on the suggested action not happening.

If you don't / Unless you **study hard, you will fail your exams.**

FURTHER EXAMPLES

If you don't / Unless you **get up now, you'll be late for work.**

I'll be angry { if he doesn't **turn** / unless he **turns** } **that music down.**

30.3 FORMAL THIRD CONDITIONAL

The third conditional can be made more formal by swapping "had" with the subject and dropping "if."

If you **had** attended **the meeting, you would have met the manager.**

Had you attended **the meeting, you would have met the manager.**

FURTHER EXAMPLES

Had I worked **harder at school, I could have studied medicine.**

Had you listened **to the directions, we would have arrived on time.**

Had she woken up **earlier, she wouldn't have been late.**

Had we bought **that house, we couldn't have afforded this trip.**

31 Conditional sentences overview

31.1 TYPES OF CONDITIONAL

The zero conditional is used to talk about situations that will always happen. It is used to talk about general truths.

PRESENT SIMPLE

If you play the violin out of tune, it sounds terrible.

PRESENT SIMPLE

The second conditional is used to talk about hypothetical situations that are very unlikely to happen, but are usually still possible.

PAST SIMPLE

If I practiced more, that song would sound better.

"WOULD" + BASE FORM

31.2 USING COMMAS IN CONDITIONAL SENTENCES

When the action comes before the result, a comma separates the two clauses of the conditional sentence. However, when the result comes first, no comma is used.

A comma is used if the action comes first.

When you freeze water, ice forms.

Ice forms when you freeze water.

The result can come at the beginning of the sentence.

"If" or "when" can sit between the action and result, without a comma.

There are four types of conditional sentences. The zero conditional refers to real situations, but the first, second, and third conditionals all refer to hypothetical situations.

See also:
Present simple **1**   Past simple **7**
Past perfect simple **13**   Modal verbs **56**

The first conditional is used to talk about hypothetical situations that are likely to happen.

PRESENT SIMPLE

If I practice really hard, this song will sound great.

"WILL" + BASE FORM

The third conditional is used to talk about hypothetical situations that definitely will not happen. The result is no longer possible because of the imaginary cause in the past.

PAST PERFECT

If I had practiced more, I would have sounded better.

"WOULD" + "HAVE" + PAST PARTICIPLE

⚠ **COMMON MISTAKES** USING OTHER TENSES IN CONDITIONAL SENTENCES

"Will," "would," and "would have" should not be used in the "if" clause when forming conditional sentences.

If I will work really hard, this piece will sound great. ✗

"Will" doesn't go in the "if" clause.

If I would practice more, that piece would sound better. ✗

"Would" doesn't go in the "if" clause.

If I would have practiced more, I would have sounded better. ✗

"Would have" doesn't go in the "if" clause.

32 Future possibilities

There are many ways to talk about imaginary future situations. Different structures can be used to indicate whether a situation is likely or unlikely.

See also:
Present simple **1**   Past simple **7**
Past perfect simple **13**

32.1 LIKELY FUTURE POSSIBILITIES

"What if" or "suppose" followed by the present tense can be used to express a future outcome that is likely to happen.

"What if" means "what would happen if an imagined situation occurred?"

What if
Suppose } **I fail my exams? I won't be able to go to college.**

Present tense shows the speaker believes this is likely to happen.

"Suppose" refers to the consequences of an imagined situation.

FURTHER EXAMPLES

What if the computer crashes?
I will lose all my work.

Suppose they assess our coursework.
We will have to keep a portfolio.

32.2 UNLIKELY FUTURE POSSIBILITIES

"What if" or "suppose" followed by the past simple can be used to express a future outcome that is possible, but unlikely to happen.

The past tense shows the speaker thinks this is unlikely to happen.

Just imagine! { **What if**
Suppose } **we all got 100% on our exams?**

FURTHER EXAMPLES

Suppose I got caught cheating.
My parents would be furious.

What if our flight was canceled?
We'd be stuck here!

32.3 THINGS THAT COULD HAVE HAPPENED

"What if" and "suppose" can also be used with the past perfect to describe situations that were possible in the past, but that didn't happen, or might not have happened.

That was so dangerous! { What if / Suppose } you had broken your leg?

The past perfect shows that this didn't happen, but it was possible.

FURTHER EXAMPLES

We were lucky to catch that plane! What if it hadn't been delayed?

Suppose you had taken the job. We would have had to move.

32.4 IN CASE

"In case" or "just in case" plus the present tense are used to show planning for a possible future situation.

Make sure the windows are shut in case the cat tries to escape.

Present tense.

FURTHER EXAMPLES

You should take an umbrella with you in case it rains later.

We should start organizing our project work, just in case they want to see it.

You should write these instructions down in case you forget what to do.

You should leave for the airport early, just in case the traffic is bad.

"Just" is added to "in case" to talk about preparation for a situation that is less likely.

33 Wishes and regrets

English uses the verb "wish" to talk about present and past regrets. The tense of the verb that follows "wish" affects the meaning of the sentence.

See also:
Past simple **7**   Past perfect simple **13**
Modal verbs **56**

33.1 "WISH" AND PAST SIMPLE

"Wish" is used with the past simple to express regrets and desires about the present, which could still happen or come true.

I wish I earned more money.

The past simple is used here to talk about the present.

FURTHER EXAMPLES

Mike's apartment is too small. He wishes he lived in a bigger house.

They wish the weather was better so they could go to the beach.

You're always busy, I wish you didn't have to work so hard.

Sandra hates her job. She wishes she worked on a farm.

HOW TO FORM

SUBJECT	"WISH"	SUBJECT	PAST SIMPLE	REST OF SENTENCE
I	wish	I	earned	more money.

"Wish" or "wishes," depending on the subject.

The past simple expresses wishes or regrets about the present.

"WISH" AND PAST PERFECT

"Wish" is used with the past perfect to talk about regrets about the past. This form is used when it is too late for the wish to come true.

I've failed my exams. I wish I had studied harder.

The past perfect is used to talk about a regret in the past.

FURTHER EXAMPLES

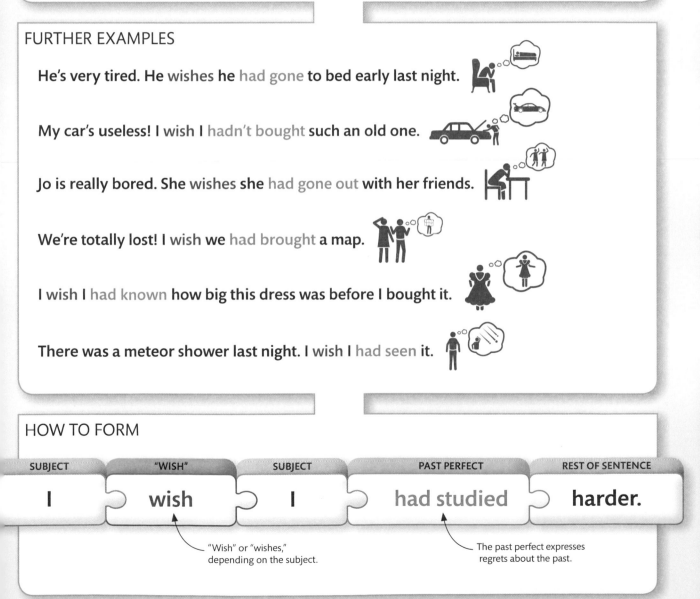

He's very tired. He wishes he had gone to bed early last night.

My car's useless! I wish I hadn't bought such an old one.

Jo is really bored. She wishes she had gone out with her friends.

We're totally lost! I wish we had brought a map.

I wish I had known how big this dress was before I bought it.

There was a meteor shower last night. I wish I had seen it.

HOW TO FORM

SUBJECT	"WISH"	SUBJECT	PAST PERFECT	REST OF SENTENCE
I	wish	I	had studied	harder.

"Wish" or "wishes," depending on the subject.

The past perfect expresses regrets about the past.

33.3 "WISH" FOR FUTURE HOPES

"Wish" can also be used to talk about hopes for the future. "Wish" with "could" is usually used when someone is expressing a desire to do something themselves.

I wish I could move somewhere warm.

[I would like to be able to move somewhere warmer.]

"Wish" with "would" is used when someone is expressing a desire for someone else to do something.

She wishes her teacher would give her less work.

[She wants her teacher to give out less homework in the future.]

FURTHER EXAMPLES

I wish I could get a new job in a different department.

Colin is always talking about cars. I wish he would stop.

I wish I could go to the concert with my friends this evening.

I wish they wouldn't make it so hard to buy tickets online.

Irene wishes she could find her diamond necklace.

Jenny's mother wishes she would clean her room.

Matteo wishes he could play the violin.

Noel wishes Adrienne would stop singing.

He wishes he could understand his homework.

Madge wishes Greg wouldn't drive so fast.

33.4 ANOTHER WAY TO SAY "I WISH"

PRESENT REGRETS

Stronger regrets about the present can be expressed by using "if only" and the past simple.

These mountains are incredible!
If only I knew **how to ski.**

PAST REGRETS

Stronger regrets about the past can be expressed by using "if only" and the past perfect.

I really wanted to take pictures.
If only I'd charged **the battery.**

FURTHER EXAMPLES

I love the sound of the guitar.
If only I played **it better.**

I'm sure the teacher explained this. If only I remembered **it!**

The show is completely sold out!
If only I'd arrived **sooner.**

I couldn't finish the marathon.
If only I had trained **harder.**

33.5 PAST REGRETS

"Should have" or "ought to have" are used to express regret that something did or didn't happen in the past.

Past participle.

This bill is so big. I { **should have** / **ought to have** } **used less electricity.**

FURTHER EXAMPLES

Maybe I should have used energy-saving light bulbs.

The negative form "ought not to have" is rarely used in UK English and never used in US English.

I shouldn't have fallen asleep with the TV on.

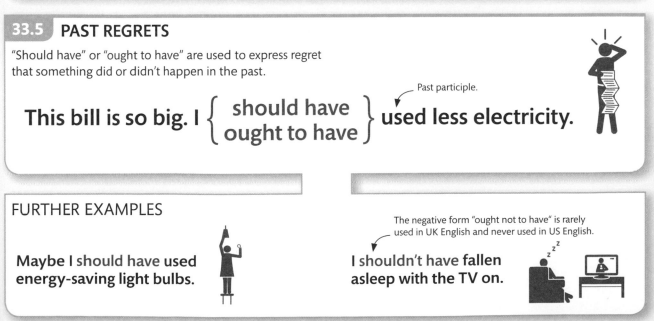

34 Forming questions

If a statement uses "be" or an auxiliary verb, its question form is made by inverting that verb and the subject. Any other question is formed by adding "do" or "does."

See also:
Present simple **1**   Types of verbs **49**
Modal verbs **56**

34.1 QUESTIONS WITH "BE"

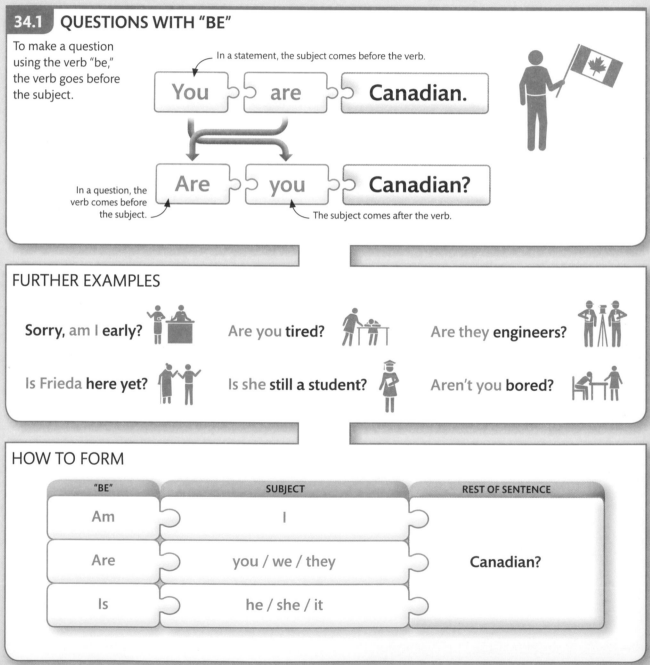

To make a question using the verb "be," the verb goes before the subject.

In a statement, the subject comes before the verb.

You — are — Canadian.

Are — you — Canadian?

In a question, the verb comes before the subject.

The subject comes after the verb.

FURTHER EXAMPLES

Sorry, am I **early?**

Are you **tired?**

Are they **engineers?**

Is Frieda **here yet?**

Is she **still a student?**

Aren't you **bored?**

HOW TO FORM

"BE"	SUBJECT	REST OF SENTENCE
Am	I	
Are	you / we / they	Canadian?
Is	he / she / it	

34.2 QUESTIONS WITH "BE" IN THE PAST

To ask questions about the past using the verb "be," the subject and verb swap places.

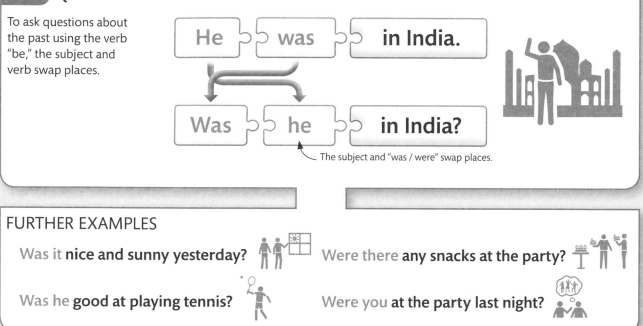

He was in India.

Was he in India?

The subject and "was / were" swap places.

FURTHER EXAMPLES

Was it **nice and sunny yesterday?**

Were there **any snacks at the party?**

Was he **good at playing tennis?**

Were you **at the party last night?**

34.3 QUESTIONS WITH AUXILIARY VERBS

For questions including an auxiliary verb, such as "have," "will," and "could," the subject and the auxiliary verb swap places. The main verb stays where it is.

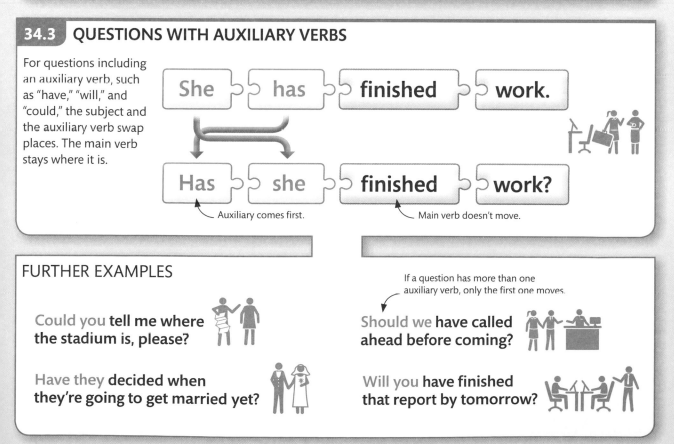

She has finished work.

Has she finished work?

Auxiliary comes first.

Main verb doesn't move.

FURTHER EXAMPLES

Could you **tell me where the stadium is, please?**

If a question has more than one auxiliary verb, only the first one moves.

Should we **have called ahead before coming?**

Have they **decided when they're going to get married yet?**

Will you **have finished that report by tomorrow?**

QUESTIONS WITH "DO" AND "DOES"

Questions in the present simple without the verb "be" or an auxiliary verb start with "do" or "does" and have the main verb in its base form. The subject and main verb do not swap around.

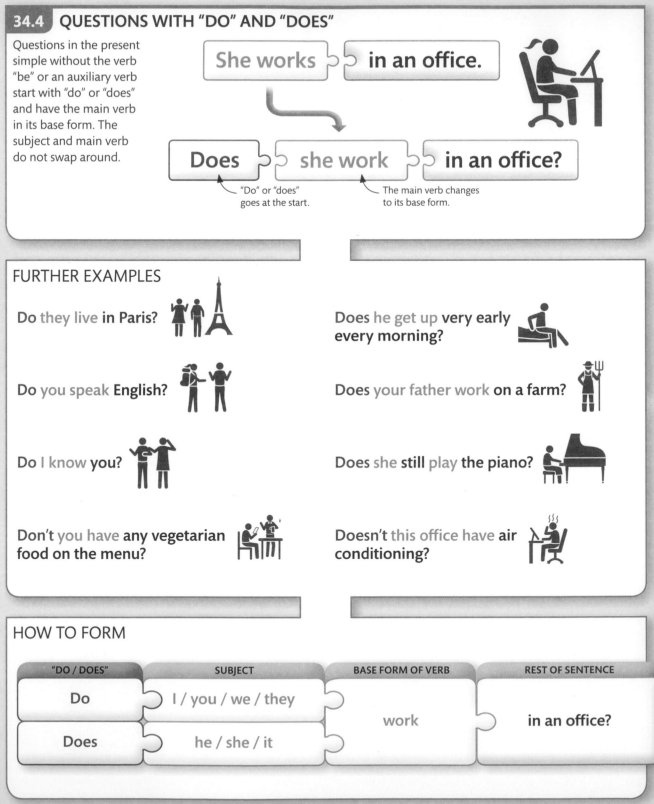

She works ᗡᑐ in an office.

Does ᗡᑐ she work ᗡᑐ in an office?

"Do" or "does" goes at the start.

The main verb changes to its base form.

FURTHER EXAMPLES

Do they live in Paris?

Do you speak English?

Do I know you?

Don't you have any vegetarian food on the menu?

Does he get up very early every morning?

Does your father work on a farm?

Does she still play the piano?

Doesn't this office have air conditioning?

HOW TO FORM

"DO / DOES"	SUBJECT	BASE FORM OF VERB	REST OF SENTENCE
Do	I / you / we / they	work	in an office?
Does	he / she / it		

QUESTIONS WITH "DID"

Questions in the past simple without the verb "be" or an auxiliary verb start with "did" and have the main verb in its base form. The subject and main verb do not swap places.

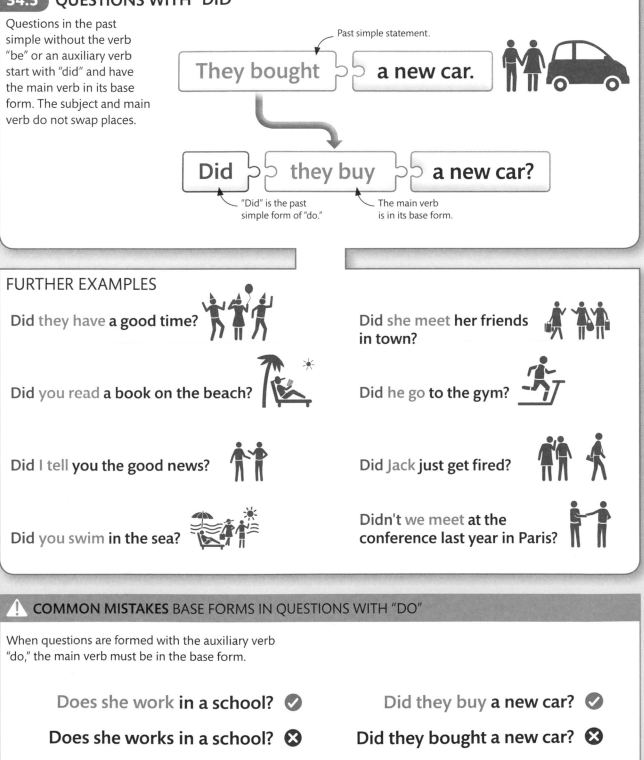

Past simple statement.

They bought ⌇ a new car.

Did ⌇ they buy ⌇ a new car?

"Did" is the past simple form of "do."

The main verb is in its base form.

FURTHER EXAMPLES

Did they have **a good time?**

Did you read **a book on the beach?**

Did I tell **you the good news?**

Did you swim **in the sea?**

Did she meet **her friends in town?**

Did he go **to the gym?**

Did Jack **just get fired?**

Didn't we meet **at the conference last year in Paris?**

⚠ **COMMON MISTAKES** BASE FORMS IN QUESTIONS WITH "DO"

When questions are formed with the auxiliary verb "do," the main verb must be in the base form.

Does she work **in a school?** ✓

Does she works **in a school?** ✗

Did they buy **a new car?** ✓

Did they bought **a new car?** ✗

35 Question words

Open questions are questions that do not have simple "yes" or "no" answers. In English, they are formed by using question words.

See also:
Forming questions **34**
Prepositions of time **107**

35.1 QUESTION WORDS

There are nine common question words in English.

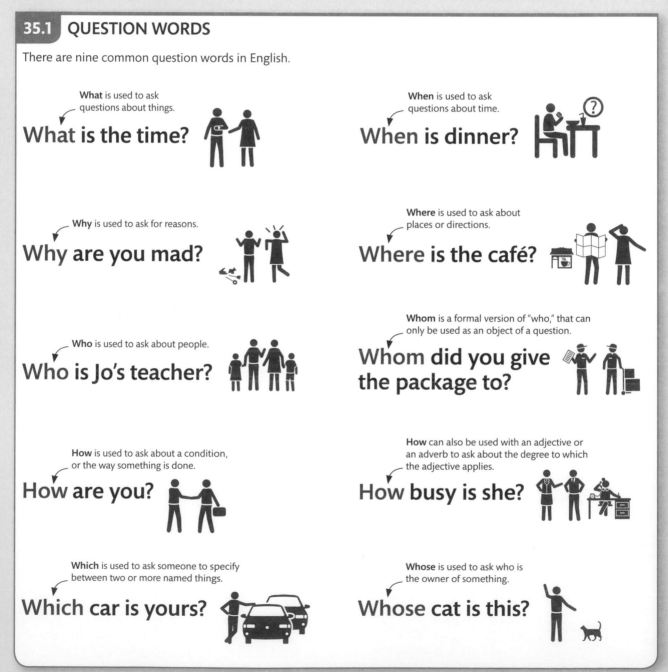

What is used to ask questions about things.

What is the time?

When is used to ask questions about time.

When is dinner?

Why is used to ask for reasons.

Why are you mad?

Where is used to ask about places or directions.

Where is the café?

Who is used to ask about people.

Who is Jo's teacher?

Whom is a formal version of "who," that can only be used as an object of a question.

Whom did you give the package to?

How is used to ask about a condition, or the way something is done.

How are you?

How can also be used with an adjective or an adverb to ask about the degree to which the adjective applies.

How busy is she?

Which is used to ask someone to specify between two or more named things.

Which car is yours?

Whose is used to ask who is the owner of something.

Whose cat is this?

35.2 "WHAT / WHICH"

"What" is used when the question is general. "Which" is used when there are two or more possibilities in the question.

There are no choices in the question.

What is the tallest building in the world?

The question includes a choice of possible answers.

Which building is taller, Big Ben or the Eiffel Tower?

FURTHER EXAMPLES

What is the highest mountain in the Alps?

What sort of food do you like?

Which mountain is higher, the Matterhorn or Mont Blanc?

Which do you prefer, the red skirt or the blue skirt?

35.3 "HOW OFTEN" AND "WHEN"

"How often" is used to ask about the frequency with which someone does an activity.
"When" is used to ask about the specific time that they do something.

"How often" asks about frequency.

How often do you go on vacation?

I usually go on vacation once a year.

"When" asks about the specific time something happens.

When do you go running?

I go on Thursday nights.

FURTHER EXAMPLES

How often do you go to the beach?

Not very often.

When do you go to the gym?

On Tuesdays and Fridays.

36 Open questions

Open questions can't be answered with "yes" or "no."
They are formed differently depending on the
main verb of the question.

See also:
Present simple **1**   Question words **35**
Types of verbs **49**

36.1 OPEN QUESTIONS WITH "BE"

If the main verb of the
sentence is "be," the
question word goes at
the beginning of the
question and the form of
"be" goes straight after it.

**My name is Sarah.
What is your name?**

"Be" comes after
the question word.

The question is "open"
because it can't be
answered "yes" or "no."

FURTHER EXAMPLES

What is Ruby's job?

Where were you last night?

What is this thing?

How was the concert?

Why are we all here?

Why aren't you at school?

HOW TO FORM

QUESTION WORD	"BE"	REST OF SENTENCE
What	**is** / **was**	**your name?**

36.2 OPEN QUESTIONS WITH OTHER VERBS

For all questions except those formed with "be," the question word is followed by an auxiliary verb. If there is already an auxiliary verb in the sentence, it is also used in the question. If there is no auxiliary verb, a form of "do" is added.

This auxiliary verb is already in the sentence, so it stays in the question.

Who should I call?

Auxiliary "do" follows the question word.

When do you eat lunch?

The question word goes at the beginning.

The main verb changes to its base form.

HOW TO FORM

QUESTION WORD	AUXILIARY VERB	SUBJECT	MAIN VERB
When	do / did / should	you	eat lunch?

FURTHER EXAMPLES

Where do **you go swimming?**

What does **she do on the weekend?**

Which **car** do **you drive to work?**

When does **he finish work?**

Why did **you stay up so late?**

Where could **he have gone?**

How did **this happen?**

Who can **speak English here?**

What should **I do now?**

When did **you get a cat?**

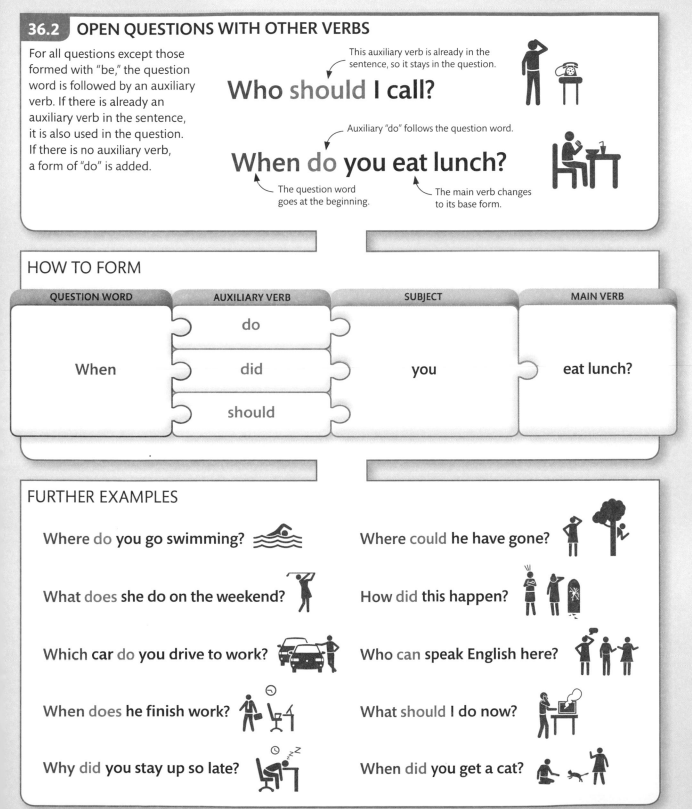

37 Object and subject questions

There are two kinds of question: object questions and subject questions. They are formed in different ways and are used to ask about different things.

See also:
Present simple **1** Types of verbs **49**
Verbs with objects **53**

37.1 OBJECT QUESTIONS

Use object questions to ask who received an action, not who did the action. They are called object questions because the question word is the object of the main verb.

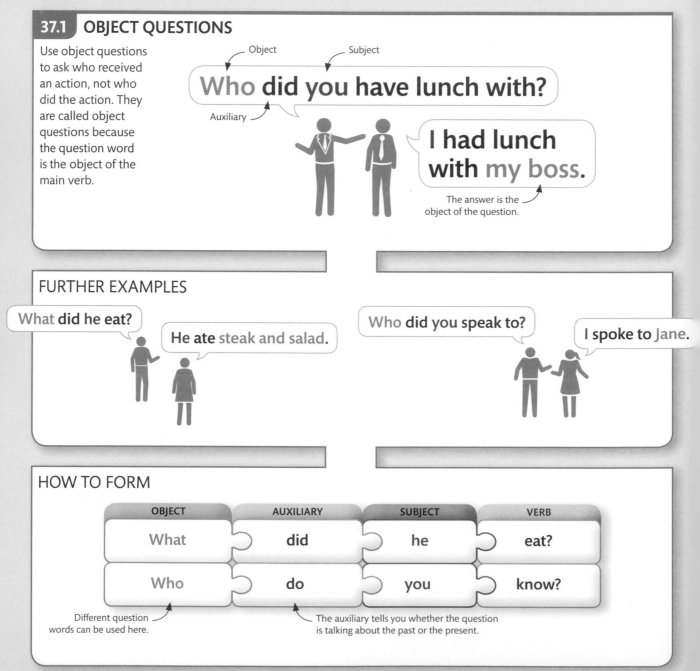

Object

Subject

Who **did you have lunch with?**

Auxiliary

I had lunch with **my boss.**

The answer is the object of the question.

FURTHER EXAMPLES

What **did he eat?**

He ate **steak and salad.**

Who **did you speak to?**

I spoke to **Jane.**

HOW TO FORM

OBJECT	AUXILIARY	SUBJECT	VERB
What	did	he	eat?
Who	do	you	know?

Different question words can be used here.

The auxiliary tells you whether the question is talking about the past or the present.

37.2 SUBJECT QUESTIONS

Subject questions are used to ask who did an action. They are called subject questions because the question word is the subject of the main verb. They do not use the auxiliary verb "do."

Question doesn't use "did."

Who called the bank**?**

Ben called the bank**.**

The answer is the subject of the question.

FURTHER EXAMPLES

Who paid the staff**?**

The boss paid the staff**.**

What broke the window**?**

The ball broke the window**.**

HOW TO FORM

"Who" and "what" are the most common pronouns used in subject questions.

SUBJECT	VERB	OBJECT
Who	**called**	**the bank?**

⚠ COMMON MISTAKES OBJECT AND SUBJECT QUESTIONS

Object questions must use a form of the auxiliary "do."

"Did" is the auxiliary verb in this object question.

What did you see? ✓

What saw you? ✗

Do not use inversion to form object questions.

Subject questions do not use an auxiliary verb and the word order stays the same as in a normal statement.

The word order stays the same as a normal statement.

Who called the bank? ✓

Who did call the bank? ✗

"Do" is only used as an auxiliary verb when forming object questions.

103

38 Indirect questions

Indirect questions are more polite than direct questions. They are very common in formal spoken English, particularly when asking for information.

See also:
Present simple **1**   Forming questions **34**
Types of verbs **49**

38.1 INDIRECT OPEN QUESTIONS

Indirect questions often start with a polite opening phrase. After the question word, the word order in indirect questions is the same as in positive statements.

Where is the station?

Do you know
Could you tell me
} **where the station is?**

Indirect questions start with an opening phrase. ⟶

The verb comes after the subject. ⟶

FURTHER EXAMPLES

Do you know **how much** the tickets will cost?

Could you tell me **why you were late?**

Could you tell me **what time** the stores close?

Indirect questions leave out the auxiliary verb "do."

HOW TO FORM

OPENING PHRASE	QUESTION WORD	SUBJECT	VERB
Do you know	where	the station	is?
Could you tell me			

A polite opening phrase comes first.

INDIRECT CLOSED QUESTIONS

Indirect closed questions are formed using "if" or "whether." In this context, "if" and "whether" mean the same thing.

Is it raining outside?

Could you tell me { if / whether } it is raining outside?

Polite opening phrase

The subject comes before the verb.

FURTHER EXAMPLES

Do you know if **that restaurant is expensive?**

Could you tell me whether **the train is on time?**

HOW TO FORM

OPENING PHRASE	"IF / WHETHER"	SUBJECT	VERB	REST OF SENTENCE
Do you know	if	it	is	raining outside?

A polite opening phrase comes first.

⚠ COMMON MISTAKES WORD ORDER WITH INDIRECT QUESTIONS

When a question has an opening phrase, the word order in indirect questions is the same as in a statement. There is no inversion, and "do" is not added.

Could you tell me **where the station is?** ✓
Could you tell me where is the station? ✗

Could you tell me **when you close?** ✓
Could you tell me when do you close? ✗

39 Question tags

In spoken English, small questions are often added to the ends of sentences. These are called question tags, and they are most often used to invite someone to agree.

See also:
Present simple **1**   Past simple **7**
Types of verbs **49**   Modal verbs **56**

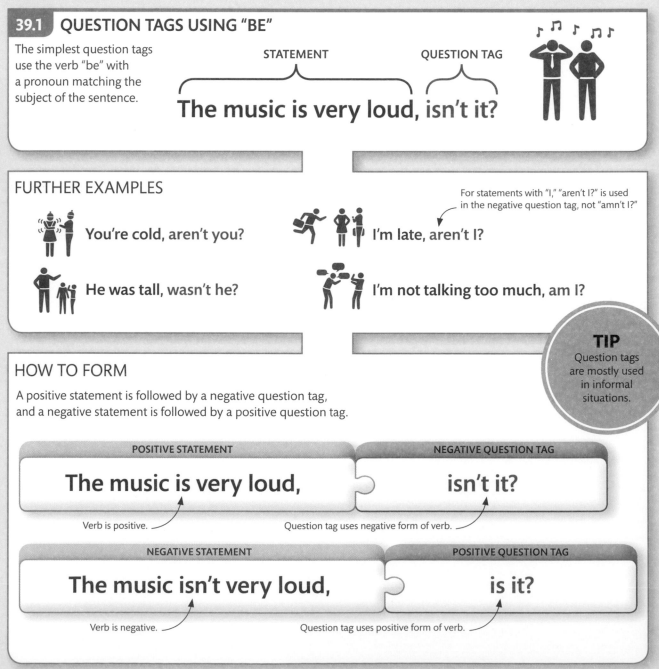

39.1 QUESTION TAGS USING "BE"

The simplest question tags use the verb "be" with a pronoun matching the subject of the sentence.

STATEMENT   QUESTION TAG

The music is very loud, isn't it?

FURTHER EXAMPLES

You're cold, aren't you?

He was tall, wasn't he?

For statements with "I," "aren't I?" is used in the negative question tag, not "amn't I?"

I'm late, aren't I?

I'm not talking too much, am I?

TIP
Question tags are mostly used in informal situations.

HOW TO FORM

A positive statement is followed by a negative question tag, and a negative statement is followed by a positive question tag.

POSITIVE STATEMENT	NEGATIVE QUESTION TAG
The music is very loud,	**isn't it?**

Verb is positive.   Question tag uses negative form of verb.

NEGATIVE STATEMENT	POSITIVE QUESTION TAG
The music isn't very loud,	**is it?**

Verb is negative.   Question tag uses positive form of verb.

39.2 QUESTION TAGS USING AUXILIARY VERBS

For most verbs other than "be," a present simple statement is followed by a question tag with "do" or "does."

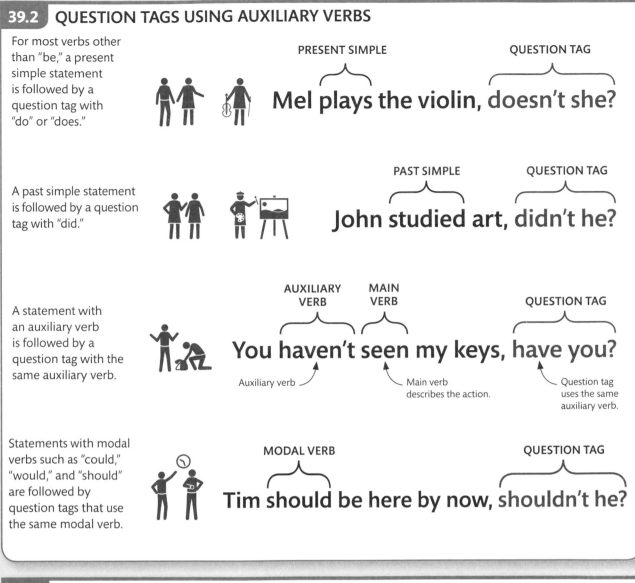

PRESENT SIMPLE   QUESTION TAG

Mel plays the violin, doesn't she?

A past simple statement is followed by a question tag with "did."

PAST SIMPLE   QUESTION TAG

John studied art, didn't he?

A statement with an auxiliary verb is followed by a question tag with the same auxiliary verb.

AUXILIARY VERB   MAIN VERB   QUESTION TAG

You haven't seen my keys, have you?

Auxiliary verb

Main verb describes the action.

Question tag uses the same auxiliary verb.

Statements with modal verbs such as "could," "would," and "should" are followed by question tags that use the same modal verb.

MODAL VERB   QUESTION TAG

Tim should be here by now, shouldn't he?

39.3 INTONATION WITH QUESTION TAGS

If the intonation goes up at the end of the question tag, it is a question requiring an answer.

You'd like to move offices, wouldn't you?

[I am asking whether or not you would like to move offices.]

If the intonation goes down at the end of a question tag, the speaker is just inviting the listener to agree.

You've already met Evelyn, haven't you?

[I already know you've met Evelyn.]

40 Short questions

Short questions are a way of showing interest during conversation. They're used to keep conversation going, rather than to ask for new information.

> **See also:**
> Present simple **1**   Forming questions **34**
> Types of verbs **49**

40.1 SHORT QUESTIONS

Short questions must be in the same tense as the statement they're responding to.
If the statement is positive, the short question should be positive and vice versa.
The subject from the statement is replaced with the relevant pronoun.

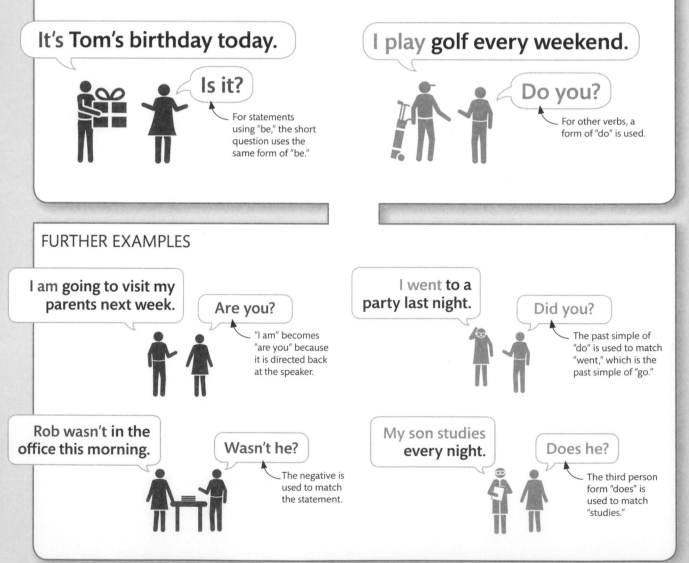

It's Tom's birthday today.

Is it?

For statements using "be," the short question uses the same form of "be."

I play golf every weekend.

Do you?

For other verbs, a form of "do" is used.

FURTHER EXAMPLES

I am going to visit my parents next week.

Are you?

"I am" becomes "are you" because it is directed back at the speaker.

I went to a party last night.

Did you?

The past simple of "do" is used to match "went," which is the past simple of "go."

Rob wasn't in the office this morning.

Wasn't he?

The negative is used to match the statement.

My son studies every night.

Does he?

The third person form "does" is used to match "studies."

40.2 SHORT QUESTIONS WITH AUXILIARY VERBS

If a statement contains an auxiliary verb, including modal verbs, that auxiliary verb is repeated in the short question.

I have **just come back from Hawaii.**

Have you?

Here, "have" is an auxiliary verb forming the present perfect.

FURTHER EXAMPLES

I couldn't **wait to come to work today.**

Couldn't you?

I've **been working since 7am.**

Have you?

The train should **be here by now.**

Should it?

I can't **find my car keys.**

Can't you?

40.3 SHORT QUESTIONS IN US ENGLISH

In US English, short questions are sometimes not inverted.

Roger is **starting a new job tomorrow.**

He is?

The subject and verb are not inverted, but this is said with a rising intonation.

My team didn't win **the game last night.**

They didn't?

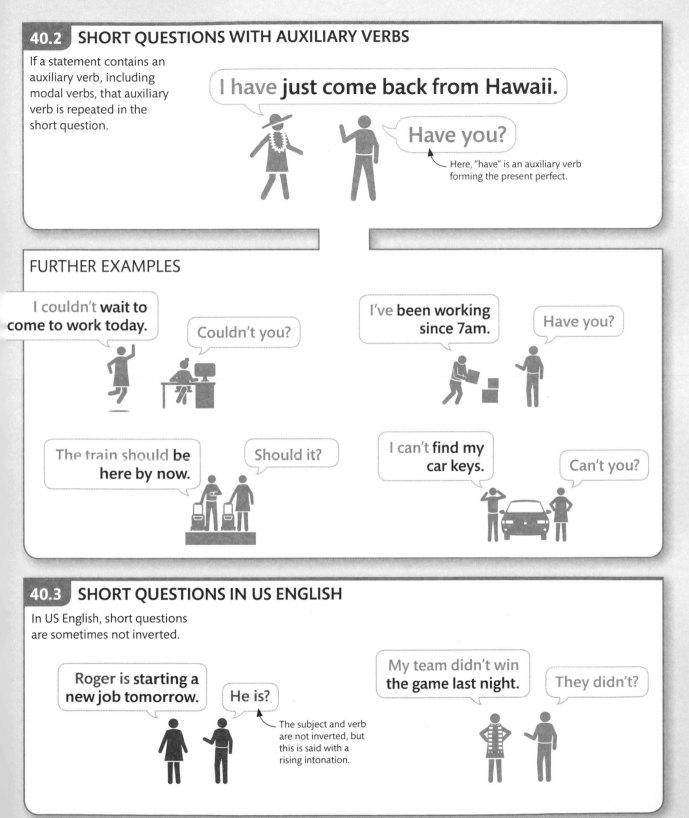

41 Short answers

When answering closed questions in English, some words can often be left out to make responses shorter. These short answers are often used in spoken English.

See also:
Present simple **1**   Types of verbs **49**
Modal verbs **56**   "There" **85**

41.1 SHORT ANSWERS

When the question uses the verb "be," "be" is used in the same tense in the short answer. When the question uses the auxilary verb "do," "do" is used in the same tense in the short answer.

Question uses "be."

Are you a doctor?

Yes, I am.

No, I'm not.

"A doctor" doesn't need to be repeated in the answer.

Question uses "do."

Do you **like coffee?**

Yes, I do.

No, I don't.

"Like coffee" doesn't need to be repeated in the answer.

FURTHER EXAMPLES

Is your name **Sophie?**   Yes, it is.

Are you **having fun?**   Yes, I am.

Was the train on time?   No, it wasn't.

Does he **live here?**   Yes, he does.

Do you **like cake?**   Yes, I do.

Did you **enjoy the play?**   No, I didn't.

41.2 SHORT ANSWERS WITH AUXILIARY VERBS

When the question uses an auxiliary verb, including modal verbs, the same auxiliary verb is used in the short answer.

Can you **ride a bicycle?**

Yes, I can.

No, I can't.

FURTHER EXAMPLES

Would you **like to play chess?**

Yes, I would.

Have they **bought a new car?**

No, they haven't.

Should I **sell my house?**

Yes, you should.

Will he **be at the party later?**

No, he won't.

⚠ COMMON MISTAKES SHORT ANSWERS WITH AUXILIARY VERBS

If a question uses an auxiliary verb, including modal verbs, it must be used in the short answer. The main verb should not be used at all.

Can you **ride a bicycle?**

Yes, I can. ✓

Yes, I ride. ✗

41.3 SHORT ANSWERS WITH "THERE"

When the question uses "there," it is also used in the answer.

Is there **a hotel in the town?**

Yes, there is.

No, there isn't.

Short for: "No, there isn't a hotel in the town."

Are there **hotels in the town?**

Yes, there are.

No, there aren't.

42 Questions overview

42.1 FORMING QUESTIONS

Questions in English are formed either by swapping the positions of the subject and the verb, or by using the auxiliary verb "do."

Tania is a pharmacist.

Is Tania a pharmacist?

The subject and "be" swap places.

42.2 SUBJECT AND OBJECT QUESTIONS

Questions in English are formed differently depending on whether they are asking who or what did an action or who or what received an action.

STATEMENT

Subject   Object

Ben called the bank.

Subject questions ask who did an action. The question word is the subject of the main verb. They do not use the auxiliary verb "do."

SUBJECT QUESTION

Question doesn't use "did."

Who called the bank?

Ben.

Object questions ask who received an action. The question word is the object of the question. They usually use the auxiliary verb "do."

OBJECT QUESTION

Question uses "did."

Who did Ben call?

The bank.

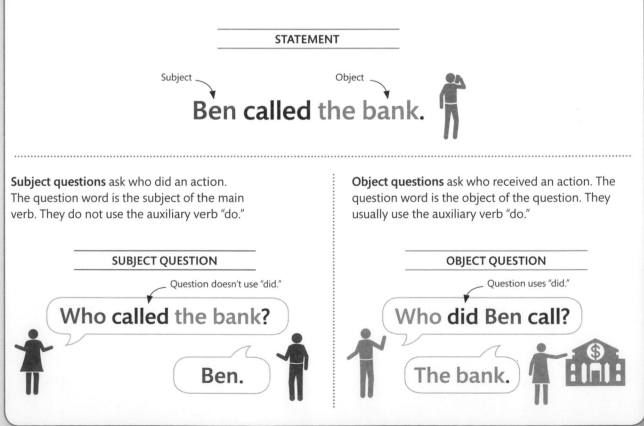

Questions in English are formed in different ways depending on the main verb. Open and closed questions are formed differently, and spoken with different intonation.

See also:
Forming questions **34** Question words **35**
Question tags **39** Short questions **40**

Joe has been to Paris.

Has Joe been to Paris?

The subject and the auxiliary verb swap places.

Tom likes pizza.

Does Tom like pizza?

A form of "do" goes before the subject. The main verb goes in its base form.

42.3 QUESTION TAGS AND SHORT QUESTIONS

Question tags are added to the end of a question, usually to ask someone to agree with you. A positive statement is followed by a negative question tag, and vice versa.

Short questions are used to show that someone is listening to the speaker. They are positive for positive statements and negative for negative statements.

You like skiing, don't you?

Yes, I go skiing twice a year.

Do you?

42.4 CLOSED AND OPEN QUESTIONS

Closed questions can only be answered with "yes" or "no." When they are spoken, the voice often rises at the end of the question.

Does Stevie work in an office?

Open questions are formed by adding question words to the start of the question. They can be answered in many different ways. The tone of the speaker's voice usually falls at the end of open questions.

Where does Stevie work?

43 Reported speech

The words that people say are called direct speech.
Reported speech is often used to describe what
someone said at an earlier point in time.

See also:
Present simple **1**   Past simple **7**
Types of verbs **49**

43.1 REPORTED SPEECH

The main verb in reported
speech is usually "said."
The reported verb is
usually in a different tense
from the direct speech.

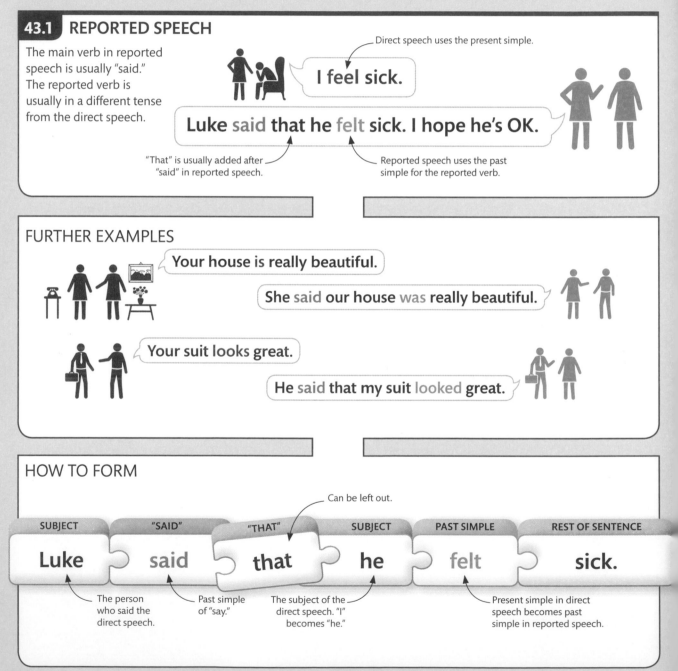

Direct speech uses the present simple.

I feel sick.

Luke said that he felt sick. I hope he's OK.

"That" is usually added after
"said" in reported speech.

Reported speech uses the past
simple for the reported verb.

FURTHER EXAMPLES

Your house is really beautiful.

She said our house was really beautiful.

Your suit looks great.

He said that my suit looked great.

HOW TO FORM

Can be left out.

SUBJECT	"SAID"	"THAT"	SUBJECT	PAST SIMPLE	REST OF SENTENCE
Luke	**said**	**that**	**he**	**felt**	**sick.**

The person
who said the
direct speech.

Past simple
of "say."

The subject of the
direct speech. "I"
becomes "he."

Present simple in direct
speech becomes past
simple in reported speech.

43.2 "TELL" IN REPORTED SPEECH

In reported speech, "tell" can also be used as the main verb. It must be followed by an object, which shows who someone is talking to.

I want to learn to drive.

"Say" does not need to be followed by an object.

He { said / told me } that he wanted to learn to drive.

"Tell" must be followed by an object.

FURTHER EXAMPLES

She told me that she was at the party.

She told me that she had a very stressful job.

He told us he arrived late to the meeting.

They told us they bought a new house.

"That" can also be left out in reported speech with "told."

I told her that I went abroad last year.

We told them that we didn't want it.

⚠ **COMMON MISTAKES** "SAY" AND "TELL" IN REPORTED SPEECH

He said that he had a fast car. ✓

"Told" must have an object.

He told me that he had a fast car. ✓

He said me that he had a fast car. ✗

He told that he had a fast car. ✗

"Said" cannot have an object.

44 Tenses in reported speech

In reported speech, the reported verb usually "goes back" a tense. Time and place references and pronouns sometimes also change.

See also:
Present continuous **4**   Past continuous **10**
Past perfect simple **13**   Modal verbs **56**

44.1 REPORTED SPEECH IN DIFFERENT TENSES

The tense used in reported speech is usually one tense back in time from the tense in direct speech.

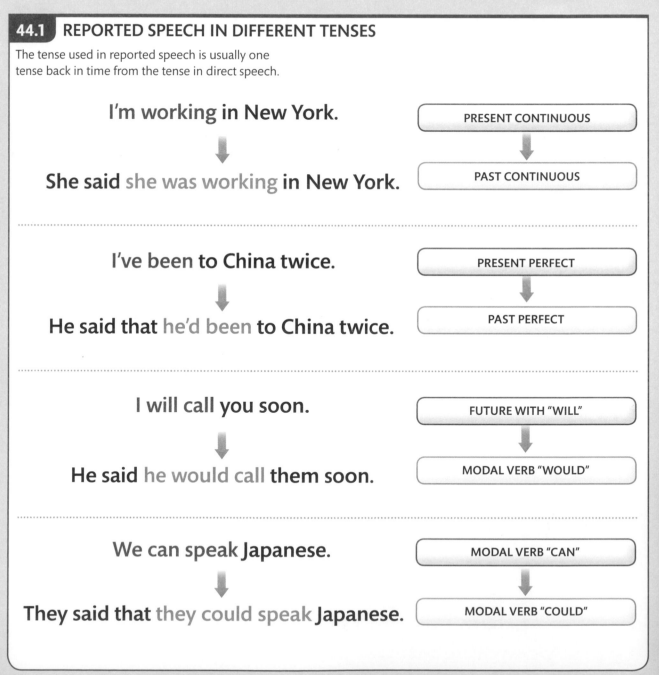

I'm working in New York.

PRESENT CONTINUOUS

She said she was working in New York.

PAST CONTINUOUS

I've been to China twice.

PRESENT PERFECT

He said that he'd been to China twice.

PAST PERFECT

I will call you soon.

FUTURE WITH "WILL"

He said he would call them soon.

MODAL VERB "WOULD"

We can speak Japanese.

MODAL VERB "CAN"

They said that they could speak Japanese.

MODAL VERB "COULD"

44.2 REPORTED SPEECH AND THE PAST SIMPLE

The past simple in direct speech can either stay as the past simple or change to the past perfect in reported speech. The meaning is the same.

I arrived in Delhi on Saturday.

DIRECT SPEECH WITH PAST SIMPLE

He said { he arrived / he'd arrived } **in Delhi on Saturday.**

REPORTED SPEECH WITH PAST SIMPLE OR PAST PERFECT

44.3 REPORTED SPEECH WITHOUT CHANGE OF TENSE

If the situation described is ongoing, the verb does not have to change tense in reported speech.

I like eating cake.

Amelia said that she likes eating cake.

Amelia still likes eating cake.

FURTHER EXAMPLES

Your hat looks great.

He said that my hat looks great.

I love your tie.

He said that he loves my tie.

44.4 TIME AND PLACE REFERENCES

If speech is reported some time after it was said, words used to talk about times and places may need to change.

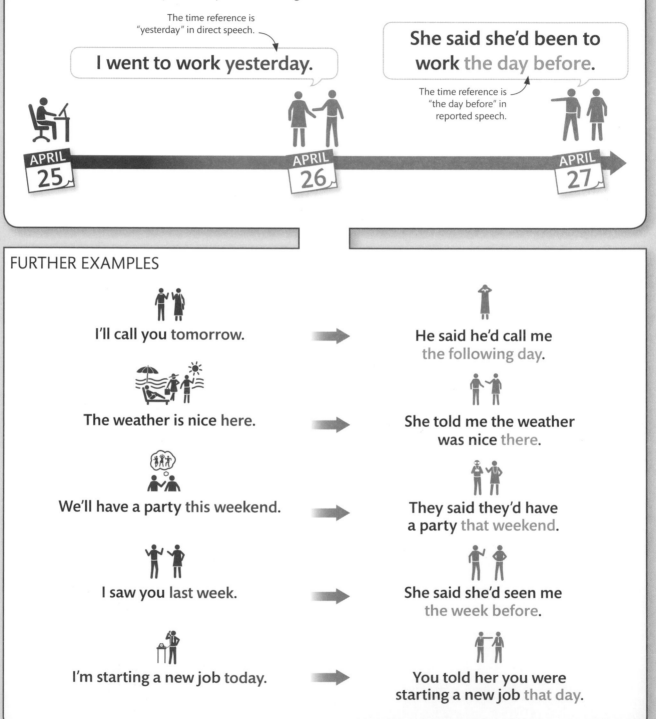

The time reference is "yesterday" in direct speech.

I went to work yesterday.

She said she'd been to work the day before.

The time reference is "the day before" in reported speech.

APRIL 25   APRIL 26   APRIL 27

FURTHER EXAMPLES

I'll call you tomorrow. ➡ He said he'd call me the following day.

The weather is nice here. ➡ She told me the weather was nice there.

We'll have a party this weekend. ➡ They said they'd have a party that weekend.

I saw you last week. ➡ She said she'd seen me the week before.

I'm starting a new job today. ➡ You told her you were starting a new job that day.

44.5 OTHER CHANGES IN REPORTED SPEECH

In reported speech, pronouns may also need to be
changed to ensure they refer to the correct person or thing.

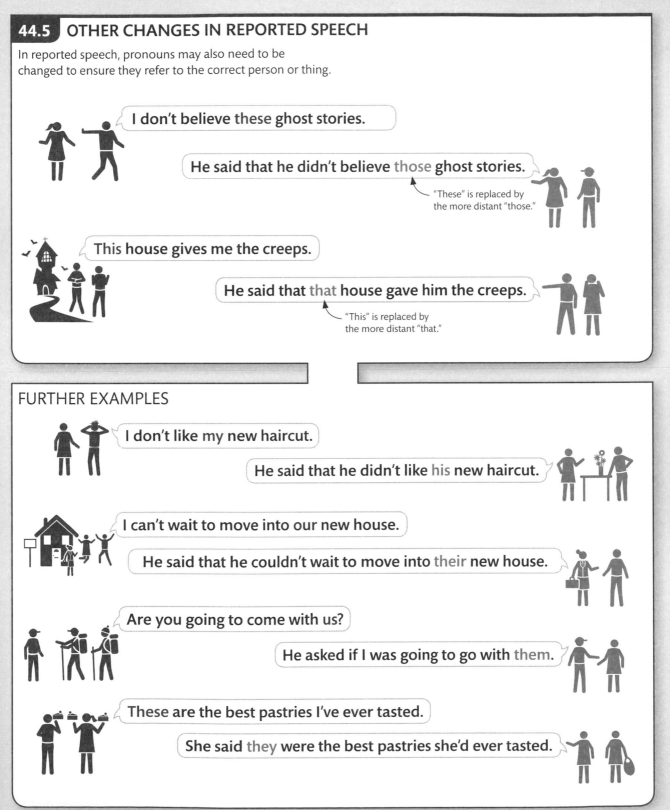

I don't believe these ghost stories.

He said that he didn't believe those ghost stories.

"These" is replaced by
the more distant "those."

This house gives me the creeps.

He said that that house gave him the creeps.

"This" is replaced by
the more distant "that."

FURTHER EXAMPLES

I don't like my new haircut.

He said that he didn't like his new haircut.

I can't wait to move into our new house.

He said that he couldn't wait to move into their new house.

Are you going to come with us?

He asked if I was going to go with them.

These are the best pastries I've ever tasted.

She said they were the best pastries she'd ever tasted.

45 Reporting verbs

In reported speech, "said" can be replaced with a wide variety of verbs that give people more information about how someone said something.

See also:
Present simple **1**   Past simple **7**
Types of verbs **49**

45.1 REPORTING VERBS WITH "THAT"

"Say" and "tell" do not give any information about the speaker's manner. They can be replaced with other verbs that suggest the speaker's mood or reason for speaking.

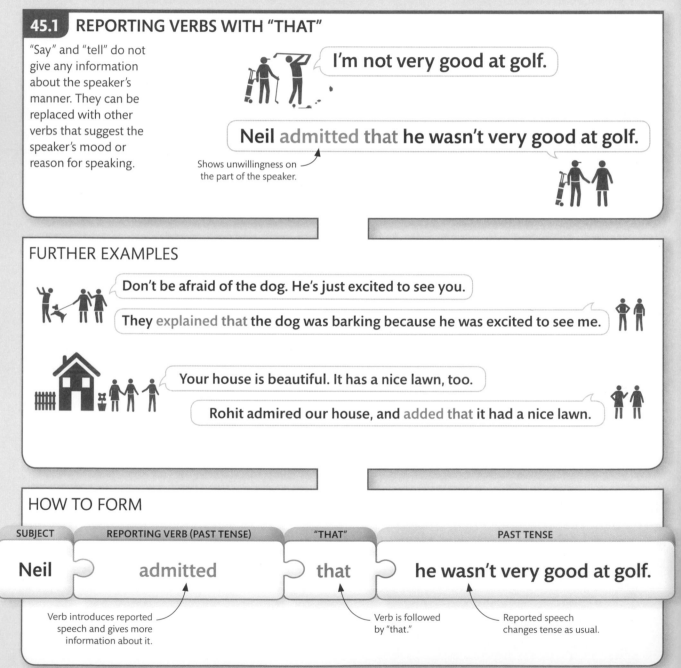

I'm not very good at golf.

Neil admitted that **he wasn't very good at golf.**

Shows unwillingness on the part of the speaker.

FURTHER EXAMPLES

Don't be afraid of the dog. He's just excited to see you.

They explained that **the dog was barking because he was excited to see me.**

Your house is beautiful. It has a nice lawn, too.

Rohit admired our house, and added that **it had a nice lawn.**

HOW TO FORM

SUBJECT	REPORTING VERB (PAST TENSE)	"THAT"	PAST TENSE
Neil	**admitted**	**that**	**he wasn't very good at golf.**

Verb introduces reported speech and gives more information about it.

Verb is followed by "that."

Reported speech changes tense as usual.

45.2 REPORTING VERBS WITH OBJECT AND INFINITIVE

Some reporting verbs are followed by an object and an infinitive. English often
uses these verbs to report orders, advice, and instructions.

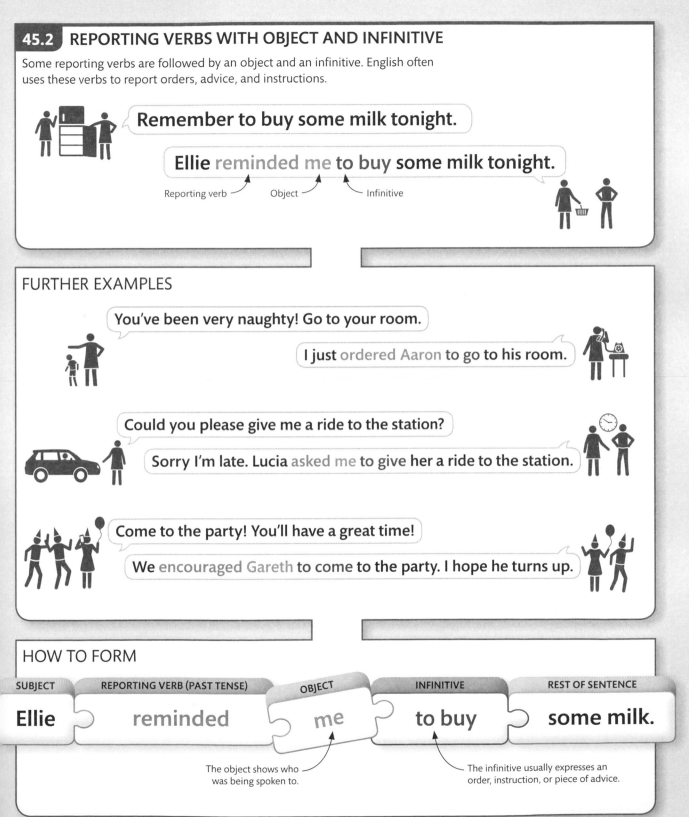

Remember to buy some milk tonight.

Ellie reminded me **to buy some milk tonight.**

Reporting verb   Object   Infinitive

FURTHER EXAMPLES

You've been very naughty! Go to your room.

I just ordered Aaron to go to his room.

Could you please give me a ride to the station?

Sorry I'm late. Lucia asked me to give her a ride to the station.

Come to the party! You'll have a great time!

We encouraged Gareth to come to the party. I hope he turns up.

HOW TO FORM

SUBJECT	REPORTING VERB (PAST TENSE)	OBJECT	INFINITIVE	REST OF SENTENCE
Ellie	reminded	me	to buy	some milk.

The object shows who
was being spoken to.

The infinitive usually expresses an
order, instruction, or piece of advice.

46 Reported speech with negatives

Negatives in reported speech are formed in the same way as negatives in direct speech. "Not" is used with the auxiliary, or with the main verb if there is no auxiliary.

See also:
Present simple negative **2**
Past simple negative **8**   Types of verbs **49**

46.1   REPORTING NEGATIVE AUXILIARIES

When the direct speech is negative using "do not," "is not," and "has not," "do," "is," or "has" changes tense, rather than the main verb.

I don't work on weekends.

Present simple negative.

He said he didn't work on weekends.

Past simple negative.

FURTHER EXAMPLES

I don't want to drive. I'd rather walk.

Sue said she didn't want to drive. She'd rather walk.

The car isn't starting.

They told me the car wasn't starting.

They haven't arrived on time because of the car.

Fay said they hadn't arrived on time because of the car.

46.2 REPORTING OTHER VERBS WITH NEGATIVES

If a reporting verb is followed by an object and an infinitive, "not" goes between the object and the infinitive to form the negative.

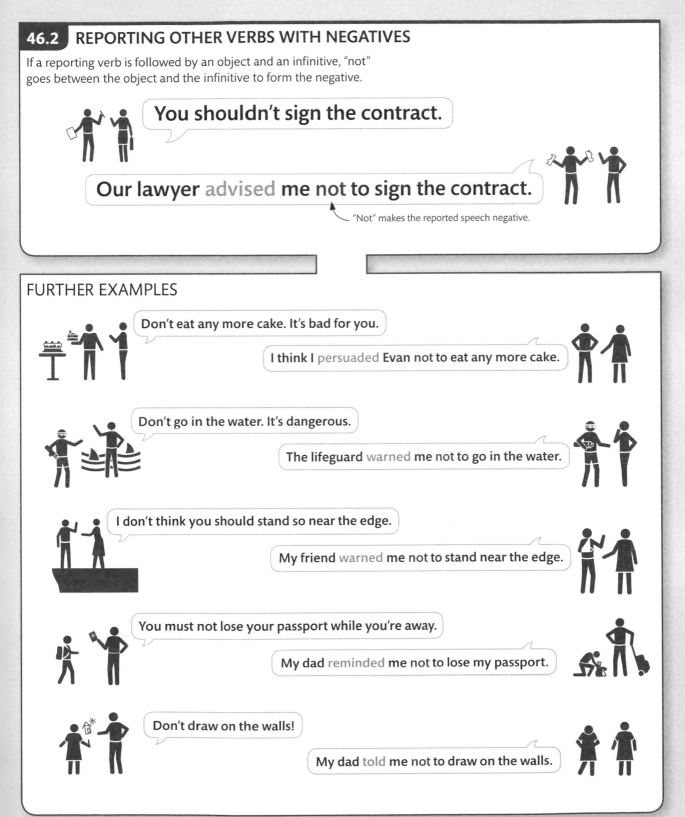

You shouldn't sign the contract.

Our lawyer advised me not to sign the contract.

"Not" makes the reported speech negative.

FURTHER EXAMPLES

Don't eat any more cake. It's bad for you.

I think I persuaded Evan not to eat any more cake.

Don't go in the water. It's dangerous.

The lifeguard warned me not to go in the water.

I don't think you should stand so near the edge.

My friend warned me not to stand near the edge.

You must not lose your passport while you're away.

My dad reminded me not to lose my passport.

Don't draw on the walls!

My dad told me not to draw on the walls.

47 Reported questions

Reported questions are used to describe questions that someone has asked. Direct questions and reported questions use different word orders.

See also:
Forming questions **34**
Open questions **36**   Types of verbs **49**

47.1 REPORTED OPEN QUESTIONS

Direct open questions are reported by swapping the order of the subject and the verb.

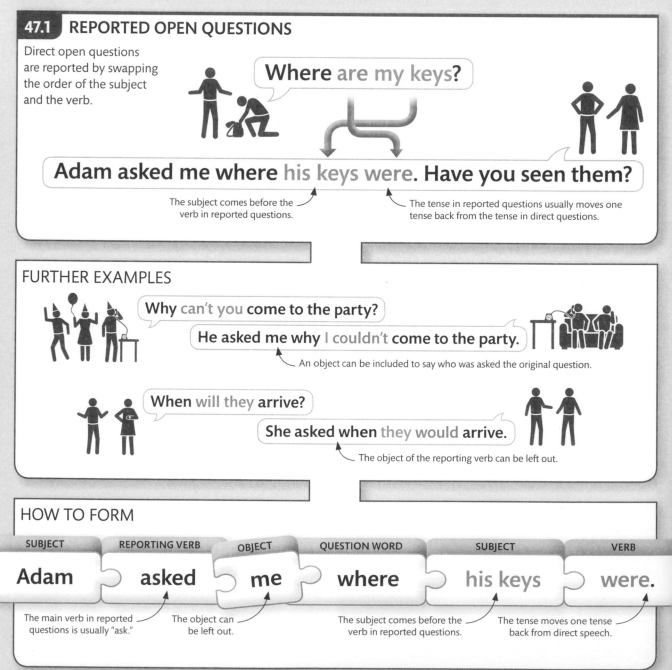

Where are my keys?

Adam asked me where his keys were. Have you seen them?

The subject comes before the verb in reported questions.

The tense in reported questions usually moves one tense back from the tense in direct questions.

FURTHER EXAMPLES

Why can't you come to the party?

He asked me why I couldn't come to the party.

An object can be included to say who was asked the original question.

When will they arrive?

She asked when they would arrive.

The object of the reporting verb can be left out.

HOW TO FORM

SUBJECT	REPORTING VERB	OBJECT	QUESTION WORD	SUBJECT	VERB
Adam	**asked**	**me**	**where**	**his keys**	**were.**

The main verb in reported questions is usually "ask."

The object can be left out.

The subject comes before the verb in reported questions.

The tense moves one tense back from direct speech.

47.2 REPORTING QUESTIONS WITH "DO"

When a direct question uses the verb "do," this is left out of reported questions.

Let's bake a cake. What **do we need**?

He asked me what **we needed**.

Reported questions leave out the auxiliary verb "do."

The past form of the verb is usually used.

FURTHER EXAMPLES

Why **do you want** to work for us?

They asked me why I **wanted** to work for them.

What **do you think**?

He asked me what I **thought**.

What **does a florist do**?

James asked me what a florist **does**.

The tense doesn't always change.

Where **do Jay and Seb live**?

Paul asked me where Jay and Seb **live**.

Who **do you know** at work?

She asked who I **knew** at work.

What **do you usually knit**?

He asked me what I usually **knit**.

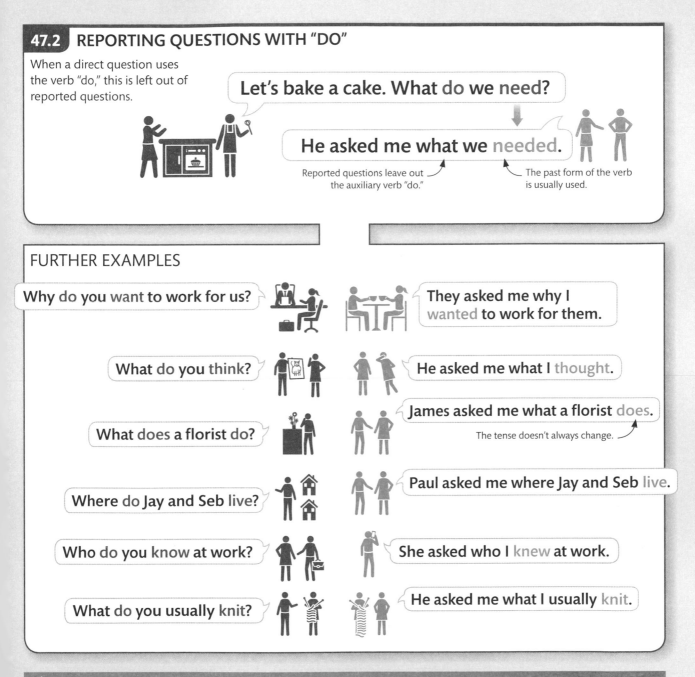

⚠ COMMON MISTAKES WORD ORDER IN REPORTED QUESTIONS

It is incorrect to swap the verb and subject in reported questions.

He asked me where **the station is**. ✔

He asked me where **is the station**. ✘

REPORTED CLOSED QUESTIONS

If the answer to a question in direct speech is "yes" or "no," "if" or "whether" is used to report the question. "Whether" is more formal than "if."

Direct question.

Are you meeting your sales targets?

My boss asked me if I was meeting my sales targets.

Reported question uses "if" or "whether."

FURTHER EXAMPLES

Will you be at the meeting on Monday?

Kara asked whether I would be at the meeting on Monday.

In reported questions with "if" and "whether," the object after "asked" can be left out.

Do you want to stay for dinner?

Ian asked me if we wanted to stay for dinner.

Reported questions with "if" and "whether" leave out the auxiliary verb "do."

HOW TO FORM

SUBJECT	"ASKED"	OBJECT	"IF / WHETHER"	SUBJECT	VERB	REST OF SENTENCE
My boss	asked	me	if / whether	I	was	meeting my sales targets.

The object can be left out.

"If" and "whether" mean the same thing, but "whether" is more formal.

REPORTING QUESTIONS WITH "OR"

"If" or "whether" can also be used to report
questions that use "or" in direct speech.

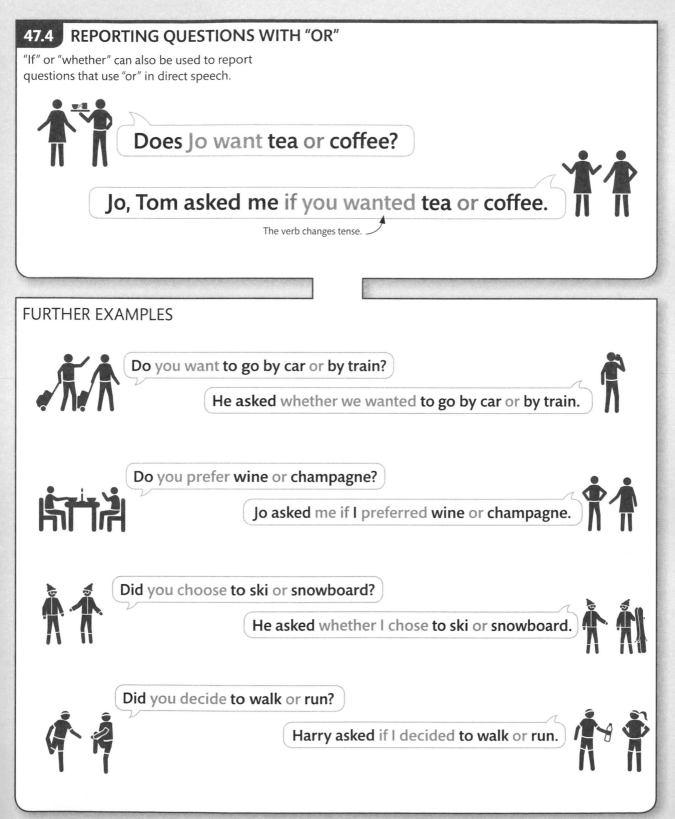

Does Jo want **tea** or **coffee?**

Jo, **Tom asked me** if you wanted **tea** or **coffee.**

The verb changes tense.

FURTHER EXAMPLES

Do you want **to go by car** or **by train?**

He asked whether we wanted **to go by car** or **by train.**

Do you prefer **wine** or **champagne?**

Jo asked me if I preferred **wine** or **champagne.**

Did you choose **to ski** or **snowboard?**

He asked whether I chose **to ski** or **snowboard.**

Did you decide **to walk** or **run?**

Harry asked if I decided **to walk** or **run.**

48 Reported speech overview

48.1 CHANGING REFERENCES IN REPORTED SPEECH

Certain words have variable reference, which means their meaning is context-dependent. In order to retain the meaning of the direct speech, reported speech usually revises tenses, pronouns, and time references.

TENSE

I **want** to become a police officer.

The tense usually moves back.

She said she **wanted** to become a police officer.

48.2 REPORTING VERBS IN THE PRESENT TENSE

The reporting verb can be in the present tense.
In this case, the tense of the sentence doesn't change.

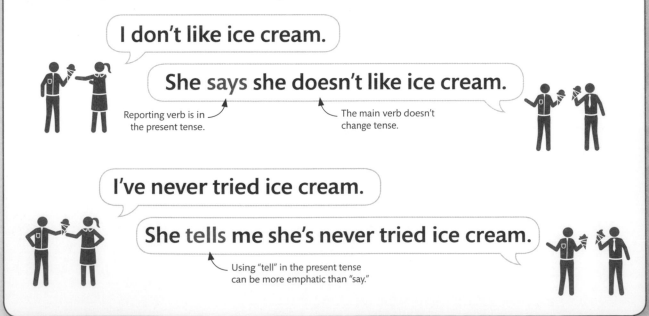

I don't like ice cream.

She **says** she **doesn't like** ice cream.

Reporting verb is in the present tense.

The main verb doesn't change tense.

I've never tried ice cream.

She **tells** me she's never tried ice cream.

Using "tell" in the present tense can be more emphatic than "say."

When forming reported speech from direct speech, some words change in order to keep the meaning consistent. Other words stay the same.

See also:
Present simple **1**   Past simple **7**   Tenses in reported speech **44**   Modal verbs **56**   Personal pronouns **77**

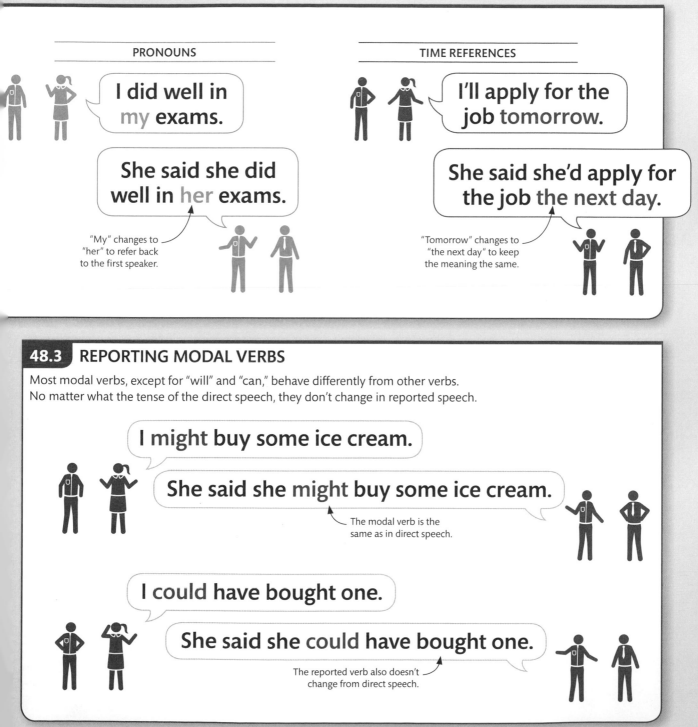

PRONOUNS

I did well in my exams.

She said she did well in her exams.

"My" changes to "her" to refer back to the first speaker.

TIME REFERENCES

I'll apply for the job tomorrow.

She said she'd apply for the job the next day.

"Tomorrow" changes to "the next day" to keep the meaning the same.

48.3 REPORTING MODAL VERBS

Most modal verbs, except for "will" and "can," behave differently from other verbs. No matter what the tense of the direct speech, they don't change in reported speech.

I might buy some ice cream.

She said she might buy some ice cream.

The modal verb is the same as in direct speech.

I could have bought one.

She said she could have bought one.

The reported verb also doesn't change from direct speech.

49 Types of verbs

Verbs can be described as main verbs or auxiliary verbs.
Main verbs describe actions, occurrences, or states of being.
Auxiliary verbs modify the meaning of main verbs.

> **See also:**
> Present perfect simple **11**
> Modal verbs **56**

49.1 MAIN VERBS

Main verbs are the most important verbs in a sentence. They can describe actions or states, or they can be used to link a subject to a description.

"Play" is the main verb that describes an action.

I play tennis every Wednesday evening.

49.2 AUXILIARY VERBS

Auxiliary verbs are used with main verbs to modify their meaning. Auxiliary verbs are used very frequently to form different tenses.

PRESENT PERFECT

SUBJECT	AUXILIARY VERB	PARTICIPLE	OBJECT
Paul	has	bought	a new shirt.

"Has" is an auxiliary verb here. It's being used to form the present perfect.

The auxiliary verb "do" is used to make questions and negatives of statements that don't already have an auxiliary verb.

SUBJECT	AUXILIARY VERB	MAIN VERB	OBJECT
Cian	didn't	pass	his exam.

AUXILIARY VERB	SUBJECT	MAIN VERB	OBJECT
Did	Cian	pass	his exam?

Modal verbs are also auxiliary verbs. They modify the meaning of the main verb, expressing various notions such as possibility or obligation.

SUBJECT	MODAL VERB	MAIN VERB	OBJECT
Jake	might	sell	his car.

49.3 LINKING VERBS

Linking verbs express a state of being or becoming. They link a subject to a complement, which renames or describes the subject.

The children are happy.

Subject

Complement

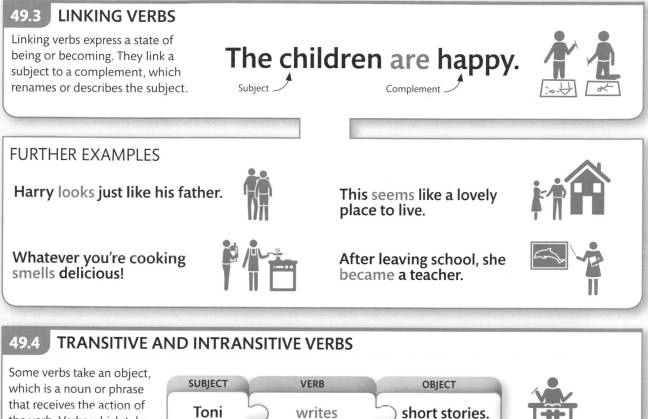

FURTHER EXAMPLES

Harry looks **just like his father.**

This seems **like a lovely place to live.**

Whatever you're cooking smells **delicious!**

After leaving school, she became **a teacher.**

49.4 TRANSITIVE AND INTRANSITIVE VERBS

Some verbs take an object, which is a noun or phrase that receives the action of the verb. Verbs which take an object are known as **transitive verbs**.

SUBJECT	VERB	OBJECT
Toni	writes	short stories.

Some verbs never take an object. These verbs are known as **intransitive verbs**.

SUBJECT	VERB
The bus	arrived.

Some verbs can be either **transitive or intransitive**.

"Read" can be used with or without an object.

SUBJECT	VERB	OBJECT
Jake	was reading	a book.

Some verbs can take **two objects**, a direct object and an indirect object.

SUBJECT	VERB	INDIRECT OBJECT	DIRECT OBJECT
Ronda	gave	her cat	some food.

The indirect object benefits from the action.

The direct object is what the verb "gave" refers to.

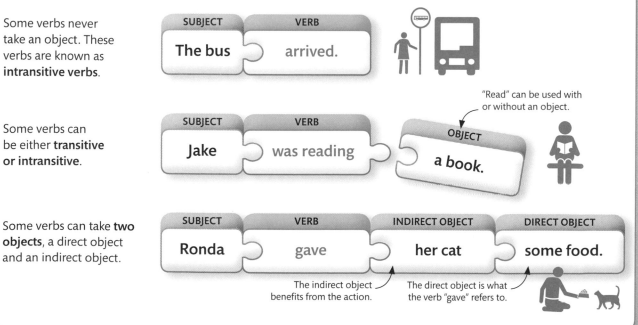

50 Action and state verbs

Verbs that describe actions or events are known as "action" or "dynamic" verbs, whereas those that describe states are known as "state" or "stative" verbs.

See also:
Present simple **1**   Present continuous **4**
Past simple **7**   Past continuous **10**

50.1 ACTION AND STATE VERBS

Action verbs usually describe what people or things do.
State verbs usually say how things are or how someone feels.

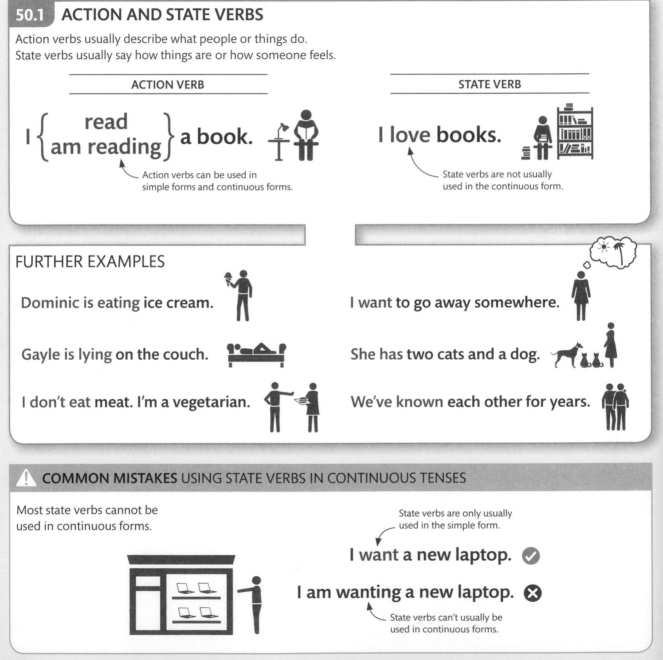

ACTION VERB

I {read, am reading} a book.

Action verbs can be used in simple forms and continuous forms.

STATE VERB

I love books.

State verbs are not usually used in the continuous form.

FURTHER EXAMPLES

Dominic is eating **ice cream.**

Gayle is lying **on the couch.**

I don't eat **meat. I'm a vegetarian.**

I want **to go away somewhere.**

She has **two cats and a dog.**

We've known **each other for years.**

⚠ COMMON MISTAKES USING STATE VERBS IN CONTINUOUS TENSES

Most state verbs cannot be used in continuous forms.

State verbs are only usually used in the simple form.

I want **a new laptop.** ✓

I am wanting **a new laptop.** ✗

State verbs can't usually be used in continuous forms.

USING STATE VERBS IN CONTINUOUS FORMS

Some verbs can be both action and state verbs. When these verbs are describing an action, they can be used in continuous forms.

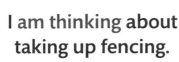

ACTION	STATE

 I am thinking about taking up fencing.
[Right now, I'm considering taking up fencing.]

 I think fencing is a great sport.
[In my opinion, fencing is a great sport.]

 **The chef was tasting his soup.**
[The chef is testing the soup's flavor.]

 This soup tasted disgusting!
[The soup has a disgusting flavor.]

 I'm seeing some friends for lunch tomorrow.
[I'm meeting some friends tomorrow.]

 I saw some birds at the park yesterday.
[There were some birds at the park.]

A few state verbs can be used in continuous forms, keeping their stative meaning.
The use of a continuous form emphasizes a change, development, or temporary situation.

CONTINUOUS FORM	SIMPLE FORM

 Are you feeling better today? You seemed sick yesterday.

 How do you feel about modern art?

We're sounding much better than usual!

 I wish they'd stop. They sound terrible!

 My leg is really hurting this morning.

My leg hurts. Maybe I should go to the doctor.

51 Infinitives and participles

Infinitives and participles are forms of verbs that are rarely used on their own, but are important when making other forms or constructions.

> **See also:**
> Present continuous **4**
> Present perfect simple **11**

51.1 INFINITIVES

The infinitive is the simplest form of the verb. English verbs have two types of infinitive.

Sometimes the infinitive is formed with "to" plus the verb. This is sometimes known as a "full" or "to" infinitive.

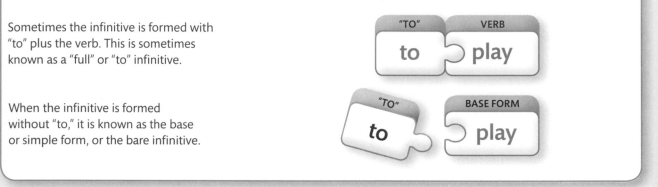

When the infinitive is formed without "to," it is known as the base or simple form, or the bare infinitive.

51.2 PRESENT PARTICIPLES AND GERUNDS

Present participles and gerunds are formed by adding "-ing" to the base form of the verb. They are spelled the same, but they perform different functions in a sentence.

Present participles are most commonly used with auxiliary verbs to form continuous tenses.

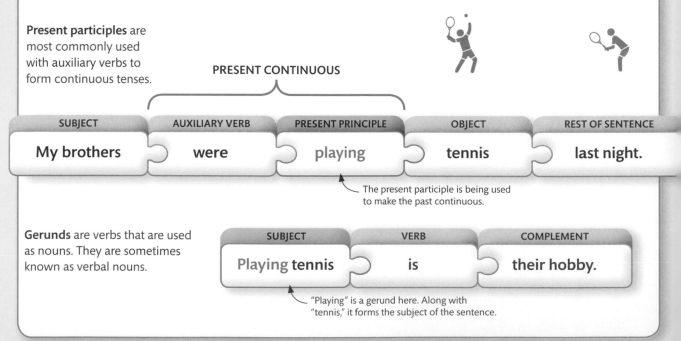

| SUBJECT | AUXILIARY VERB | PRESENT PRINCIPLE | OBJECT | REST OF SENTENCE |
| My brothers | were | playing | tennis | last night. |

The present participle is being used to make the past continuous.

Gerunds are verbs that are used as nouns. They are sometimes known as verbal nouns.

| SUBJECT | VERB | COMPLEMENT |
| Playing tennis | is | their hobby. |

"Playing" is a gerund here. Along with "tennis," it forms the subject of the sentence.

51.3 PRESENT PARTICIPLE AND GERUND SPELLING RULES

All present participles and gerunds are formed by adding "-ing" to the base form of the verb. The spelling of some base forms changes slightly before adding "-ing."

Main verb.

wear

"-ing" is added to form regular present participles.

wearing

Last letter is a silent "-e."

choose

The "-e" is left out and "-ing" is added.

choosing

Last letters are "-ie."

tie

"-ie" changes to "y."

tying

Last letters are consonant–vowel–consonant and the final syllable is stressed.

forget

The last letter doubles, unless it's "w," "x," or "y."

forgetting

FURTHER EXAMPLES

The last letter is not doubled because "per" is not stressed.

They're whispering to each other.

The last letter of the verb doesn't double if it's "y."

I'm enjoying my vacation.

The last letter is doubled because the pattern is consonant–vowel–consonant.

She's swimming in the ocean.

The "-e" is dropped from the verb.

He's making a cake.

Connor went walking in the hills.

Paul was told off for lying.

Sarah loves riding her horse.

The audience started clapping.

Stop wasting so much paper!

She started looking for a new job.

The children were sitting on the floor.

I'm choosing the new intern.

51.4 PAST PARTICIPLES

Past participles are used with auxiliary verbs to form perfect simple tenses, such as the present perfect simple.

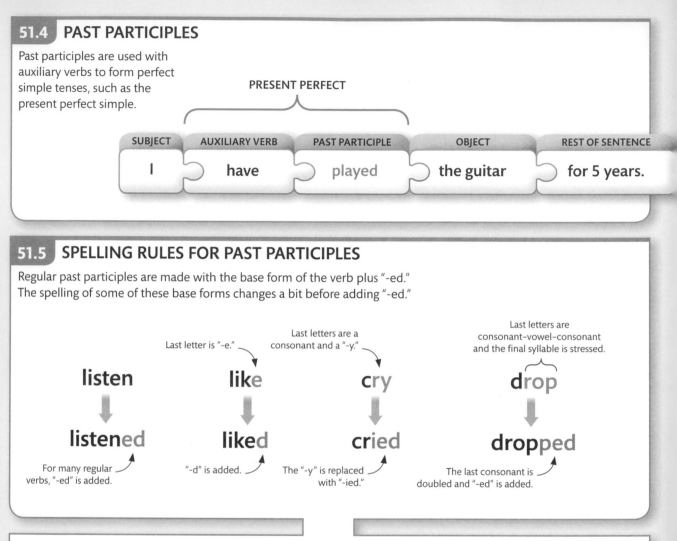

PRESENT PERFECT

SUBJECT	AUXILIARY VERB	PAST PARTICIPLE	OBJECT	REST OF SENTENCE
I	have	played	the guitar	for 5 years.

51.5 SPELLING RULES FOR PAST PARTICIPLES

Regular past participles are made with the base form of the verb plus "-ed."
The spelling of some of these base forms changes a bit before adding "-ed."

Last letter is "-e."

Last letters are a consonant and a "-y."

Last letters are consonant–vowel–consonant and the final syllable is stressed.

listen → **listened**
For many regular verbs, "-ed" is added.

like → **liked**
"-d" is added.

cry → **cried**
The "-y" is replaced with "-ied."

drop → **dropped**
The last consonant is doubled and "-ed" is added.

FURTHER EXAMPLES

I should have covered my work. Susanna has copied all my answers.

You haven't passed the exam this time, but at least you have improved.

I had planned to take the kids to the beach, but the weather's terrible.

By this time next week, I will have finished all of my assignments.

My boss has asked me to come in early again tomorrow. I'm so tired!

IRREGULAR PAST PARTICIPLES

Many verbs in English have irregular past participle forms. They often look quite different from their base form.

I buy new clothes every month.

⬇

I have just bought a new coat.

PAST PARTICIPLE

FURTHER EXAMPLES

BASE FORM	PAST PARTICIPLE	SAMPLE SENTENCE
be	been	You're late. Where have you been?
become	become	This has become a real problem.
begin	begun	The class has already begun, so be quiet.
choose	chosen	Which subjects have you chosen to study?
do	done	My son has done a lot for the local community.
feel	felt	I haven't felt very well for over a week now.
know	known	Sonia would have known how to solve this problem.
find	found	The police have found the suspect.
forget	forgotten	My husband has forgotten our anniversary again.
go	gone	Helen has gone to Peru. She'll be back next week.
have	had	You look so different! Have you had a haircut?
make	made	I have made a cake for your birthday.
say	said	Jerry has said he'll be making a presentation.
see	seen	After this evening, I'll have seen this show six times.
sing	sung	This will be the first time she's sung in public.
tell	told	Has anyone told you the news? Kate's pregnant!
understand	understood	Has everyone understood the instructions?
write	written	I sent the email as soon as I had written it.

52 Verb patterns

Some verbs in English can only go with a gerund or an infinitive. Some verbs can go with either. These verbs often describe wishes, plans, or feelings.

See also:
Types of verbs **49**
Infinitives and participles **51**

52.1 VERBS WITH INFINITIVES

English uses the infinitive with "to" after certain verbs that describe someone's plans or wishes to do an activity.

VERB   INFINITIVE

They arranged to play tennis.

Main verb describes a plan or wish to do an activity.

Infinitive with "to" describes the activity.

FURTHER EXAMPLES

The infinitive doesn't change no matter what the tense of the main verb is.

I'm waiting to play badminton, but my friend is running late.

My car broke down, but my friend offered to drive me home.

We wanted to play baseball yesterday, but it was raining.

Ron decided to learn how to play the trombone.

OTHER VERBS FOLLOWED BY INFINITIVES

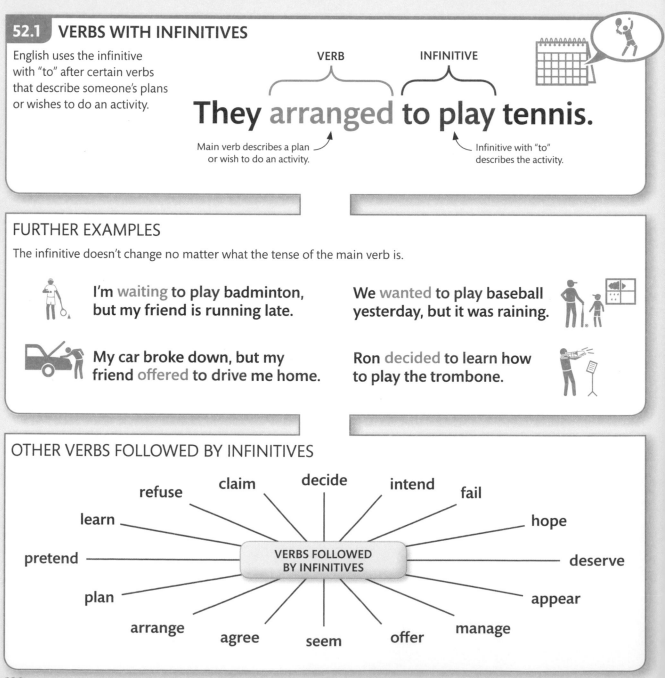

refuse   claim   decide   intend   fail

learn   hope

pretend   **VERBS FOLLOWED BY INFINITIVES**   deserve

plan   appear

arrange   agree   seem   offer   manage

52.2 VERBS WITH GERUNDS

English uses gerunds after certain verbs that say how a person feels about an activity.

VERB   GERUND

I enjoy swimming.

The verb describes feelings about an activity.

The word for the activity is in gerund form.

FURTHER EXAMPLES

He doesn't feel like playing tennis tonight.

Do you miss skiing now that summer is here?

Would you consider applying for a promotion?

We really dislike jogging. We're so out of shape!

I really enjoy running marathons.

He doesn't mind staying late at work when he has to.

OTHER VERBS FOLLOWED BY GERUNDS

mind   enjoy   allow

admit   consider

risk   dislike

discuss   VERBS FOLLOWED BY GERUNDS   finish

delay   deny

appreciate   suggest

miss   avoid   keep

52.3 VERBS FOLLOWED BY INFINITIVE OR GERUND (NO CHANGE IN MEANING)

Some verbs can be followed by a gerund (an "-ing" form)
or a "to" infinitive, with little or no change in meaning.
You can often use both forms interchangeably.

I like $\left\{ \begin{array}{l} \textbf{to work} \\ \textbf{working} \end{array} \right\}$ in an open-plan office with a team.

FURTHER EXAMPLES

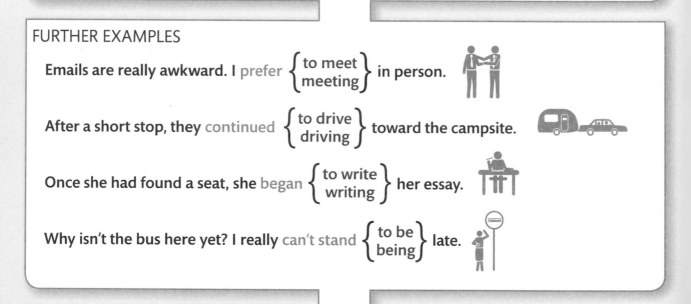

Emails are really awkward. I prefer $\left\{ \begin{array}{l} \text{to meet} \\ \text{meeting} \end{array} \right\}$ in person.

After a short stop, they continued $\left\{ \begin{array}{l} \text{to drive} \\ \text{driving} \end{array} \right\}$ toward the campsite.

Once she had found a seat, she began $\left\{ \begin{array}{l} \text{to write} \\ \text{writing} \end{array} \right\}$ her essay.

Why isn't the bus here yet? I really can't stand $\left\{ \begin{array}{l} \text{to be} \\ \text{being} \end{array} \right\}$ late.

OTHER VERBS FOLLOWED BY INFINITIVE OR GERUND (NO CHANGE IN MEANING)

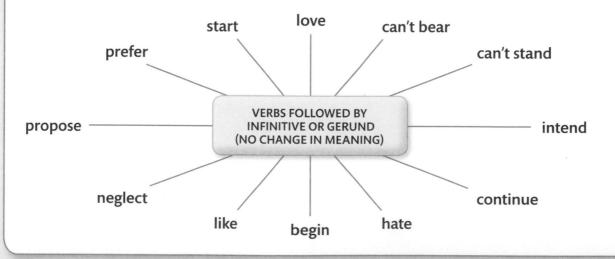

start
love
can't bear
prefer
can't stand

propose

VERBS FOLLOWED BY INFINITIVE OR GERUND (NO CHANGE IN MEANING)

intend

neglect
continue
like
begin
hate

52.4 VERBS FOLLOWED BY INFINITIVE OR GERUND (CHANGE IN MEANING)

Some verbs change their meaning depending on the form of the verb that follows them. The infinitive is used to describe the purpose of the main verb's action. The gerund is often used to talk about the action which is happening around the same time as the main verb's action.

He stopped to talk to her in the office before lunch.

[He was walking around the office, and he stopped walking so that he could talk to her.]

She stopped talking to him and rushed to a meeting.

[She was talking to him, and she stopped talking in order to do something else.]

FURTHER EXAMPLES

VERB + INFINITIVE

She forgot to send the email, so her team never received the update.

[She did not send the email.]

He went on to write the report once the meeting had finished.

[He finished a meeting and then wrote the report.]

I regret to tell you the unhappy news. Your flight has been delayed.

[I have to tell you unhappy news, and I am sorry about this.]

Did you remember to meet David? Your meeting was scheduled for today.

[You were supposed to meet David. Did you remember to do that?]

VERB + GERUND

She forgot sending the email, so she sent it a second time.

[She forgot that she had already sent the email.]

He went on writing the report all evening. It took hours.

[He was writing the report, and continued to do so.]

I regret telling you the unhappy news. I can see it has upset you.

[I wish I hadn't told you the unhappy news because you are very upset now.]

Did you remember meeting David? I'd forgotten that we had already met him.

[You had met David before. Did you remember that?]

53 Verb patterns with objects

Some verbs, known as transitive verbs, have objects. When these verbs are followed by infinitives or gerunds, the object must come between the verb and the infinitive or gerund.

See also:
Types of verbs **49**
Infinitives and participles **51**

53.1 VERB WITH OBJECT AND INFINITIVE

Some verbs that are followed by an infinitive must also have an object before that infinitive.

VERB + OBJECT + INFINITIVE

My computer **allows** me **to work** on two screens at once.

HOW TO FORM

SUBJECT	VERB	OBJECT	INFINITIVE	REST OF SENTENCE
My computer	allows	me	to work	on two screens.

FURTHER EXAMPLES

Emma's brother wants her **to turn down the television.**

Giorgio bought a new suit **to wear to his brother's wedding.**

The building manager will tell you **to leave the building if there's a fire.**

Helena's mother is **always** reminding her **to do the dishes.**

Jonathan's teacher expects him **to do better next time.**

I've asked my boyfriend **to buy some bread and milk on his way home.**

⚠ COMMON MISTAKES VERB PATTERNS WITH "WANT"

When the verb "want" is followed by an object and an infinitive, it is not formed with a "that" clause.

"Want" should be followed by an object and infinitive.

I **want him** to come to the exhibit with me. ✔

I **want that** he comes to the exhibit with me. ✘

"Want" can't be followed by a "that" clause.

53.2 VERB + OBJECT + GERUND PATTERNS

Some verbs that are followed by a gerund must also have an object before that gerund.

VERB + OBJECT + GERUND

Hayley heard the boss interviewing **the new secretary.**

HOW TO FORM

SUBJECT	VERB	OBJECT	GERUND	REST OF SENTENCE
Hayley	heard	the boss	interviewing	the new secretary.

FURTHER EXAMPLES

I remember Arnold **leaving the house at around 10 o'clock.**

Jeremy spends every winter **snowboarding in the Alps.**

I really don't like anyone **talking to me while I'm trying to study.**

My sister loves science. I can see her **becoming a doctor one day.**

53.3 DOUBLE OBJECT VERBS

The direct object is the person or thing that an action happens to. The indirect object receives the same action. If the indirect object is the focus of the sentence, it comes after the direct object plus "to" or "for."

DIRECT OBJECT   INDIRECT OBJECT

She lent some money to her son.

She lent her son some money.

The preposition is dropped when the order of the objects is reversed.

FURTHER EXAMPLES

Carolina sold
- her house **to** her younger brother.
- her younger brother her house.

Federico bought
- a car **for** his parents.
- his parents a car.

53.4 USING DOUBLE OBJECT VERBS WITH PRONOUNS

If the direct object is a pronoun, it must come before the indirect object.

She lent it to her son. ✓

She lent her son it. ✗

If the indirect object is a pronoun, it can come before or after the direct object.

She lent some money to him. ✓

She lent him some money. ✓

FURTHER EXAMPLES

Carolina sold
- it **to** her younger brother.
- it **to** him.
- him her house.

Federico bought
- it **for** his parents.
- it **for** them.
- them a car.

144

54 Verb patterns with prepositions

Some verb patterns include prepositions. Prepositions cannot be followed by infinitives, so these verb patterns only use gerunds.

See also:
Infinitives and participles **51**
Verb patterns **52**   Prepositions **105**

54.1 VERB WITH PREPOSITION AND GERUND

If a preposition is followed by a verb, the verb must be a gerund (the "-ing" form).

Jasmine decided **against taking the job.**

Gerund

FURTHER EXAMPLES

Zac and Penny are thinking **about taking a trip around the world.**

My grandmother is always worrying **about forgetting her house keys.**

54.2 VERB WITH OBJECT, PREPOSITION, AND GERUND

If a verb takes an object, that object must come between the verb and the preposition.

He congratulated her on **winning the competition.**

FURTHER EXAMPLES

Hilda stopped her dog **from running away.**

I asked my mother **about buying a new computer, but she said no.**

55 Phrasal verbs

Some verbs in English have two or more words in them, and usually have a new meaning when they are used together. These are called phrasal verbs.

See also: Verb patterns with objects **53**
Prepositions **105** Separable phrasal verbs **R20**
Inseparable phrasal verbs **R21**

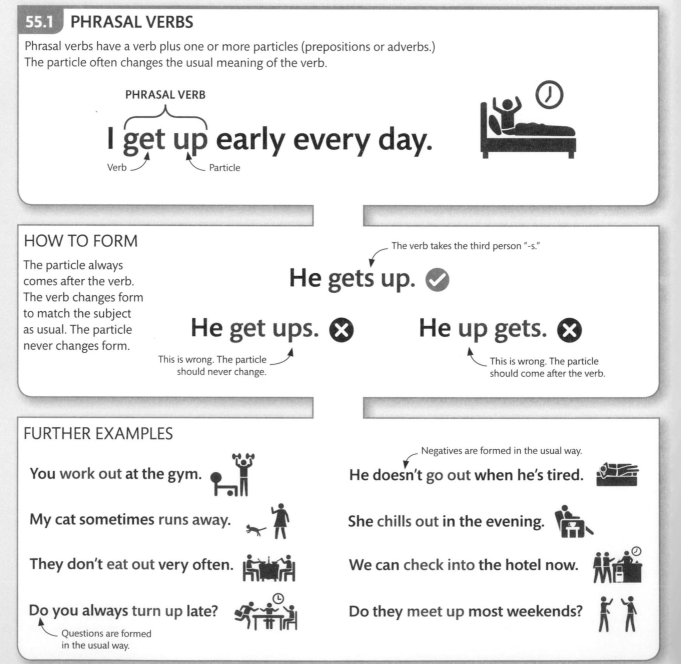

55.1 PHRASAL VERBS

Phrasal verbs have a verb plus one or more particles (prepositions or adverbs.)
The particle often changes the usual meaning of the verb.

PHRASAL VERB

I get up early every day.

Verb — Particle

HOW TO FORM

The particle always comes after the verb. The verb changes form to match the subject as usual. The particle never changes form.

The verb takes the third person "-s."

He gets up. ✓

He get ups. ✗

This is wrong. The particle should never change.

He up gets. ✗

This is wrong. The particle should come after the verb.

FURTHER EXAMPLES

You work out at the gym.

My cat sometimes runs away.

They don't eat out very often.

Do you always turn up late?

Questions are formed in the usual way.

Negatives are formed in the usual way.

He doesn't go out when he's tired.

She chills out in the evening.

We can check into the hotel now.

Do they meet up most weekends?

146

PHRASAL VERBS IN DIFFERENT TENSES

When phrasal verbs are used in different tenses, the verb changes, but the particle remains the same.

The particle never changes.

| PRESENT SIMPLE | I work out every week. |

| PAST SIMPLE | I worked out yesterday. |

| PRESENT CONTINUOUS | I am working out right now. |

| FUTURE WITH "WILL" | I will work out tomorrow. |

FURTHER EXAMPLES

 I cleaned up the kitchen last night.

 Their car is always breaking down.

I think we're lost! We should have looked up the route.

 She doesn't dress up very often.

You should go over your answers again.

 I am counting on Rajiv to give the presentation next week.

 I can't believe she turned down the job.

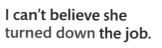 I met up with my friends last weekend.

 I'm still getting over the flu.

 When will they grow up?

55.3 SEPARABLE PHRASAL VERBS

If a phrasal verb has a direct object, it can sometimes go between the verb and the particle. Phrasal verbs that do this are called "separable" phrasal verbs.

The object can go after the particle.

He is picking up litter.

He is picking litter up.

The object can also go between the verb and the particle.

He is picking it up.

FURTHER EXAMPLES

I turned on **the light**.　　I turned **the light** on.

Can you pick up **that box**?　　Can you pick **that box** up?

You should throw away **those old shoes**.　　You should throw **those old shoes** away.

I was annoyed because he woke up **the baby**.　　I was annoyed because he woke **her** up.

I always fill up **the water jug** when it's empty.　　I always fill **it** up when it's empty.

⚠ **COMMON MISTAKES** SEPARABLE PHRASAL VERBS

If the direct object of a separable phrasal verb is a pronoun, it must go between the verb and the particle.

Pronoun

He picked it up. ✔

The pronoun cannot go at the end of the sentence.

He picked up it. ✘

55.4 INSEPARABLE PHRASAL VERBS

Some phrasal verbs cannot be separated. The object must always come after the particle; it can never sit between the particle and the verb. This is true whether the object is a noun or a pronoun.

The verb and the particle must stay together.

We had to run to get on the train. ✓

We had to run to get the train on. ✗

This is wrong. The object can't sit between the verb and the particle.

FURTHER EXAMPLES

I need to go over my notes.

Susan really takes after her father, they're very similar.

I've come across a new recipe.

I'm taking care of my sister's children tonight.

It's great to hear from you!

Caterpillars turn into butterflies.

He has fallen behind the rest of the class this year.

I ran into her at the supermarket.

Drop by the house any time you like.

He sleeps in most Saturdays.

They will have to do without a trip this summer.

Get on this bus for the beach.

Get off that bicycle if you don't have a helmet.

I am looking into visiting somewhere warm.

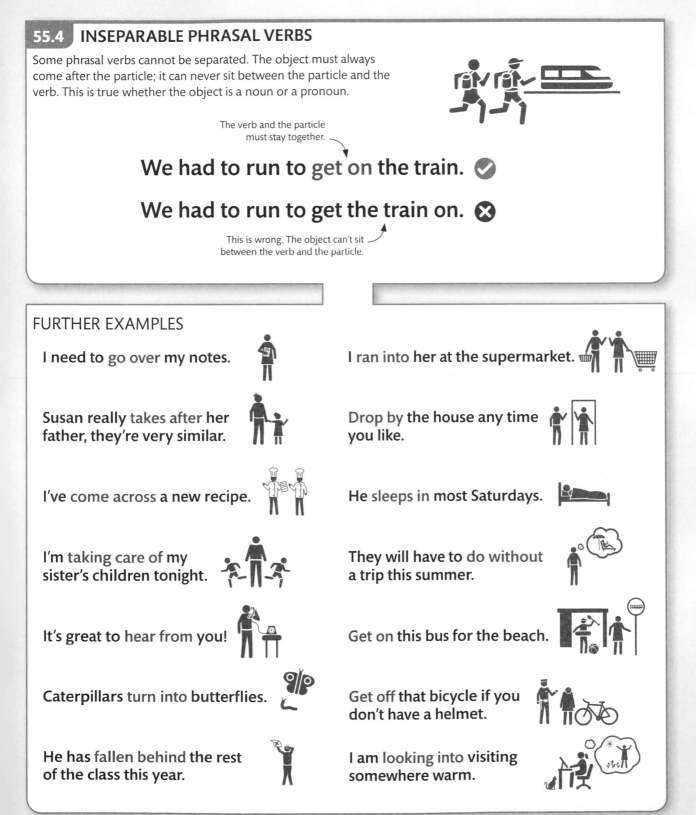

55.5 THREE-WORD PHRASAL VERBS

Three-word phrasal verbs have a verb, a particle, and a preposition. The particle and preposition often change the usual meaning of the verb.

VERB + PARTICLE + PREPOSITION

He looks up to his brother.

The verb changes with the subject.

The particle and preposition never change form.

INTONATION

In spoken English, the stress is on the middle word of a three-word phrasal verb.

look **up** to   get **along** with   look **forward** to

FURTHER EXAMPLES

We have run <u>out</u> of coffee, so I'll get some more.

You're walking too fast, I can't keep <u>up</u> with you.

I must have dropped my keys when I was getting <u>out</u> of the car.

TIP
Most, but not all, three-word phrasal verbs are inseparable.

55.6 "GET BACK FROM"

"Get back from" can be separable or inseparable depending on the context.

When "get back from" means "to return from," it is always **inseparable**.

I got <u>back</u> from Italy yesterday.

When "get back from" means "to retrieve from" it is **separable**. The object must go between "get" and "back."

I need to get the lawn mower <u>back</u> from Tina.

55.7 NOUNS BASED ON PHRASAL VERBS

Some nouns are made from phrasal verbs, often formed
by joining the verb and the particle together. When
these words are spoken, the stress is usually on the verb.

Verb   Particle

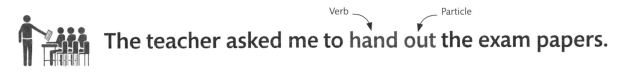

The teacher asked me to hand out the exam papers.

The teacher gave us a <u>hand</u>out for the lesson.

Stress is on the
first syllable.

Sometimes, the noun is formed by putting the particle in front
of the verb. In these cases, the spoken stress is usually on the particle.

Oh no! It was sunny and now it's pouring down.

We have a rainy season with daily <u>down</u>pours.

Stress is on the
first syllable.

FURTHER EXAMPLES

The company is trying to
cut back on staff expenses.

Not another <u>cut</u>back! The company
must be in serious trouble.

It's a shame that he wants
to drop out of school.

We've had a surprisingly high
percentage of <u>drop</u>outs in the class.

We want to get away and go
somewhere sunny this winter.

A trip to Australia sounds like
a fabulous <u>get</u>away.

56 Modal verbs

Modal verbs are very common in English. They are used to talk about a variety of things, particularly possibilities, obligations, and deductions.

See also:
Present simple negative **2**
Forming questions **34**   Types of verbs **49**

56.1 USES OF MODAL VERBS

English has many modal verbs. Each modal verb can can be used in several different contexts.

ABILITY	I can speak three languages. I can't read Latin because it's too difficult. I couldn't study it when I was at school.
PERMISSION	You can have more cake if you want. You may take as much as you like. Could I have another slice of cake?
REQUESTS	Can / Could you give me a ride home later? Would you email James for me, please? Will you lock up the office tonight?
OFFERS	Can I help you with those? May I take one of those for you? Shall I carry some of your bags?
SUGGESTIONS AND ADVICE	You should / ought to go to the doctor. You could try the new medicine.
OBLIGATION	You must arrive on time for work. You must not be late for work.
LOGICAL DEDUCTIONS	It can't be Jane because she's on vacation. It could / might / may be Dave. I don't know. It must be Tom, since nobody else ever calls.

MODAL VERB FORMATIONS

Modal verbs share certain characteristics. They don't change form to match the subject, and they are always followed by a main verb in its base form. Their question and negative forms are made without "do."

SUBJECT	MODAL VERB	BASE FORM	REST OF SENTENCE
I / You / He / She / It / We / They	can	play	the piano quite well.

The modal verb stays the same for any subject.

The main verb stays in its base form.

Negatives are formed by adding "not" between the modal verb and main verb.

You should **run a marathon.**

You should not **run a marathon.**

Questions are usually formed by swapping the subject and the modal verb.

They should **visit the castle.**

Should they **visit the castle?**

"Ought to" and "have to" are exceptions because they use "to" before the base form. "Ought to" is a more formal way of saying "should," and "have to" means "must." They both act like normal verbs.

You { ought to / have to } **learn how to drive.**

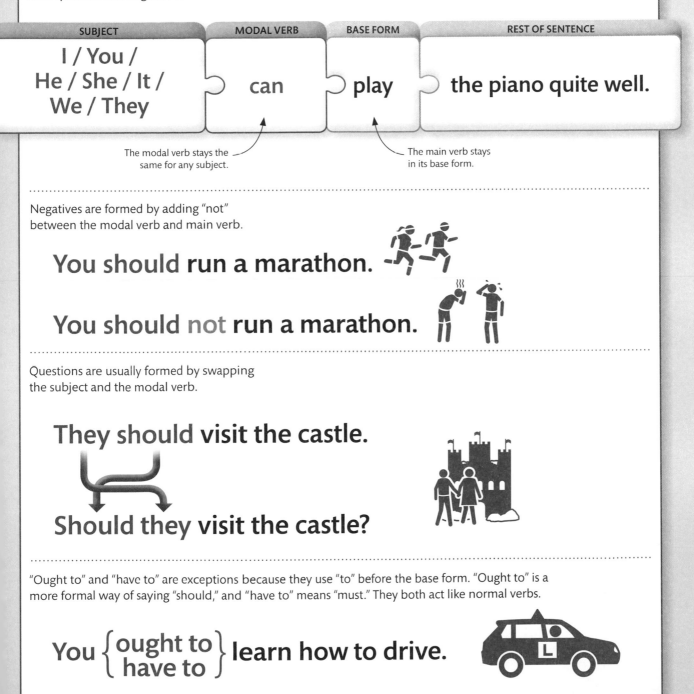

57 Ability

"Can" is a modal verb that describes what someone is able to do. It is used in different forms to describe past and present abilities.

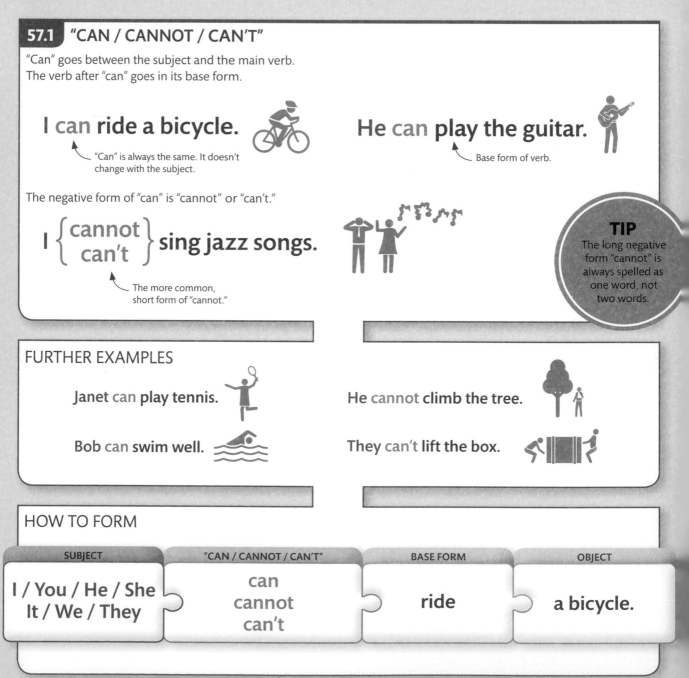

See also:
Present simple **1**
Future with "will" **18**

57.1 "CAN / CANNOT / CAN'T"

"Can" goes between the subject and the main verb.
The verb after "can" goes in its base form.

I can ride a bicycle.

"Can" is always the same. It doesn't change with the subject.

He can play the guitar.

Base form of verb.

The negative form of "can" is "cannot" or "can't."

I { cannot / can't } sing jazz songs.

The more common, short form of "cannot."

TIP
The long negative form "cannot" is always spelled as one word, not two words.

FURTHER EXAMPLES

Janet can play tennis.

Bob can swim well.

He cannot climb the tree.

They can't lift the box.

HOW TO FORM

SUBJECT	"CAN / CANNOT / CAN'T"	BASE FORM	OBJECT
I / You / He / She It / We / They	can cannot can't	ride	a bicycle.

154

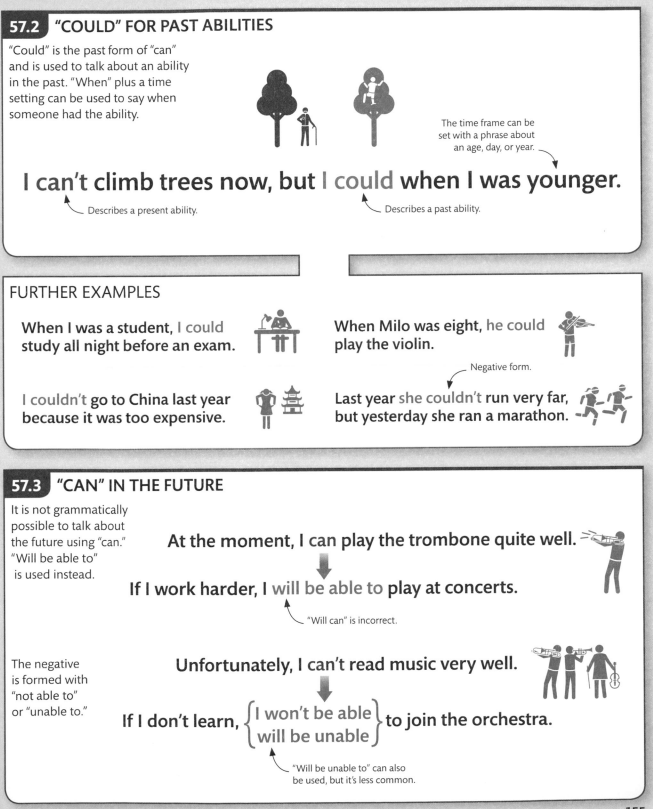

57.2 "COULD" FOR PAST ABILITIES

"Could" is the past form of "can" and is used to talk about an ability in the past. "When" plus a time setting can be used to say when someone had the ability.

The time frame can be set with a phrase about an age, day, or year.

I can't climb trees now, but I could when I was younger.

Describes a present ability.

Describes a past ability.

FURTHER EXAMPLES

When I was a student, I could study all night before an exam.

When Milo was eight, he could play the violin.

Negative form.

I couldn't go to China last year because it was too expensive.

Last year she couldn't run very far, but yesterday she ran a marathon.

57.3 "CAN" IN THE FUTURE

It is not grammatically possible to talk about the future using "can." "Will be able to" is used instead.

At the moment, I can play the trombone quite well.

If I work harder, I will be able to play at concerts.

"Will can" is incorrect.

The negative is formed with "not able to" or "unable to."

Unfortunately, I can't read music very well.

If I don't learn, { I won't be able / will be unable } **to join the orchestra.**

"Will be unable to" can also be used, but it's less common.

"Can," "could," and "may" are used to ask permission to do something, or to ask someone to do something for you. They can also be used to offer to help someone.

See also:
Types of verbs 49
Modal verbs 56

58.1 ASKING PERMISSION AND MAKING REQUESTS

"**Can**" is the most common modal verb used to ask permission or to make a request.

Can I have some popcorn?

Yes, you can.

Informal answers use "can" as well.

"**Could**" replaces "can" for more formal situations, such as in business or to talk to strangers.

Excuse me, could I sit here, please?

"Please" is used in polite requests.

I'm sorry, but that seat is taken.

Negative answers can be more polite by adding "I'm sorry" or "I'm afraid."

"**May**" can also be used in formal situations.

May I make an appointment?

Of course.

FURTHER EXAMPLES

Can I borrow your pen?

Can I have this in a smaller size?

Excuse me, could you open the door for me?

May I reserve a table for 7pm?

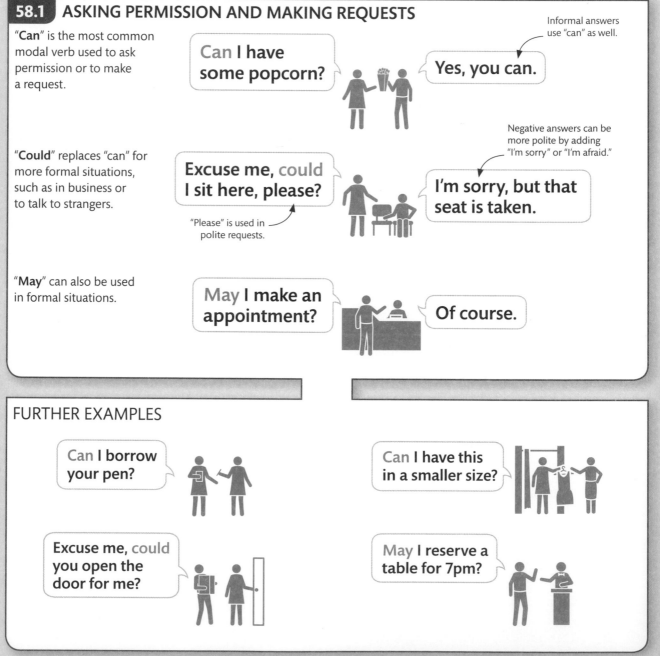

58.2 MAKING OFFERS

"Can" and "may" can also be used to offer to do something for someone.

Can I help you carry those?

Yes, please.

"May" is only used for formal situations.

May I take your coat?

Yes, thank you.

FURTHER EXAMPLES

Can I get you a drink?

That would be lovely.

My computer's broken again!

Can I help at all?

Good evening. May I take your order?

Yes, please.

Which way is the elevator?

It's on the left. May I help you with your bags?

58.3 SHALL FOR OFFERS AND SUGGESTIONS

"Shall" is used to find out if someone thinks a certain suggestion is a good idea. This is not often used in US English.

That bag looks heavy. Shall I carry it for you?

Yes, please.

Shall I open the window?

Good idea. It's far too hot in here.

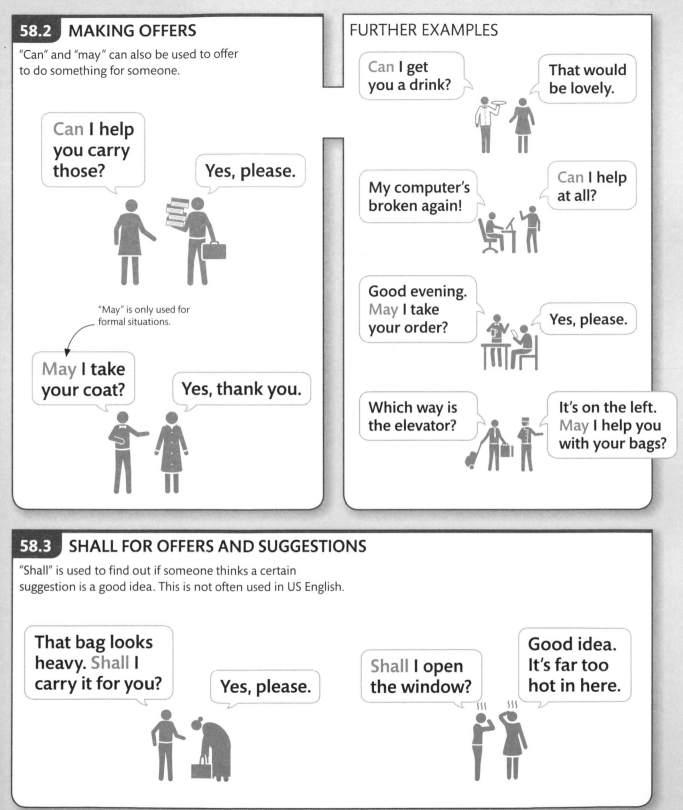

59 Suggestions and advice

The modal verb "could" can be used to offer suggestions. "Could" is not as strong as "should." It communicates gentle advice.

See also:
Conditional sentences **29** Types of verbs **49**
Modal verbs **56**

59.1 "SHOULD" FOR ADVICE

"Should" is used when the speaker wants to make a strong suggestion.

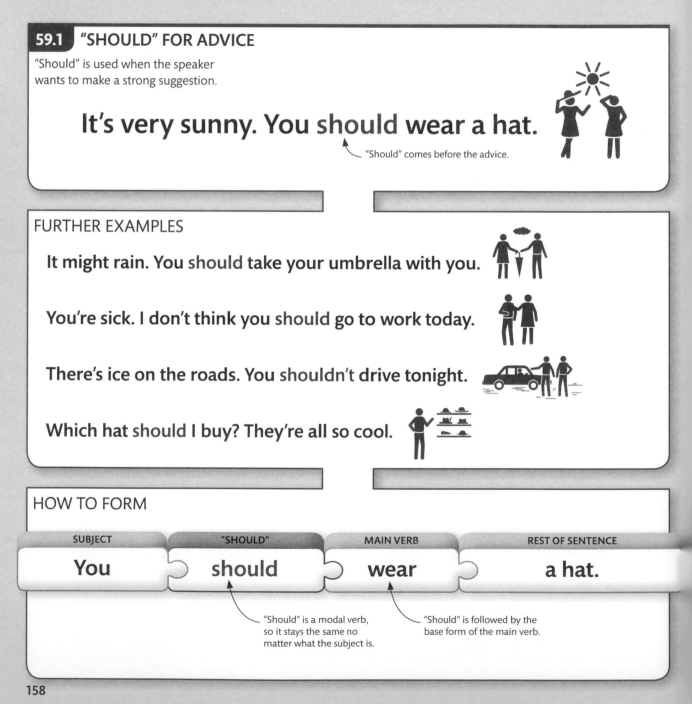

It's very sunny. You should wear a hat.

"Should" comes before the advice.

FURTHER EXAMPLES

It might rain. You should take your umbrella with you.

You're sick. I don't think you should go to work today.

There's ice on the roads. You shouldn't drive tonight.

Which hat should I buy? They're all so cool.

HOW TO FORM

SUBJECT	"SHOULD"	MAIN VERB	REST OF SENTENCE
You	should	wear	a hat.

"Should" is a modal verb, so it stays the same no matter what the subject is.

"Should" is followed by the base form of the main verb.

59.2 "OUGHT TO" FOR ADVICE

"Ought to" is a more formal and less common way to say "should."
It is not usually used in the negative or question forms.

You { should / ought to } wear a scarf. It's very cold outside.

59.3 "IF I WERE YOU"

English uses "if I were you" to give advice in second conditional sentences. The advice is expressed using "I would."

I don't know if I should take this job.

English uses "were," not "was," in this context.

If I were you, I would take it.

The advice comes after "I would."

FURTHER EXAMPLES

I'm going to the concert tonight.

If I were you, I'd leave early. The traffic is awful.

The suggestion can come first without changing the meaning.

I think I'll buy this shirt.

I wouldn't buy it if I were you. I don't like the pattern.

There is no comma before "if."

59.4 "HAD BETTER"

"Had better" can also be used to give very strong or urgent advice that can have a negative consequence if it is not followed.

{ You had better / You'd better } leave for school! It's already 8.45.

59.5 "COULD" FOR SUGGESTIONS

"Could" is often used to suggest a solution to a problem. It states a possible course of action without necessarily recommending it.

"Could" means that the action is a possibility; a choice that might solve the problem.

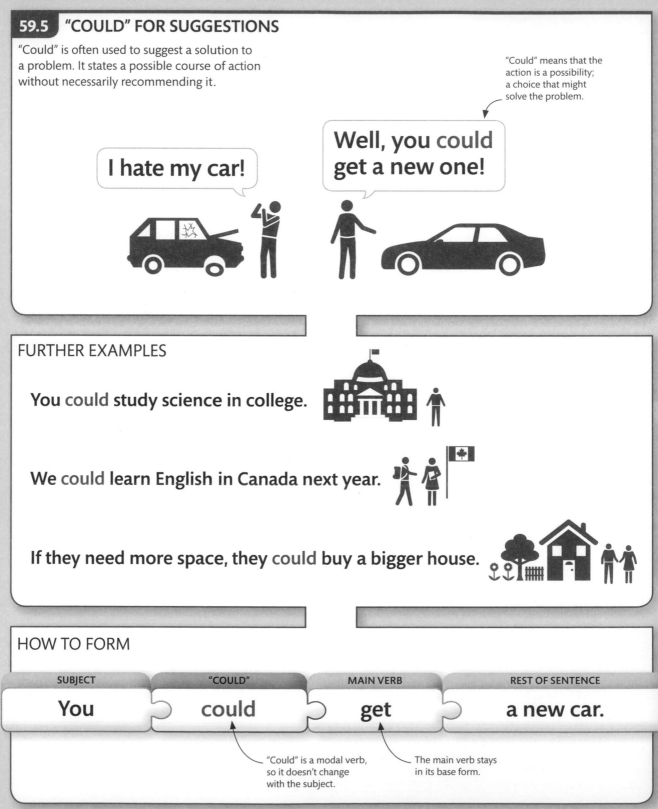

I hate my car!

Well, you could get a new one!

FURTHER EXAMPLES

You could study science in college.

We could learn English in Canada next year.

If they need more space, they could buy a bigger house.

HOW TO FORM

SUBJECT	"COULD"	MAIN VERB	REST OF SENTENCE
You	could	get	a new car.

"Could" is a modal verb, so it doesn't change with the subject.

The main verb stays in its base form.

59.6 "COULD" AND "OR" FOR SUGGESTIONS

When people give suggestions using "could," they often give more than one option to choose from.

Our friends are coming over for dinner, but the oven's broken.

We could make a salad or we could order a pizza.

"Or" is used to give an alternative suggestion.

FURTHER EXAMPLES

I can't decide what to make for dinner tonight.

Well, you could make a curry or lasagne.

The modal verb doesn't have to be repeated after "or."

What should I wear to Jan's wedding?

You could wear your new dress or a skirt.

If the main verb is the same for both suggestions, it isn't repeated after "or."

59.7 MAKING RECOMMENDATIONS

One of the most common ways of recommending something or making a suggestion is to use modal verbs.

TIP
Emphasis can be added by putting "really" in front of "should," "ought to," and "must."

General suggestion.

You { could / might } visit the park. It's beautiful.

Stronger suggestion.

You { should / ought to } visit the castle. It's great.

Very strong suggestion.

You must visit the palace. It is beautiful!

60 Obligations

In English, "have to" or "must" are used when talking about obligations or things that are necessary. They are often used to give important instructions.

See also:
Future with "will" **18**   Types of verbs **49**
Modal verbs **56**

60.1 OBLIGATIONS

"**Must**" and "**have to**" both express a strong need or obligation to do something.

You { must / have to } rest, or your leg won't heal.

"**Must not**" is a strong negative obligation. It means something is not allowed.

You **must not** get your bandage wet, or your leg might not heal properly.

"**Don't have to**" means something is not necessary, or there is no obligation.

You **don't have** to come again. Your leg is better.

FURTHER EXAMPLES

He **must** take two pills each morning and evening for the next two weeks.

She **must not** go back to work until her back is better.

Do I have to go back to the doctor again? I'm feeling so much better now.

HOW TO FORM

"Must" does not change with the subject, but "have to" becomes "has to" in the third person singular. Both forms are followed by the base form of the main verb.

SUBJECT	"MUST / HAVE TO"	MAIN VERB	REST OF SENTENCE
She	must has to must not doesn't have to	take	this medicine.

⚠ COMMON MISTAKES "MUST NOT" AND "DON'T HAVE TO"

"Must not" and "don't have to" do not mean the same thing. "Must not" is used to give an instruction that forbids someone from doing something. "Don't have to" is used to tell someone that it is not necessary that they do something.

You **must not** use a calculator during this exam.

[It is against the rules to use a calculator during this exam.]

You **don't have to** use a calculator, but it might be useful.

[You are allowed to use a calculator, but it is not required.]

60.2 "MUST" AND "HAVE TO" IN THE FUTURE

There is no future form of "must." The future of "have to" is formed with the auxiliary verb "will."

In some countries, people { **must** / **have to** } recycle. It's the law.

In the future, I think everyone will have to recycle.

"Will must" is incorrect.

"Must not" does not have a future form. "Don't have to" can be used in the future by changing "don't" to "will not" or "won't."

One day, I hope I will not have to work so hard.

60.3 "MUST" AND "HAVE TO" IN THE PAST

There is no past form of "must." The past tense of "have to" is used instead.

For most jobs, you { **must** / **have to** } use a computer.

In the past, you didn't have to use a computer.

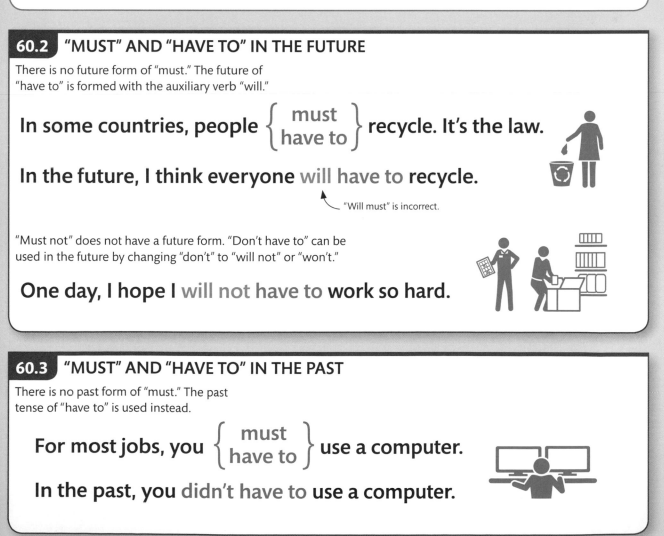

61 Making deductions

Modal verbs can also be used to talk about how likely or unlikely something is. They can be used to guess and make deductions about what has happened or is happening now.

See also:
Types of verbs **49**
Infinitives and participles **51** Modal verbs **56**

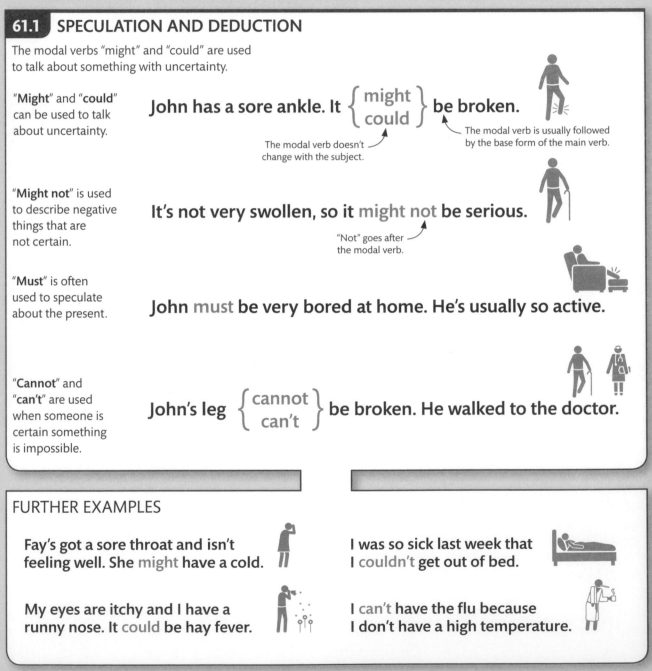

61.1 SPECULATION AND DEDUCTION

The modal verbs "might" and "could" are used to talk about something with uncertainty.

"**Might**" and "**could**" can be used to talk about uncertainty.

John has a sore ankle. It { might / could } be broken.

The modal verb doesn't change with the subject.

The modal verb is usually followed by the base form of the main verb.

"**Might not**" is used to describe negative things that are not certain.

It's not very swollen, so it might not be serious.

"Not" goes after the modal verb.

"**Must**" is often used to speculate about the present.

John must be very bored at home. He's usually so active.

"**Cannot**" and "**can't**" are used when someone is certain something is impossible.

John's leg { cannot / can't } be broken. He walked to the doctor.

FURTHER EXAMPLES

Fay's got a sore throat and isn't feeling well. She might have a cold.

I was so sick last week that I couldn't get out of bed.

My eyes are itchy and I have a runny nose. It could be hay fever.

I can't have the flu because I don't have a high temperature.

SPECULATION AND DEDUCTION ABOUT THE PAST

"**Must have**" with a past participle is used to speculate about the past when the speaker is sure something happened.

He just disappeared. Aliens must have taken him.

Past participle

"**May**," "**might**," or "**could**" can replace "must" when the speaker is not sure whether something happened or not.

They { might may could } have taken him to another planet.

"**Can't**" or "**couldn't**" can be used to refer to something that the speaker is certain did not happen.

It { can't couldn't } have been aliens. They don't exist.

FURTHER EXAMPLES

Bethan didn't return my call yesterday. She must have been busy.

She might have forgotten to call me back.

She might not have written down my number correctly.

Paula can't have been at the party last night, she was at work.

I didn't see who knocked on the door, but it may have been the mailman.

What happened to my vase? The cat must have knocked it over.

62 Possibility

Modal verbs can be used to talk about possibility, or to express uncertainty. "Might" is the most common modal verb used for this purpose.

See also:
Present simple **1**   Infinitives and participles **51**
Modal verbs **56**

62.1 "MIGHT" FOR POSSIBILITY

"Might" can be added to different phrases to refer to past, present, or future possibilities.

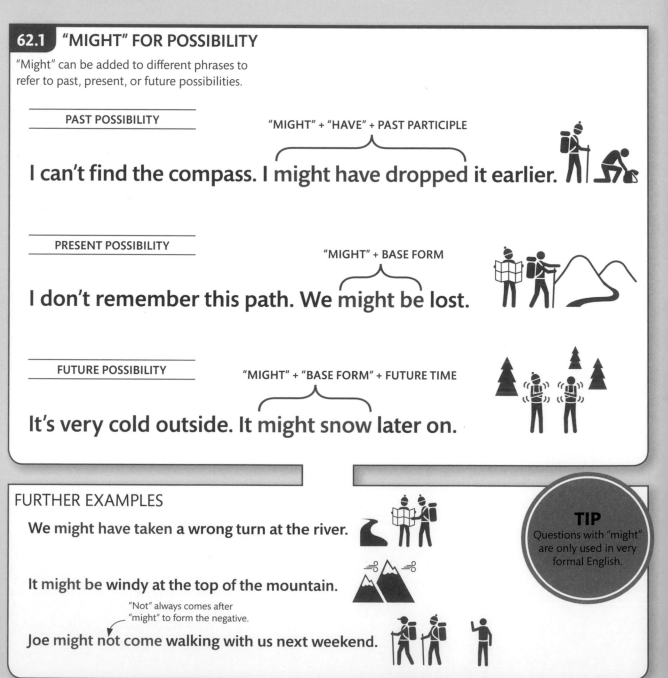

PAST POSSIBILITY

"MIGHT" + "HAVE" + PAST PARTICIPLE

I can't find the compass. I might have dropped it earlier.

PRESENT POSSIBILITY

"MIGHT" + BASE FORM

I don't remember this path. We might be lost.

FUTURE POSSIBILITY

"MIGHT" + "BASE FORM" + FUTURE TIME

It's very cold outside. It might snow later on.

FURTHER EXAMPLES

We might have taken a wrong turn at the river.

It might be windy at the top of the mountain.

"Not" always comes after "might" to form the negative.

Joe might not come walking with us next weekend.

TIP
Questions with "might" are only used in very formal English.

"MIGHT" WITH UNCERTAINTY

Other phrases can be added to sentences with "might" to emphasize uncertainty about something.

 I might take the bus home. I'm not sure.

I don't know. **I might have more pizza.**

62.3 **PAST POSSIBILITY**

As well as "might," other modal verbs can be used to talk about something that possibly happened in the past.

The copier isn't working. It $\begin{Bmatrix} \text{might} \\ \text{may} \\ \text{could} \end{Bmatrix}$ **have run out of paper.**

[He thinks it is possible that the copier has run out of paper.]

These constructions can be used to talk about something that possibly did not happen in the past.

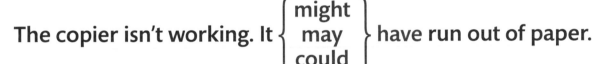

You $\begin{Bmatrix} \text{might not} \\ \text{may not} \end{Bmatrix}$ **have plugged it in correctly.**

[He thinks it is possible that the printer wasn't plugged in correctly.]

"Could not" can only be used when the speaker is certain that something did not happen.

You couldn't have changed the ink correctly.

[He is certain that the ink wasn't changed correctly.]

63 Articles

Articles are short words which come before nouns to show whether they refer to a general or a specific object. There are several rules telling which article, if any, should be used.

See also:
Singular and plural nouns **69**   Countable and uncountable nouns **70**   Superlative adjectives **97**

63.1   THE INDEFINITE ARTICLE

The indefinite article "a" or "an" is used to talk about something in general.

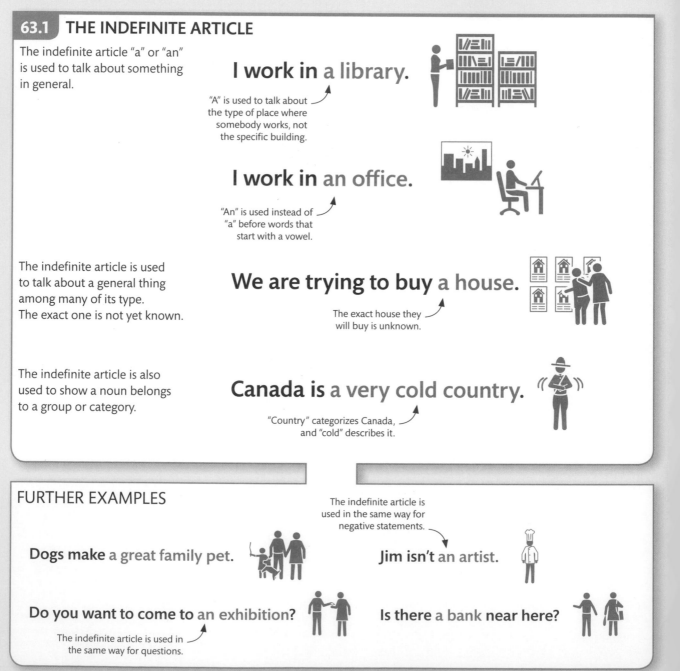

I work in a library.

"A" is used to talk about the type of place where somebody works, not the specific building.

I work in an office.

"An" is used instead of "a" before words that start with a vowel.

The indefinite article is used to talk about a general thing among many of its type. The exact one is not yet known.

We are trying to buy a house.

The exact house they will buy is unknown.

The indefinite article is also used to show a noun belongs to a group or category.

Canada is a very cold country.

"Country" categorizes Canada, and "cold" describes it.

FURTHER EXAMPLES

Dogs make a great family pet.

The indefinite article is used in the same way for negative statements.

Jim isn't an artist.

Do you want to come to an exhibition?

The indefinite article is used in the same way for questions.

Is there a bank near here?

63.2 "SOME"

"Some" replaces "a" or "an" in sentences with plural nouns.

Use "a" and "an" to talk about one thing.

"Hotel" is singular.

There is a hotel in the town.

There are some hotels in the town.

Use "some" to talk about more than one thing.

"Hotels" is plural.

FURTHER EXAMPLES

There are some banks on Main Street.

There are some children in the park.

63.3 "SOME" AND "ANY" WITH QUESTIONS AND NEGATIVES

"Some" is replaced by "any" to form questions and negatives.

There are some cafés in the town.

Are there any cafés in the town?

There are some children in the park.

There aren't any children in the park.

FURTHER EXAMPLES

Are there any museums?

There aren't any parks.

Are there any swimming pools?

There aren't any factories.

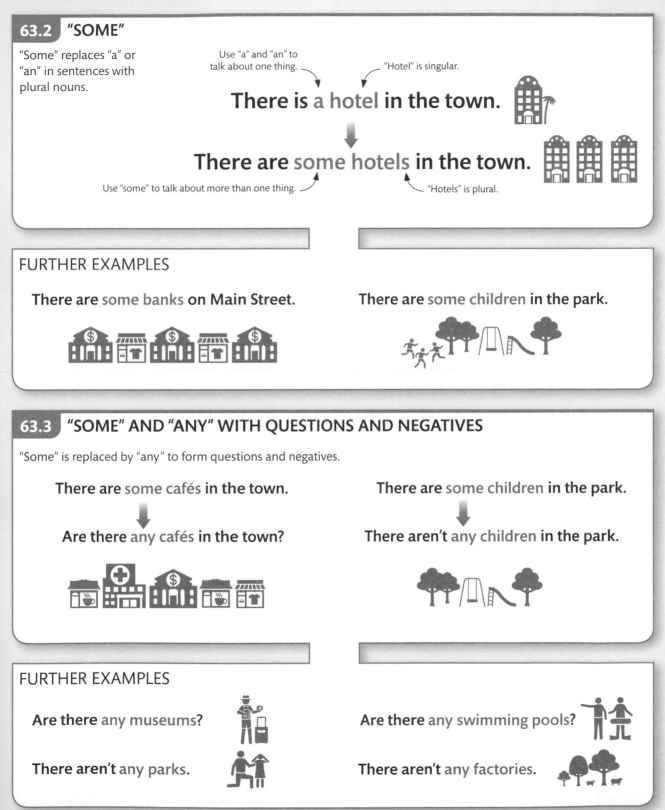

63.4 THE DEFINITE ARTICLE

The definite article "the" is used to talk about a specific person or thing that everyone understands.

We went on a tour and the guide was excellent.

It is clear from the context that this means the tour guide.

When a person or thing has been mentioned already, "the" is used the next time the thing or person is talked about.

There's a bus trip or a lecture. I'd prefer the bus trip.

The bus trip has already been mentioned.

The definite article is used before superlatives.

The Colosseum is probably the most famous site in Rome.

Superlative phrase.

The definite article is also used with unique objects.

I'm going to the Trevi Fountain before I leave.

There is only one Trevi Fountain.

It is also used for people with unique titles.

"Pope" is a title.

The Pope is visiting another country this week.

FURTHER EXAMPLES

What is the biggest country in the world?

I never take the first train to work in the morning.

I love this restaurant. The waiters are great.

I went to Paris and climbed the Eiffel Tower.

Did you buy those shoes from the shoe shop on Broad Lane?

The President will be speaking on TV tonight.

63.5 USING "THE" TO SPECIFY

"The" can be followed by a prepositional phrase or a defining relative clause to specify which thing someone is talking about.

The pictures on the wall are beautiful.

This makes it clear which pictures are being referred to.

The dog that I saw earlier was adorable.

This makes it clear which dog is being talked about.

FURTHER EXAMPLES

The computers in this office are all too slow.

The books that I bought yesterday are for my son's birthday.

The students in my classes are very intelligent and dedicated.

The pastries that they sell here are absolutely delicious.

63.6 "THE" WITH ADJECTIVES FOR CERTAIN GROUPS

Some adjectives can be used with the definite article to refer to a group or class of people.

Rich people have bought most of the new houses in this town.

Almost all the houses here are owned by the rich.

FURTHER EXAMPLES

Emergency treatment for the injured is essential.

The media sometimes portrays the young as lazy.

Many charities try to protect the poor.

The elderly often need the support of their families.

> **TIP**
> These phrases are plural in meaning, but it's incorrect to say "the youngs," etc.

63.7 THE ZERO ARTICLE

An article is not needed with uncountable and plural nouns used in a general context. This is known as the zero article.

I don't like the beach. I get sand everywhere.

Uncountable noun.

Plural noun.

You can see famous sights all over New York City.

The zero article is also used with some places and institutions when it is clear what their purpose is.

Liz is seven. She goes to school now.

She goes there to study, which is the purpose of schools, so no article is used.

Larry works at the school in Park Street.

The definite article is used to talk about the specific school where he works.

FURTHER EXAMPLES

Coffee is one of Colombia's major exports.

Kangaroos are common in Australia.

I am studying Engineering in college in Chicago.

Liz goes to school at 8am.

In the UK, children start school when they are five years old.

I've got so many books.

Paris is the capital of France.

Names of places often take the zero article.

Go to bed, Tom!

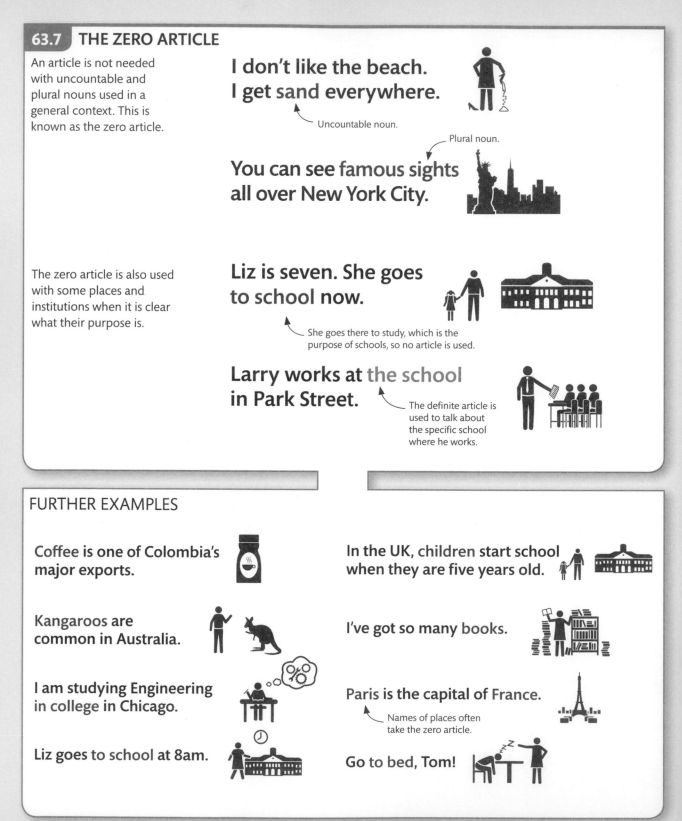

63.8 THE ZERO ARTICLE AND GENERIC "THE"

The zero article can be used with plural nouns to talk about a class of things in general. This can also be done with the definite article, plus a singular noun.

Referring to an invention, not an individual telescope.

Telescopes
The telescope } **changed the way we see the night sky.**

Referring to a species of animal, not an individual animal.

Cheetahs
The cheetah } **can run faster than any other land animal.**

Referring to a type of musical instrument, not an individual instrument.

Violins are
The violin is } **often the key instrument in an orchestra.**

63.9 DEFINITE AND INDEFINITE ARTICLES WITH NAMES

The zero article is normally used with the name of a person.

This is my uncle, Neil Armstrong.

In this case, "the" is pronounced "thee."

The definite article is used before a person's name to differentiate them from another person with the same name.

He's not the Neil Armstrong, is he?
[He isn't the famous person with that name, is he?]

The indefinite article is used when the focus is on a particular name, rather than the person.

I'm afraid there isn't a "Joseph Bloggs" on the list.
[The particular name given is not on the list.]

64 Articles overview

64.1 USING ARTICLES

SINGULAR NOUNS

Singular nouns must be used with an article. The definite article ("the") or indefinite article ("a / an") can be used, depending on whether the object is being spoken about in general or specific terms.

INDEFINITE ARTICLE

"A" refers to cars in general, not the car he wants to buy.

He wants to buy a new car. ✅

I've got a beautiful green coat. ✅

"A" is used because the green coat is something new that is being introduced.

PLURAL NOUNS

The indefinite article "a / an" cannot be used with plural nouns. "Some" is used instead for plural nouns when referring to an indefinite quantity of something.

The indefinite article cannot be used for plural nouns.

Sam bought a new shoes today. ❌

I've just planted some roses. ✅

"Some" suggests a limited number of roses, but the exact number is unknown.

UNCOUNTABLE NOUNS

The indefinite article is not usually used with uncountable nouns. The definite article is used to talk about uncountable nouns in specific terms, and the zero article is used to talk about them in general terms.

"A / an" cannot be used with uncountable nouns.

I left a money on the table. ❌

Children should drink a milk. ❌

The definite and indefinite articles are used in different situations, and this can depend on whether they are being used with a singular, plural, or uncountable noun.

See also:
Singular and plural nouns 69
Countable and uncountable nouns 70

DEFINITE ARTICLE

"The" is used to talk about a specific car that the speaker and listener both know about.

Is the red car outside yours? ✓

I want to buy the green coat hanging in the window. ✓

The definite article is used to talk about plural nouns in specific terms.

The shoes Sam bought were very expensive. ✓

The roses you planted outside are beautiful. ✓

The speaker is referring to specific money that the listener already knows about, so the definite article is used.

I left the money on the table. ✓

Children should drink the milk. ✗

Milk is an uncountable noun which is being spoken about in general terms, so the definite article can't be used.

ZERO ARTICLE

This is wrong. Singular countable nouns must have an article.

I've got new car. ✗

I've got beautiful green coat. ✗

No article is used because "shoes" is a plural noun being spoken about in a general context.

Sam is always buying shoes. ✓

Roses are a type of flower. ✓

Roses are being spoken about in general terms. There's no idea of a number.

No article is used because "money" is being spoken about in a general sense.

She earns a lot of money. ✓

Children should drink milk. ✓

65 "This / that / these / those"

"This," "that," "these," and "those" can be used as determiners before a noun to specify which noun is being talked about. They can also be used as pronouns to replace a noun in a sentence.

See also:
Singular and plural nouns **69**
Personal pronouns **77**   Possession **80**

65.1 "THIS" AND "THAT" AS DETERMINERS

"This" and "that" are only used with singular nouns. "This" is used for something close, and "that" for something farther away.

This house is too big.
The house is close to you.

That house is too small.
The house is farther away from you.

"This" can also be used for something current or present, and "that" can be used for something absent or in the past.

This job is great.
"This" refers to the job that the speaker is currently doing.

That job was boring.
"That" refers to a job in the past that isn't being done anymore.

"Was" is in the past tense.

FURTHER EXAMPLES

This essay is proving to be really difficult.

I like this rabbit so much I want to take it home.

When I eat out I always order this rice dish.
Uncountable nouns are only used with "this" and "that," never "these" and "those."

That cake in the window looks incredible.

I'd like to see that play this weekend.

This show is great, but I didn't like that other show as much.
"Other" can be used after "that" to stress that it is different to the first noun.

"These" and "those" are only used with plural nouns. "These" is used for things close by or current. "Those" is used for things farther away or in the past.

This cake is delicious.

These cakes are delicious.

"These" is the plural of "this."

"These" and "those" go before plural nouns.

That sandwich tastes bad.

Those sandwiches look better.

"Those" is the plural of "that."

"These" and "those" go before plural nouns.

FURTHER EXAMPLES

These new shoes are hurting my feet.

I hope these exams go well.

I don't think these vegetables are very fresh.

These books are so heavy! I can't carry them.

I'd like to live in one of those big town houses.

Those sunglasses look great on you!

I like the look of those Caribbean cruises.

I'll take those apples and these bananas, please.

"THIS" AND "THAT" AS PRONOUNS

"This" and "that" can replace singular nouns in a sentence. They point out a specific thing. "This" is used for something close, and "that" is used for something farther away.

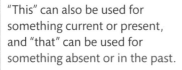

This is my dog.

The dog is close to you.

That is my dog.

The dog is farther away from you.

"This" can also be used for something current or present, and "that" can be used for something absent or in the past.

This is a great party.

"This" means the party is happening now.

"That" means the party has already happened.

That was such a fun party yesterday.

FURTHER EXAMPLES

This is a great honor. Thank you everyone for coming.

That was so exciting.

This has always been the most beautiful park.

If you could do a blow-dry, that would be great.

This is the perfect laptop for creative work.

That sounded out of tune. I'd get the piano fixed.

This is the best soup I've ever tasted.

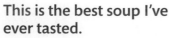

That looks great. Is the car new?

65.4 "THESE" AND "THOSE" AS PRONOUNS

"These" and "those" can replace plural nouns in a sentence. "These" is used for things close by or current. "Those" is used for things farther away or in the past.

This is my bag.

That is my bag.

"These" is the plural of "this." →

These are my bags.

"Those" is the plural of "that." →

Those are my bags.

"These" and "those" are also used for contrast. "These" things belong to one person. →

"Those" things belong to another person. →

These are my bags and those are your bags.

FURTHER EXAMPLES

These are the best kind of shoes to wear when running.

I think those will probably taste better with sauce.

These are the only clothes I own.

Those aren't very good for you. Try these instead.

65.5 SUBSTITUTING WITH "THAT" AND "THOSE"

"That" and "those" can be used in place of a noun phrase to mean "the one" or "the ones."

"That" refers to "policy." →

The new policy is better than that of before.

"Those who" means "people who." →

I disapprove of those who don't recycle.

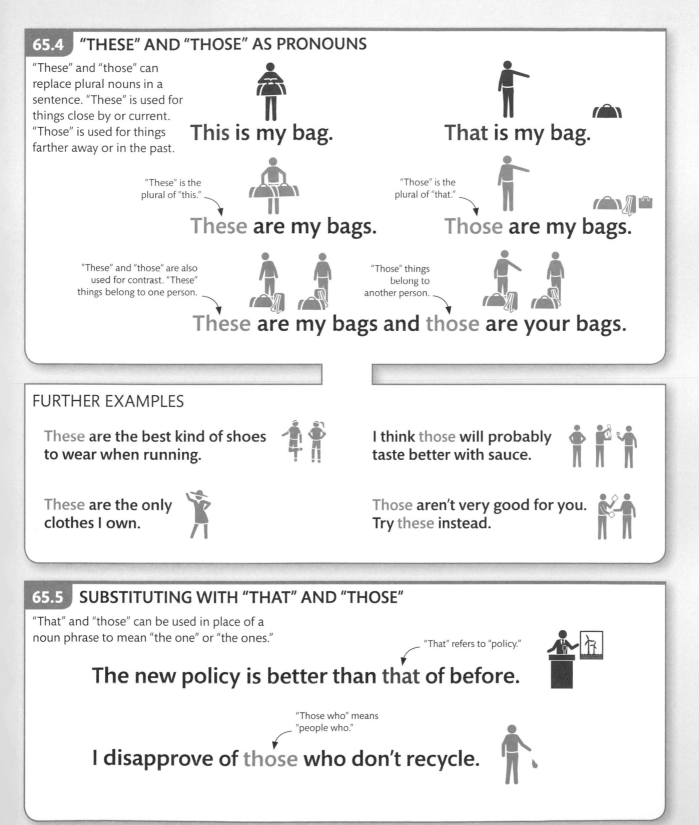

179

66 "No / none"

"No" and "none" both show the absence or lack of something. "No" is always used with a noun, whereas "none" replaces a noun in a sentence.

See also:
Singular and plural nouns **69**
Countable and uncountable nouns **70**

66.1 "NO"

"No" is only used with uncountable nouns or plural countable nouns.

Uncountable noun.

There was no time to cook a meal.

[There wasn't any time to cook a meal.]

Plural noun.

I have no ingredients in my kitchen.

[I don't have any ingredients in my kitchen.]

FURTHER EXAMPLES

This menu has no vegetarian options.

I would have booked a restaurant but there were no tables.

No waiters were available to take our order.

There are no recipes in this book that I haven't tried.

66.2 "NO" AND NOUN FOR EMPHASIS

Although "no" has the same meaning as "not any" in this context, "no" is often emphatic.

There wasn't any food left.

There was no food left!

This version of the sentence can indicate surprise or disappointment.

66.3 "NONE"

"None" can replace "no" plus noun to indicate a lack of something.

"Left" shows that there was some pizza before.

I wanted some pizza, but there was none left.

[I wanted some pizza, but there was no pizza left.]

"None of" is used before pronouns and nouns with determiners.

None of the pizza was left.

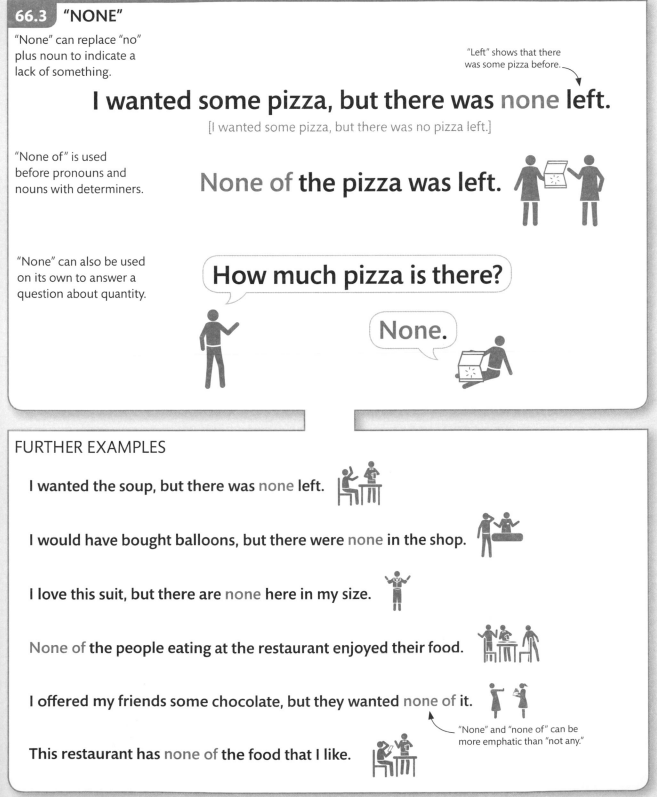

"None" can also be used on its own to answer a question about quantity.

How much pizza is there?

None.

FURTHER EXAMPLES

I wanted the soup, but there was none left.

I would have bought balloons, but there were none in the shop.

I love this suit, but there are none here in my size.

None of the people eating at the restaurant enjoyed their food.

I offered my friends some chocolate, but they wanted none of it.

"None" and "none of" can be more emphatic than "not any."

This restaurant has none of the food that I like.

67 "Each / every"

"Each" and "every" are words that go before singular nouns to refer to all members of a group of people or things.

See also:
Singular and plural nouns 69

67.1 "EACH" AND "EVERY"

In most cases, there is no difference in meaning between "each" and "every."

Means all the times.

I buy more and more { each / every } time I go shopping.

{ Each / Every } place we stopped at was beautiful.

Means all the places.

FURTHER EXAMPLES

The host made sure he greeted each guest at the party.

Last summer I went to visit my grandmother every day.

Each person on the beach was developing a bad sunburn.

I always try every kind of ice cream when I go abroad.

⚠ COMMON MISTAKES "EACH" AND "EVERY"

Unlike "each," "every" cannot be used to talk about just two things.

She had an earring in each ear. ✓

She had an earring in every ear. ✗

She only has two ears, so "every" can't be used here.

67.2 "EACH"

"Each" is used to talk separately about every member of a group.

You must check each answer carefully.

"Each" is also used when talking about small numbers.

Each pencil is a different color.

FURTHER EXAMPLES

I get more awake after each cup of coffee.

I took lots of time over each application I made.

Each player on my team contributed to our win.

Each friend who visited me brought a gift.

67.3 "EVERY"

"Every" is used when speaking about the whole group of something.

I want to eat every piece of this delicious pie.

"Every" is also used when talking about large numbers.

Every child has the right to an education.

FURTHER EXAMPLES

Every night I look up at all the stars in the sky.

My colleague says he's visited every country in the world.

Every fan in the stadium was cheering loudly.

I can't remember every hotel I've ever stayed in.

68 "Either / neither / both"

"Either," "neither," and "both" are used in situations where two options are being described. They indicate that one, two, or none of the options are possible.

See also:
Articles **63**   Singular and plural nouns **69**
Personal pronouns **77**

68.1 "EITHER," "NEITHER," AND "BOTH"

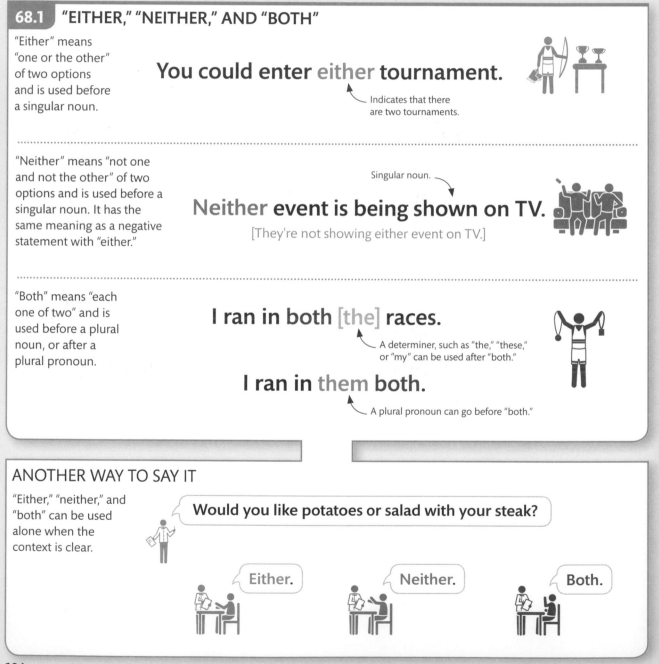

"Either" means "one or the other" of two options and is used before a singular noun.

You could enter either tournament.

Indicates that there are two tournaments.

"Neither" means "not one and not the other" of two options and is used before a singular noun. It has the same meaning as a negative statement with "either."

Singular noun.

Neither event is being shown on TV.

[They're not showing either event on TV.]

"Both" means "each one of two" and is used before a plural noun, or after a plural pronoun.

I ran in both [the] races.

A determiner, such as "the," "these," or "my" can be used after "both."

I ran in them both.

A plural pronoun can go before "both."

ANOTHER WAY TO SAY IT

"Either," "neither," and "both" can be used alone when the context is clear.

Would you like potatoes or salad with your steak?

Either.

Neither.

Both.

"Either of," "neither of," and "both of" are used before a plural pronoun or a determiner plus a plural noun.

"Bicycles" is a plural noun.

I could buy either of these bicycles, but I don't really need either of them.

"Them" is a plural pronoun.

We won neither of the races.
Neither of us trained hard enough.

"Of" is optional after "both" when a determiner is used with the noun.

We train with both (of) our coaches.
They are proud of both of us.

Plural personal pronouns "us," "you," and "them" can be used with "either of," "neither of," and "both of" as a subject as well as an object.

I danced with both of them.

"Them" is the object.

Neither of you can dance.

"You" is the subject.

FURTHER EXAMPLES

I wasn't able to get tickets for either of the first heats.

Neither of the athletes are very fit.

I'm going to watch both the equestrian events later today.

Either of them could win the contest. It's hard to call.

We thought neither of them would be able to finish.

Both of you are strong contenders. You deserve to win.

"EITHER... OR," "NEITHER... NOR," AND "BOTH... AND"

"Either... or" and "neither... nor" are used to compare options, usually noun phrases, prepositional phrases, or clauses.

I want **either** the cake **or** the cookie.

Neither the cake **nor** the cookie tasted good.

"Nor" can only be used with "neither."

"Neither" is only used with a positive verb.

"Either... or" and "neither... nor" can be used with two or more options.

The first two options are separated with a comma.

I want to play **either** tennis, badminton, **or** squash.

Neither basketball, golf, **nor** hockey are the sports for me.

"Both... and" is the opposite of "neither... nor," but can only be used with two options.

I want **both** the cake **and** the cookie.

FURTHER EXAMPLES

We'll meet up on **either** Tuesday **or** Wednesday.

My teacher told me I could **neither** paint **nor** draw.

I invited **both** my grandmother **and** my uncle.

I'm going to play **either** tennis, basketball, **or** hockey tonight.

Neither sports **nor** exercise interest me.

I went to **both** the bakery **and** the butcher shop.

68.4 AGREEMENT AFTER "EITHER... OR" AND "NEITHER... NOR"

When "either... or" or "neither... nor" are used to join two nouns,
the verb usually agrees with the second noun.

The verb agrees with the second, singular noun.

Either a tablet or a laptop is **needed for the course.**

The verb agrees with the second, plural noun.

Neither the teacher nor the children were **happy.**

If the second noun is singular and the first is plural,
either a singular verb or a plural verb can be used.

Neither the classrooms nor the office { has / have } **internet access.**

The verb can be singular or plural.

FURTHER EXAMPLES

Either a loan or a grant is **available for financial help.**

I hope either sandwiches or soup is **on the menu today.**

Either my brother or my grandparents are coming.

Either pens or pencils are suitable to use in the exam.

Neither the swimming pool nor the gym is **open on Sundays.**

Neither a shirt nor a tie is **compulsory at school.**

Neither the bread nor the cakes are ready yet.

Neither calculators nor study notes are allowed in the exam.

69 Singular and plural nouns

Nouns in English do not have a gender. They change form depending on whether they are singular, meaning there is one, or plural, meaning there is more than one.

See also:
Adjectives **92**   Articles **63**
Irregular plurals **R24**

69.1 COMMON NOUNS

Common nouns often come after articles.
Adjectives describe nouns.

car   **banana**   **skirt**   **game**   **idea**   **thought**

69.2 PROPER NOUNS

Nouns that refer to specific names of people, places, days, and months are called proper nouns, and begin with a capital letter.

Egypt **is a beautiful country.**

Egypt is a country, so it
begins with a capital letter.

"Country" is a
common noun.

FURTHER EXAMPLES

I study at Southern University.

My best friend is called Jasmine.

I can see Mars in the sky tonight.

I was born in Canada.

The Titanic sank when it hit an iceberg.

I hope to someday win an Oscar.

69.3 SPELLING RULES FOR PLURALS

To make most nouns plural, "-s" is added to the singular noun.

book → books

toy → toys

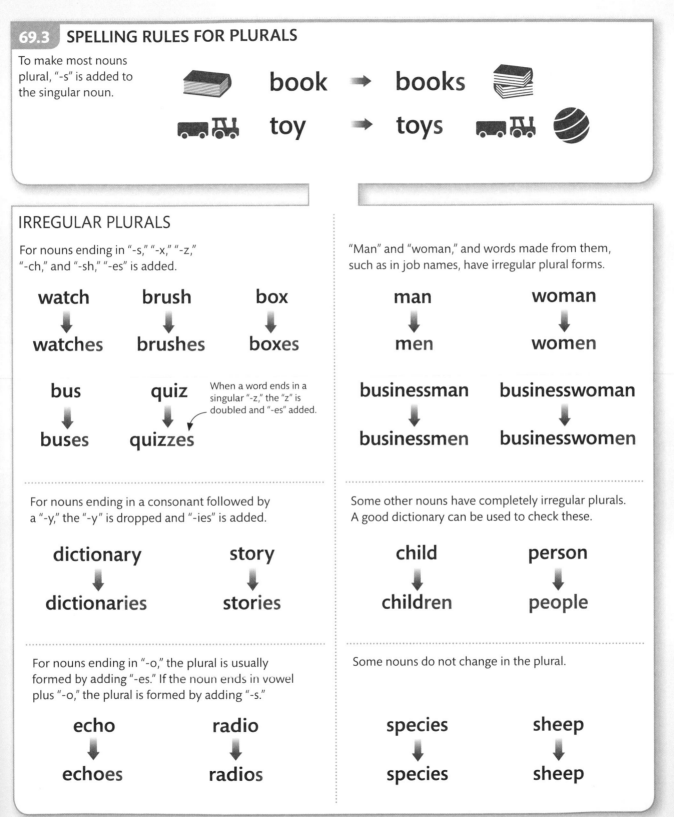

IRREGULAR PLURALS

For nouns ending in "-s," "-x," "-z," "-ch," and "-sh," "-es" is added.

watch → watches

brush → brushes

box → boxes

bus → buses

quiz → quizzes

When a word ends in a singular "-z," the "z" is doubled and "-es" added.

"Man" and "woman," and words made from them, such as in job names, have irregular plural forms.

man → men

woman → women

businessman → businessmen

businesswoman → businesswomen

For nouns ending in a consonant followed by a "-y," the "-y" is dropped and "-ies" is added.

dictionary → dictionaries

story → stories

Some other nouns have completely irregular plurals. A good dictionary can be used to check these.

child → children

person → people

For nouns ending in "-o," the plural is usually formed by adding "-es." If the noun ends in vowel plus "-o," the plural is formed by adding "-s."

echo → echoes

radio → radios

Some nouns do not change in the plural.

species → species

sheep → sheep

70 Countable and uncountable nouns

In English, nouns can be countable or uncountable.
Countable nouns can be individually counted. Objects
that aren't counted are uncountable.

> **See also:**
> Forming questions **34** Articles **63**
> Numbers **74** Quantity **75**

70.1 COUNTABLE AND UNCOUNTABLE NOUNS

"A," "an," or numbers are used to talk about countable nouns.
"Some" can be used for both countable and uncountable nouns.

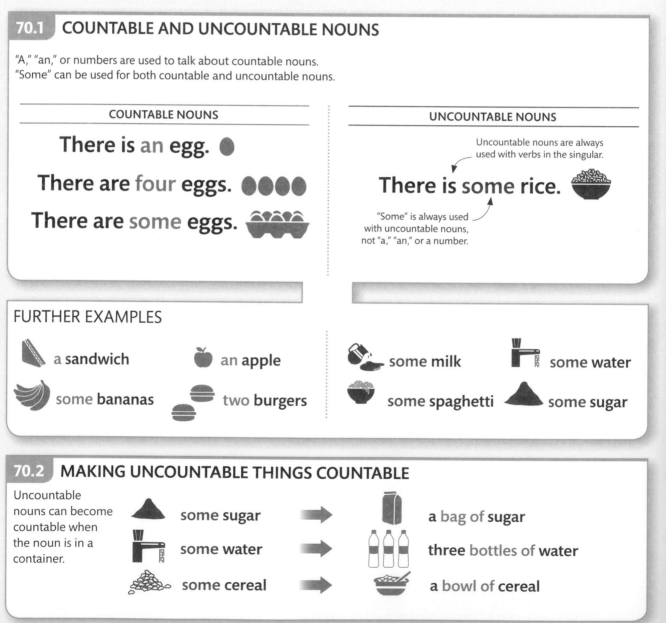

COUNTABLE NOUNS

There is an egg.

There are four eggs.

There are some eggs.

UNCOUNTABLE NOUNS

Uncountable nouns are always
used with verbs in the singular.

There is some rice.

"Some" is always used
with uncountable nouns,
not "a," "an," or a number.

FURTHER EXAMPLES

a **sandwich**

an **apple**

some **bananas**

two **burgers**

some **milk**

some **water**

some **spaghetti**

some **sugar**

70.2 MAKING UNCOUNTABLE THINGS COUNTABLE

Uncountable
nouns can become
countable when
the noun is in a
container.

some **sugar** → a bag of **sugar**

some **water** → three bottles of **water**

some **cereal** → a bowl of **cereal**

70.3 NEGATIVES

For both countable and uncountable nouns, "any" is used in negative sentences and questions.

COUNTABLE NOUNS	UNCOUNTABLE NOUNS

There are some eggs.

There is some rice.

There aren't any eggs.
The verb is plural.

There isn't any rice.
The verb is singular.

Are there any eggs?
The verb is plural.

Is there any rice?
The verb is singular.

70.4 QUESTIONS ABOUT QUANTITIES

"Many" is used to ask questions about quantities of countable nouns, and "much" to ask questions about quantities of uncountable nouns.

How many eggs are there?
The verb is plural.

How much rice is there?
The verb is singular.

FURTHER EXAMPLES

How many cupcakes are there?

How many apples are there?

How much cheese is there?

How much chocolate is there?

⚠ COMMON MISTAKES "MUCH" AND "MANY"

"Much" can only be used with uncountable nouns and the verb must always be singular.

How much pasta is there? ✓   **How many pasta are there?** ✗

71 Subject–verb agreement

One of the basic principles of English is that subjects and verbs must agree in number. Some subjects, however, can act like singular or plural nouns depending on the context.

See also:
Present simple **1**
Singular and plural nouns **69**

71.1 PLURAL NOUNS WITH SINGULAR AGREEMENT

Books and other works of art that end in a plural noun are used as singular for agreement.

Even though "tales" is plural, *The Canterbury Tales* is a single work of literature.

The Canterbury Tales was first published in the 1400s.

Other nouns look like they are plural because they end in an "-s," but have singular agreement. These include many place names and academic subjects.

Mathematics is becoming a more popular subject.

FURTHER EXAMPLES

Little Women **is a novel by Louisa May Alcott.**

The Netherlands is famous for its tulip industry.

Gymnastics was the most enjoyable sport at school.

Politics is often a topic for academic debate.

Athletics was an important part of the ancient Olympic Games.

71.2 COLLECTIVE NOUNS

Collective nouns have a singular form, but refer to a number of people or objects as a group. In US English they generally take a singular verb. In UK English they can often be used with either singular or plural verbs.

If the subject describes a singular body, then the verb form must be singular.

The team is getting a new manager next year.

[The team as a whole is getting a new manager.]

Subject describes a collection of individuals.

UK only.

The team are feeling excited about the news.

[Each individual member of the team is feeling excited.]

FURTHER EXAMPLES

The society is going to have a meeting next week.

The society are discussing how often they should meet.

The band has just released its new album.

The band have been on tour to promote their new album.

The government is located in the capital city.

The government are in talks with the US.

My family is bigger than most other families I know.

My family are going away together for the first time in years.

The company has hired some new staff.

The company have been busy baking for a charity cake sale.

72 Abstract and concrete nouns

Most abstract nouns are uncountable. Some, however, can be either countable or uncountable, and the two forms often mean slightly different things.

See also:
Singular and plural nouns **69**
Countable and uncountable nouns **70**

72.1 ABSTRACT AND CONCRETE NOUNS

Abstract nouns refer to ideas, events, concepts, feelings, and qualities that do not have a physical form. Concrete nouns are things that can be seen, touched, heard, or smelled.

He has a lot of books, but not much knowledge.

"Books" is a countable, concrete noun.

"Knowledge" is an uncountable, abstract noun.

FURTHER EXAMPLES

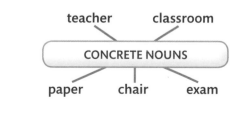

teacher   classroom

CONCRETE NOUNS

paper   chair   exam

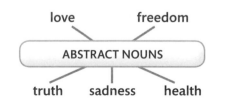

love   freedom

ABSTRACT NOUNS

truth   sadness   health

FURTHER EXAMPLES

I can't wait to prepare for this dinner party.

I'm going to get my car fixed sometime soon.

I'm having difficulty logging on to my computer.

I need to come up with better ideas to keep my boss happy.

72.2 COUNTABLE AND UNCOUNTABLE ABSTRACT NOUNS

Some abstract nouns have both countable and uncountable forms. The forms have a slight difference in meaning, with the countable form being specific and the uncountable form being more general.

COUNTABLE	UNCOUNTABLE
I've been there a few times. Each "time" is a specific occasion.	**There's plenty of time left.** "Time" refers to the concept in general.
He has had many successes. "Successes" are the specific achievements.	**Hard work leads to success.** "Success" refers to achievement in general.
It has some great qualities. "Qualities" refers to specific features.	**It has a reputation for quality.** "Quality" refers to a high standard.
We learned several new skills. These are the particular abilities learned.	**It takes skill to do that job.** "Skill" is the general ability to do somethig.
I've had some thoughts about it. These are several specific thoughts.	**The task requires thought.** "Thought" refers to the process of thinking.
This city has a great mix of cultures. This refers to several different cultures.	**The museum is filled with culture.** "Culture" refers to items of art and history.
There's a range of abilities in class. "Abilities" refers to a variety of different skill levels.	**She has great ability in writing.** "Ability" refers to general skill.

195

73 Compound nouns

Compound nouns are two or more nouns that act as a single unit. The first noun(s) modifies the last, in a similar way to an adjective.

> **See also:**
> Singular and plural nouns **69**
> Adjectives **92**

73.1 COMPOUND NOUNS

Two nouns can go together to talk about one thing.

Table tennis is a form of tennis played on a table.

On Tuesdays I play table tennis.

The first noun is usually singular, even if the meaning is plural.

A picture book is a book of pictures, but "picture" stays singular.

My baby sister loves her picture book.

Sometimes, the first noun is plural.

My brother always plays on his games console.

"Games" is plural.

Some compound nouns are written as two separate words, some as one word, and some with a hyphen between the two. There are no clear rules for this, but good dictionaries can be used to check.

toothbrush   **bus stop**   **six-pack**

Hyphen

FURTHER EXAMPLES

The meeting is in the town hall.

I eat dinner at the kitchen table.

I'm having my 44th birthday party.

I buy tickets at the ticket office.

We were in a cycle race.

I've always wanted a sailboat.

73.2 LONGER COMPOUND NOUNS

Two or more nouns can be put with another noun to modify it. This structure is common in newspaper headlines in order to save space.

I came first in the table tennis tournament.

Bank robbery ringleader capture confirmed.

This means "the capture of the ringleader of the bank robbery" has been confirmed.

73.3 PLURAL COMPOUND NOUNS

To make a compound noun plural, the final noun becomes plural.

The summer party was fun.

Summer parties are always fun.

"Party" becomes "parties."

FURTHER EXAMPLES

Restaurant chains are reliable when you need a quick meal.

I have a collection of teapots.

I organize my bookcases when they start to look messy.

I spend a lot of time waiting at bus stops.

74 Numbers

Cardinal numbers are used for counting and saying how many of something there are. Ordinal numbers give the position of something in an ordered list.

> **See also:**
> Singular and plural nouns **69**
> Quantity **75** Approximate quantity **76**

74.1 CARDINAL NUMBERS

1 one	**2** two	**3** three	**4** four	**5** five	**6** six
7 seven	**8** eight	**9** nine	**10** ten	**11** eleven	**12** twelve
13 thirteen	**14** fourteen	**15** fifteen	**16** sixteen	**17** seventeen	**18** eighteen
19 nineteen	**20** twenty	**21** twenty-one	**22** twenty-two	**30** thirty	**40** forty
50 fifty	**60** sixty	**70** seventy	**80** eighty	**90** ninety	**100** one hundred

74.2 SAYING NUMBERS

In US English, people say "zero" for the number "0," whereas in UK English, other words for "0" are possible. When listing repeated numbers, for example part of a phone number, in US English each number is said individually. In UK English, other expressions are possible.

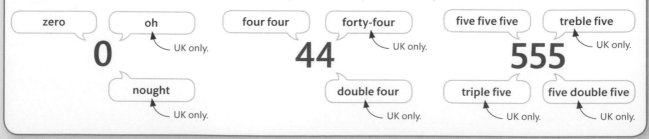

| zero | oh — UK only. | four four | forty-four — UK only. | five five five | treble five — UK only. |

0 — nought — UK only.

44 — double four — UK only.

555 — triple five — UK only. — five double five — UK only.

74.3 LARGE NUMBERS

You can say "one hundred" or "a hundred." Both are correct. Don't add "s" to "hundred," "thousand," or "million."

100 — one hundred / a hundred

101 — one hundred and one

200 — two hundred — No "s" at the end.

1,000 — one thousand / a thousand

1,200 — one thousand, two hundred

3,000 — three thousand

1,000,000 — one million / a million

1,300,000 — one million, three hundred thousand

40,000,000 — forty million

Commas are used to separate long rows of figures.

FURTHER EXAMPLES

In UK English, add "and" before the last two numbers to say numbers higher than one hundred. In US English, this is considered informal.

2,876 — two thousand, eight hundred and seventy-six

"And" goes before "seventy-six."

54,041 — fifty-four thousand and forty-one

100,922 — one hundred thousand, nine hundred and twenty-two

296,308 — two hundred and ninety-six thousand, three hundred and eight

Use commas to separate millions, thousands, and hundreds.

1,098,283 — one million, ninety-eight thousand, two hundred and eighty-three

74.4 SIMILAR SOUNDING NUMBERS

It is important to stress the correct syllable in these numbers to avoid confusion.

Stress the last syllables.

Stress the first syllables.

13 thir<u>teen</u>   30 <u>thir</u>ty

14 four<u>teen</u>   40 <u>for</u>ty

15 fif<u>teen</u>   50 <u>fif</u>ty

16 six<u>teen</u>   60 <u>six</u>ty

17 seven<u>teen</u>   70 <u>seven</u>ty

18 eigh<u>teen</u>   80 <u>eigh</u>ty

19 nine<u>teen</u>   90 <u>nine</u>ty

199

1st
first

2nd
second

3rd
third

4th
fourth

5th
fifth

6th
sixth

7th
seventh

8th
eighth

9th
ninth

10th
tenth

11th
eleventh

12th
twelfth

13th
thirteenth

14th
fourteenth

15th
fifteenth

16th
sixteenth

17th
seventeenth

18th
eighteenth

19th
nineteenth

20th
twentieth

21st
twenty-first

22nd
twenty-second

30th
thirtieth

40th
fortieth

50th
fiftieth

60th
sixtieth

70th
seventieth

80th
eightieth

90th
ninetieth

100th
one-hundredth

74.6 DATES

In the US, people often describe dates by writing cardinal numbers and saying ordinal numbers. In the UK, people use ordinal numbers to write and say dates.

His birthday is on

In US English, the number is written after the month.

May 18 (US)
May the 18th (UK)
the 18th of May (UK)

May eighteenth

May the eighteenth

the eighteenth of May

74.7 FRACTIONS

You might see fractions written out as words. Aside from "half" (½) and "quarter" (¼), the bottom number of a fraction is written or spoken as an ordinal number.

¼ — a quarter
⅓ — a third
½ — a half
⅗ — three fifths
1½ — one and a half

Use ordinal numbers for the bottom of a fraction.

Use cardinal numbers for the top of a fraction.

Use "and" to link a whole number and a fraction.

74.8 DECIMALS

Decimals are always written as numbers, not words. The decimal point is spoken as "point," and all numbers after the decimal point are spoken separately.

There are three ways of saying decimals that begin with 0.

Decimal points are written in English using a period, or full stop.

0.5 — point five / nought point five / zero point five

UK only.

1.7 — one point seven

3.97 — three point nine seven

This is not said as "three point ninety-seven."

74.9 PERCENTAGES

The % symbol is written and spoken as "percent." "Per cent" is also sometimes written in UK English. Percentages are normally written as numbers, not words.

1% — one percent
99% — ninety-nine percent
55.5% — fifty-five point five percent
12% — twelve per cent
70% — seventy per cent
100% — one hundred per cent

75 Quantity

In English there are many ways to express general or specific quantities, say whether quantities are adequate, and compare different quantities.

See also:
Singular and plural nouns **69**
Countable and uncountable nouns **70**

75.1 USING QUANTITY PHRASES

English has different phrases for quantities when the exact number is not known.

"Some" is used when there are more than one, but the exact quantity is unknown.

There are some buildings.

"A few" is used for small numbers.

There are a few buildings.

"Lots of" is used for large numbers.

There are lots of buildings.

FURTHER EXAMPLES

There are some very old trees in my local park.

There are a few items on the menu that I'd like to try.

There are a few sights that I'd like to see while I'm here.

There are lots of mountains in the Alps that I'd love to climb.

There are some vegetables that I really don't like.

There are a few cars parked outside my house.

Lots of my friends rely on trains to get to work.

There are lots of people waiting outside the gallery.

75.2 "ENOUGH / TOO MANY" WITH COUNTABLE NOUNS

"Enough," "not enough," and "too many" are used to to talk about quantities of countable nouns, which are objects or things that can be easily counted.

We need four eggs. Do we have enough?

"Enough" is used for questions.

We have two eggs. That's not enough.

Indicates there are too few.

We have four eggs. That's enough.

"Enough" is the correct amount.

Don't use five eggs. That's too many.

Indicates more than enough.

FURTHER EXAMPLES

There are enough apples here.

There aren't enough employees.

I don't have enough shoes.

You have too many clothes.

75.3 "ENOUGH / TOO MUCH" WITH UNCOUNTABLE NOUNS

"Enough," "not enough," and "too much" are used to talk about amounts of uncountable nouns, which are things that cannot easily be counted.

We need eight ounces of flour. Do we have enough?

4oz — not enough flour

Indicates too little.

8oz — enough flour

Indicates the correct amount.

12oz — too much flour

Indicates more than is needed or wanted.

FURTHER EXAMPLES

There is enough milk.

I don't have enough energy.

There isn't enough time.

There is too much food.

75.4 "A LOT OF" AND "LOTS OF"

"A lot of" and "lots of" are commonly used informally before uncountable nouns and plural countable nouns to indicate that there is a large quantity of something.

A lot of } people play sports to keep fit.
Lots of

FURTHER EXAMPLES

There was a lot of food at the event.

The event raised a lot of money.

The charity received lots of donations.

Lots of people enjoy charity events.

75.5 "LITTLE" FOR SMALL AMOUNTS

"Little" is used with uncountable nouns to say that there is not much of something in UK English. It emphasizes how small the amount is.

"A little" is used with uncountable nouns to mean "some." It emphasizes that the amount, though small, is enough.

little = not much

I have little money left. I can't afford to visit the wildlife park.

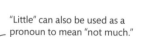

a little = some

I have a little money left. Should we visit the wildlife park?

"Little" can also be used as a pronoun to mean "not much."

Little can be done about the decreasing number of red squirrels.

Informally, "a (little) bit of" can be used instead of "a little."

There's a little bit of the park that we haven't seen yet.

75.6 "FEW" FOR SMALL NUMBERS

"Few" is used with plural countable nouns to say that there are not many of something. It emphasizes how small the number is.

"A few" is used with plural countable nouns to mean "some." It emphasizes that the number, though small, is enough.

few = not many

There are few rare birds here.
We probably won't see any.

a few = some

There are a few rare birds here.
We might see one.

FURTHER EXAMPLES

"Few" can also be used as a pronoun to mean "not many."

Few are willing to contribute to the upkeep of the national park.

"Very" can be used to stress that the number of something is even smaller.

I wanted to see an owl, but very few can be seen during the day.

75.7 "QUITE A FEW" AND "QUITE A BIT (OF)" FOR BIG QUANTITIES

The phrases "quite a bit of" and "quite a few" are understatements that actually mean "a lot" or "many."

quite a few = many

The park is home to quite a few species.

quite a bit of = a lot of

There is quite a bit of open space for the animals.

FURTHER EXAMPLES

Quite a few of the students in my class don't like History.

There are quite a few books that I'd like to read.

There's still quite a bit of snow on the ground.

She ate quite a bit of cake at her birthday party.

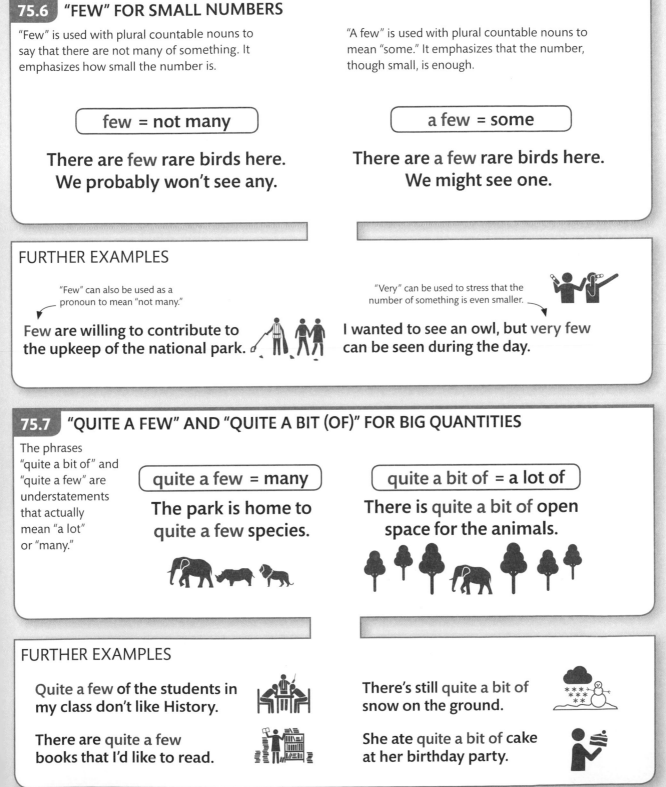

75.8 "MORE"

"More" is used to show that there is a greater quantity or amount of something. It is used with both countable and uncountable nouns.

"Cookies" is a countable noun.

I'm buying more cookies.

We need more milk.

"Milk" is an uncountable noun.

FURTHER EXAMPLES

I like spending more time with my family.

We raised even more money for charity.

"Even" can be added for emphasis.

Our new house has more space.

More and more people are donating.

"More and more" shows that the amount is increasing over time.

75.9 "FEWER" AND "LESS"

"Fewer" and "less" are used to show that there is a smaller quantity or amount or something. "fewer" belongs with plural countable nouns and "less" with uncountable nouns.

"People" is a plural countable noun.

Fewer people drive cars these days.

Traveling by bus or train uses less fuel.

"Fuel" is an uncountable noun.

FURTHER EXAMPLES

There are fewer whales in the oceans nowadays.

We need to spend less money.

Fewer people enjoy gardening these days.

There is much less traffic today.

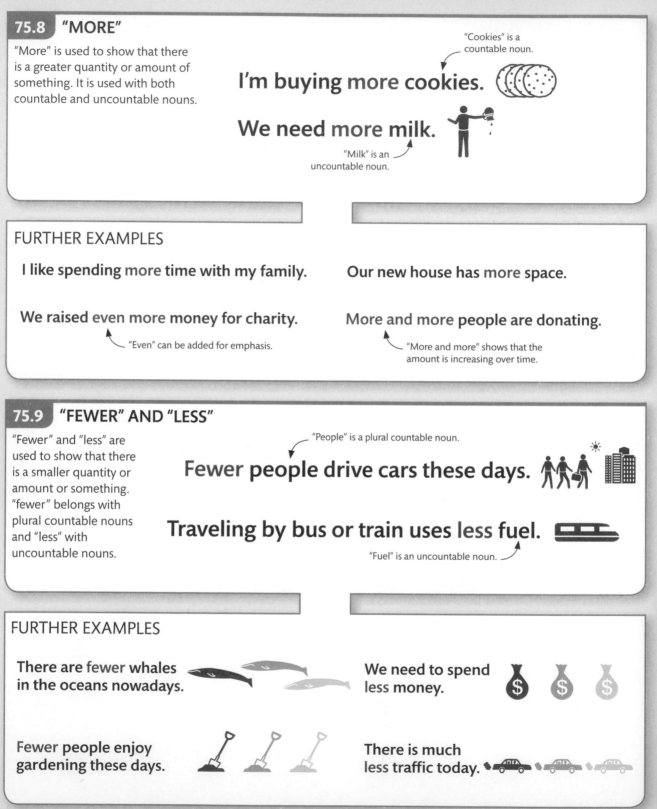

⚠ COMMON MISTAKES "FEWER" AND "LESS"

It is important to remember the distinction between countable and uncountable nouns when using "fewer" and "less."

"Fewer" is only used with plural countable nouns.

I have **fewer** potatoes than I need. ✔

"Less" is only used with uncountable nouns.

I have **less** potatoes than I need. ✖

I have **fewer** flour than the recipe requires. ✖

I have **less** flour than I need. ✔

75.10 "MORE THAN," "LESS THAN," AND "FEWER THAN"

"**More than**" is used when talking about amounts or quantities of countable and uncountable nouns.

Lions eat **more than** 15 pounds of meat each day.

"**Fewer than**" is used for groups of people or things.

There are **fewer than** 3,500 tigers in the wild.

"**Less than**" is used when talking about amounts, distances, time, and money.

The wildlife park costs **less than** $5 to visit.

FURTHER EXAMPLES

The committee holds meetings **more than** 5 times a month.

The charity survives with **fewer than** 20 volunteers.

There were **more than** 100 people at the event.

There are **fewer than** 50 tickets left for the charity concert.

Charity workers are paid on average **less than** $10 an hour.

You can donate **less than** the recommended amount.

76 Approximate quantity

If specific figures are known, it can be useful to give them. However, more general terms may be needed if figures are not known, or to avoid repetition.

See also:
Singular and plural nouns **69**
Numbers **74**   "As... as" comparisons **96**

76.1 APPROXIMATE QUANTITIES

There are certain quantifying phrases used in English when exact figures are not known, or not necessary to give.

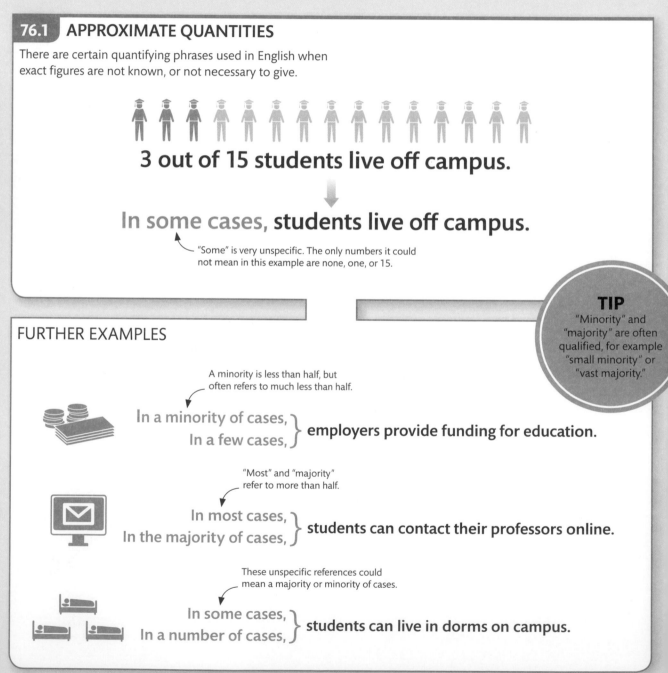

3 out of 15 students live off campus.

In some cases, students live off campus.

"Some" is very unspecific. The only numbers it could not mean in this example are none, one, or 15.

TIP
"Minority" and "majority" are often qualified, for example "small minority" or "vast majority."

FURTHER EXAMPLES

A minority is less than half, but often refers to much less than half.

In a minority of cases,
In a few cases,
} **employers provide funding for education.**

"Most" and "majority" refer to more than half.

In most cases,
In the majority of cases,
} **students can contact their professors online.**

These unspecific references could mean a majority or minority of cases.

In some cases,
In a number of cases,
} **students can live in dorms on campus.**

76.2 APPROXIMATE STATISTICS

Statistics can be made more general by modifying them with words such as "approximately," "about," "just," "well," or "almost."

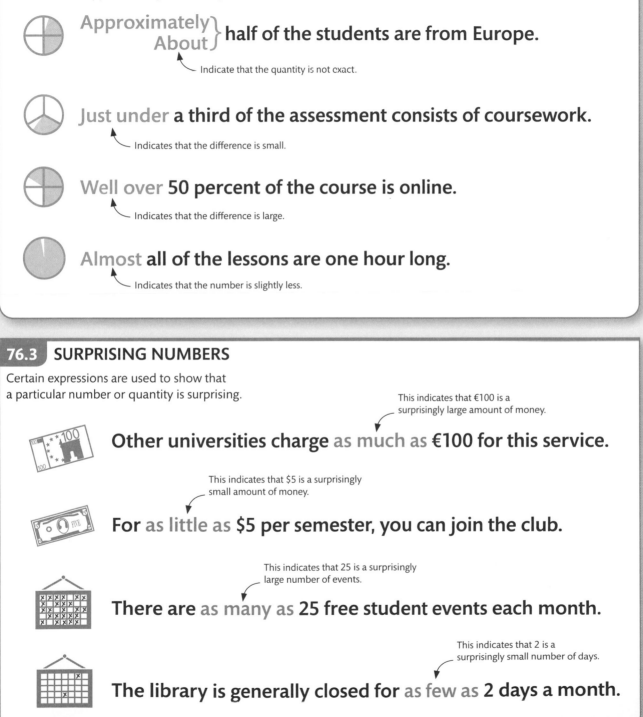

Approximately / **About** } **half of the students are from Europe.**

Indicate that the quantity is not exact.

Just under a third of the assessment consists of coursework.

Indicates that the difference is small.

Well over 50 percent of the course is online.

Indicates that the difference is large.

Almost all of the lessons are one hour long.

Indicates that the number is slightly less.

76.3 SURPRISING NUMBERS

Certain expressions are used to show that a particular number or quantity is surprising.

This indicates that €100 is a surprisingly large amount of money.

Other universities charge as much as €100 for this service.

This indicates that $5 is a surprisingly small amount of money.

For as little as $5 per semester, you can join the club.

This indicates that 25 is a surprisingly large number of events.

There are as many as 25 free student events each month.

This indicates that 2 is a surprisingly small number of days.

The library is generally closed for as few as 2 days a month.

77 Personal pronouns

Personal pronouns are used to replace nouns in a sentence. They can refer to people or things and have different forms depending on whether they are a subject or an object.

See also:
Verb patterns with objects **53**
Possession **80**   Contractions **R13**

77.1 SUBJECT PRONOUNS

Subject pronouns replace the subject of a sentence. They are used to avoid repetition, or where a name is not known. There are no formal or informal forms of pronouns in English.

Who's he?

The subject pronoun "he" is used because the speaker doesn't know the person's name.

The verbs "be" and "have" are often contracted with pronouns.

That's Andy. He's a policeman.

"He" refers to Andy to avoid repetition.

HOW TO FORM

The pronoun used depends on how many nouns it is replacing, and person (first, second, or third.)

	FIRST PERSON	SECOND PERSON	THIRD PERSON
SINGULAR	I	you	he she it
PLURAL	we	you	they

FURTHER EXAMPLES

I'm turning 25 next week.

You are a great actor.

He likes driving fast.

Stuart and I are going climbing.

They complain every time.

You make a great team.

77.2 OBJECT PRONOUNS

Object pronouns replace the object of a sentence. Most of them have a different form from the equivalent subject pronoun.

"Lizzy" is the object.

Animals love Lizzy.

Animals love her.

"Her" replaces "Lizzy."

There is no difference between direct and indirect object pronouns.

"Her" is the indirect object.

I gave her the puppy.

The puppy loves her.

"Her" is the direct object.

TIP
"You" is the same whether it is singular, plural, a subject, or an object.

HOW TO FORM

			SUBJECT			
I	we	you	he	she	it	they
↓	↓	↓	↓	↓	↓	↓
me	us	you	him	her	it	them

OBJECT

FURTHER EXAMPLES

I want to tell you that I'm sorry.

"All" can be used to show that "you" is plural.

Sam invited you all to the party.

Dave asked me to go with him.

We're sad that he won't come with us.

It was a very difficult time for them.

Georgia wanted it for Christmas.

78 Reflexive pronouns

Reflexive pronouns show that the subject of a verb is the same as its object. They can also be used in other situations to add emphasis.

> **See also:**
> Verbs patterns with objects **53**
> Personal pronouns **77**

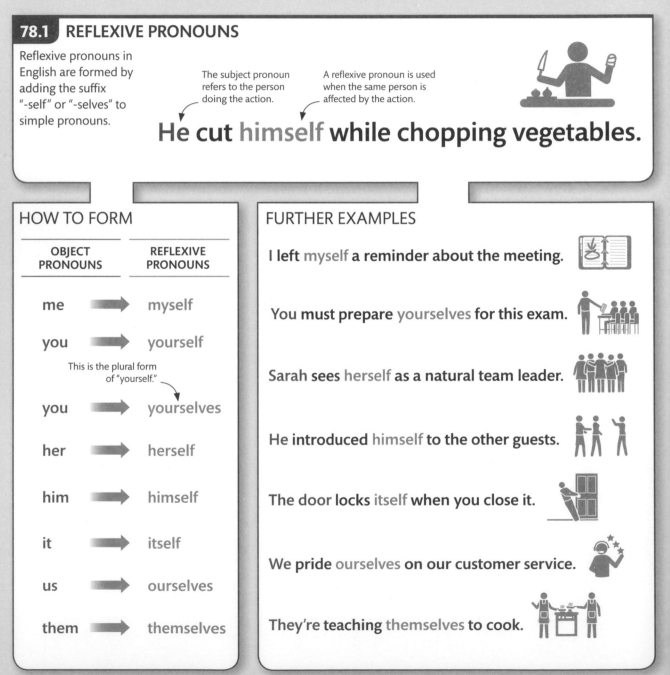

78.1 REFLEXIVE PRONOUNS

Reflexive pronouns in English are formed by adding the suffix "-self" or "-selves" to simple pronouns.

The subject pronoun refers to the person doing the action.

A reflexive pronoun is used when the same person is affected by the action.

He cut himself while chopping vegetables.

HOW TO FORM

OBJECT PRONOUNS		REFLEXIVE PRONOUNS
me	⮕	myself
you	⮕	yourself

This is the plural form of "yourself."

you	⮕	yourselves
her	⮕	herself
him	⮕	himself
it	⮕	itself
us	⮕	ourselves
them	⮕	themselves

FURTHER EXAMPLES

I **left** myself **a reminder about the meeting.**

You **must prepare** yourselves **for this exam.**

Sarah **sees** herself **as a natural team leader.**

He **introduced** himself **to the other guests.**

The door **locks** itself **when you close it.**

We **pride** ourselves **on our customer service.**

They're **teaching** themselves **to cook.**

212

78.2 VERBS THAT CANNOT BE REFLEXIVE

Several verbs that are followed by reflexive pronouns in other languages are not normally followed by a reflexive pronoun in English.

The verb "relax" is not followed by a reflexive pronoun.

I'm really stressed. I can't relax. ✓

I'm really stressed. I can't relax myself. ✗

This is wrong.

FURTHER EXAMPLES

I'll turn my music down if you can't concentrate.

He shaves every morning.

He was sick, but he's feeling better now.

She goes to bed at the same time every night.

Let's meet at the café at 2:30.

She washes her hair every evening.

I get up early every day.

I often hurry out of the house.

⚠ COMMON MISTAKES REFLEXIVE PRONOUNS

A reflexive pronoun can only be used if the subject and object of the sentence are the same. If the object is different from the subject, an object pronoun should be used instead.

The subject of the sentence is "my boss," so it is correct to use an object pronoun.

My boss invited Joe and me to the meeting. ✓

My boss invited myself and Joe to the meeting. ✗

"I" is not the subject of the sentence, so it is wrong to use a reflexive pronoun.

78.3 USING REFLEXIVE PRONOUNS FOR EMPHASIS

Sometimes reflexive pronouns are not essential to the grammar of the sentence, but can be used to add emphasis in different ways.

The company director gave the talk.

This sentence makes sense without a reflexive pronoun.

Adding the reflexive pronoun at the end of the clause emphasizes that the action was not done by someone else.

The company director gave the talk himself.

[The company director gave the talk, rather than getting someone else to do it.]

Adding the reflexive pronoun directly after the subject emphasizes its importance.

The company director himself gave the talk.

[The company director, who is an important person, gave the talk.]

FURTHER EXAMPLES

You don't have to do the dishes. I'll do them myself.

She's fixing her car herself. It's cheaper than taking it to the garage.

The meal itself wasn't very good, but it was a great evening.

The board members themselves will be at the meeting today.

I do my laundry myself, but my dad does my sister's for her.

I wanted us to build the furniture ourselves, but it's not going well.

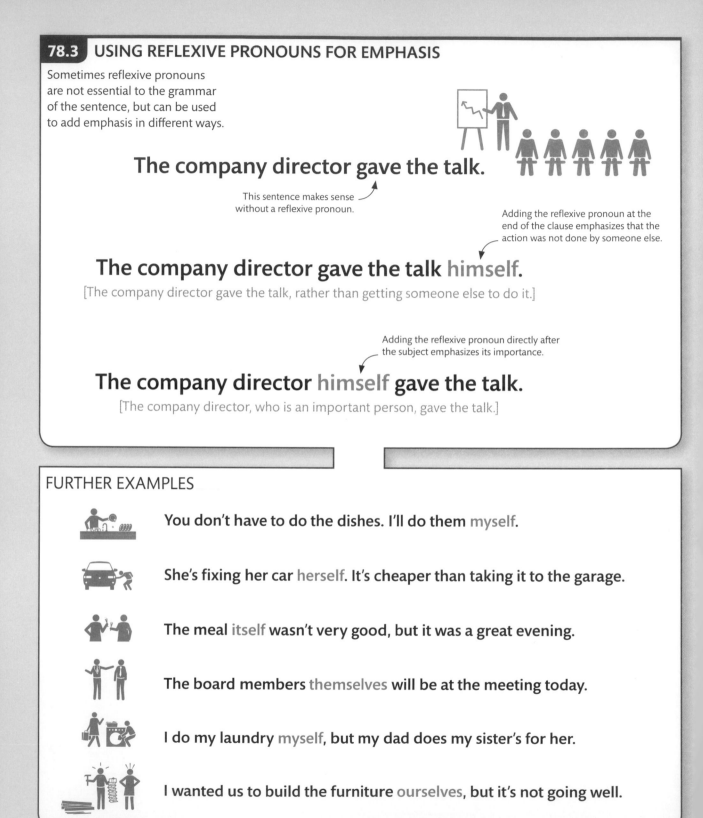

78.4 REFLEXIVE COLLOCATIONS

Many collocations contain reflexive pronouns. They often follow the pattern verb plus reflexive pronoun plus preposition.

She still has to familiarize herself with **company policy.**

FURTHER EXAMPLES

Reflexive pronouns are often used in the imperative. Here, "yourself" implies that "you" is the subject.

TIP
Sometimes the subject is not included, but is implied by the reflexive pronoun.

Are you leaving early today? Enjoy yourself!

The managers don't concern themselves with **minor issues.**

Remember to behave yourselves **when you are in public.**

Try to tear yourself away from **the computer as often as possible.**

He was sitting by himself **in the café.**

"By" is used with a reflexive pronoun to mean "alone."

78.5 "EACH OTHER"

When two or more people or things perform the same action to the other, "each other" is used instead of a reflexive pronoun.

Amy and Raj looked at each other.

[Amy looked at Raj and Raj looked at Amy.]

Amy and Raj looked at themselves in the mirror.

[Amy looked at herself in the mirror and Raj looked at himself in the mirror.]

FURTHER EXAMPLES

"One another" means the same as "each other."

They gave each other **presents.**

The children are shouting at one another.

My cats hate each other!

We're helping each other **with our homework.**

Indefinite pronouns

Indefinite pronouns, such as "anyone," "someone," and "everyone," are used to refer to a person or object, or a group of people or objects, without explaining who or what they are.

See also:
Present simple **1**
Forming questions **34**

79.1 "ANYONE" AND "SOMEONE"

"Someone" and "somebody" refer to an unspecified person in a positive statement or question. "Anyone" and "anybody" refer to an unspecified person in a question or negative statement.

Did anyone call me this morning?

Yes, someone called you at 11 o'clock.

Do you want to talk to somebody?

"Somebody" means the same as "someone," but is more informal.

No, I don't want to talk to anybody.

"Anybody" means the same as "anyone," but is more informal.

FURTHER EXAMPLES

Is someone working late?

Can somebody carry my bag?

I gave somebody a flower.

Someone gave me a present.

I didn't give anybody your name.

Did anyone buy a gift for Mrs. Tan?

I don't know anyone in this town.

Did anybody here send me this letter?

79.2 "EVERYONE" AND "NO ONE"

"Everyone" refers to a whole group of people.
"No one" means no person in a group.

"No one" is written as two words.

Why is there no one in the office?

Everyone is at the big meeting.

The singular form of the verb is used with "everyone" and "everybody."

"Everybody" means the same as "everyone," but is less formal.

Where is everybody?

I don't know, there's nobody here.

The singular form of the verb is used with "nobody" and "no one."

"Nobody" means the same as "no one."

FURTHER EXAMPLES

Nobody wants to come with me.

I'm at the park with everyone if you'd like to join us.

Everybody has some kind of special skill.

There was nobody but me at work until 10am.

⚠️ **COMMON MISTAKES** "NO ONE" AND "ANYONE"

"No one" and "nobody" go in positive statements and questions. "Anyone" and "anybody" go in negative statements and questions.

This is a negative statement, so "anyone" or "anybody" is used.

There isn't anyone here. ✓

There isn't no one here. ✗

This is a negative statement, so "no one" is incorrect.

217

"Something" and "anything" refer to an unspecified or unnamed object or thing. "Something" can only be used in questions and positive statements, whereas "anything" can be used in negative statements as well as questions and positive statements.

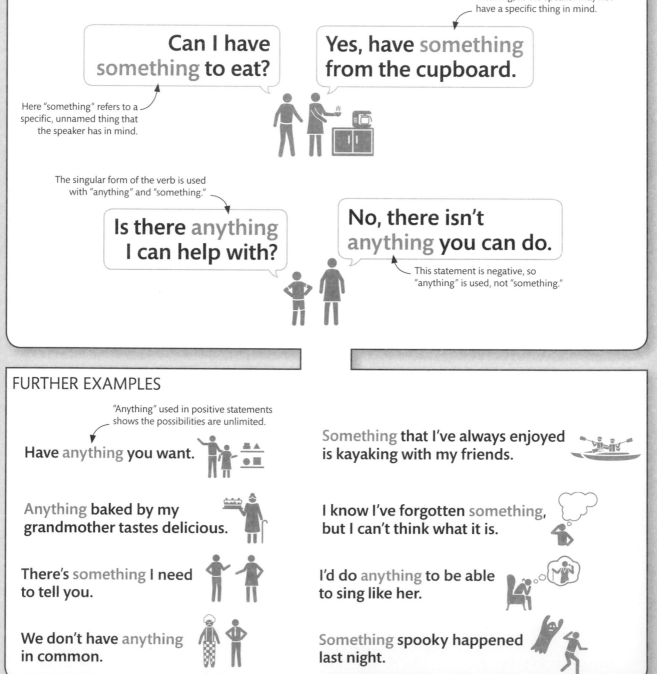

Here "something" has a more general meaning, as the speaker may not have a specific thing in mind.

Can I have something to eat?

Yes, have something from the cupboard.

Here "something" refers to a specific, unnamed thing that the speaker has in mind.

The singular form of the verb is used with "anything" and "something."

Is there anything I can help with?

No, there isn't anything you can do.

This statement is negative, so "anything" is used, not "something."

FURTHER EXAMPLES

"Anything" used in positive statements shows the possibilities are unlimited.

Have anything you want.

Anything baked by my grandmother tastes delicious.

There's something I need to tell you.

We don't have anything in common.

Something that I've always enjoyed is kayaking with my friends.

I know I've forgotten something, but I can't think what it is.

I'd do anything to be able to sing like her.

Something spooky happened last night.

79.4 "NOTHING" AND "EVERYTHING"

"**Nothing**" means that there are no available objects or things.

Tim and James have nothing in common.

There is no single thing that Tim and James have in common.

"**Everything**" means all the possible objects or things are available.

Tim and Dan do everything together.

Where "**nothing**" is used in a positive statement, "anything" can be used in a negative statement with the same meaning.

The verb is positive.

There's nothing I want to buy here.

[There isn't anything I want to buy here.]

The verb is negative.

FURTHER EXAMPLES

There's nothing I love more than a sunny day.

I want to see everything at the museum.

Everything is going well at the moment.

I know absolutely nothing about Geography.

Nothing at the exhibition was any good.

I do everything to the best of my ability.

I love that new Italian restaurant. Everything tastes so good!

Nothing interests me about politics.

80 Possession

Possessive determiners, possessive pronouns, apostrophe with "s," and the verbs "have" and "have got" are all used to express possession in English.

See also:
Forming questions **34**   Verb patterns with objects **53**   "This / that / these / those" **65**

80.1 POSSESSIVE DETERMINERS

Possessive determiners are used before a noun to show who it belongs to. They change form depending on whether the owner is singular, plural, male, or female.

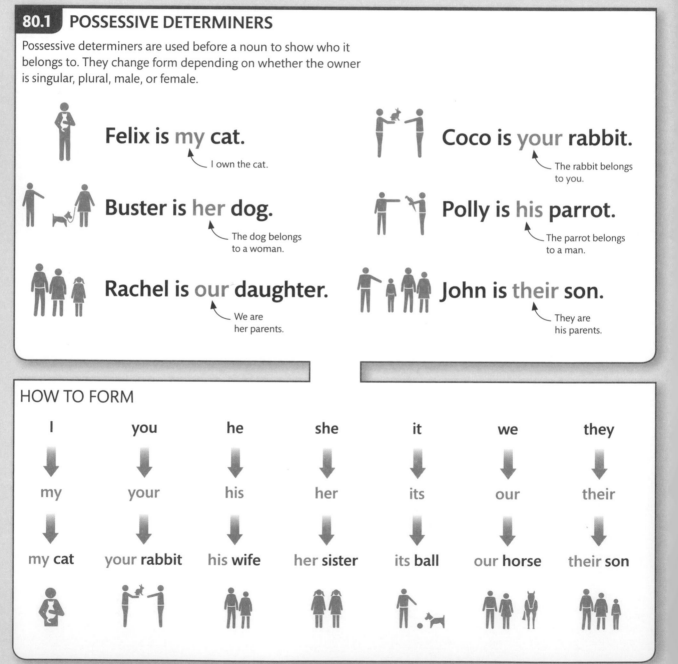

Felix is my cat.
I own the cat.

Coco is your rabbit.
The rabbit belongs to you.

Buster is her dog.
The dog belongs to a woman.

Polly is his parrot.
The parrot belongs to a man.

Rachel is our daughter.
We are her parents.

John is their son.
They are his parents.

HOW TO FORM

I	you	he	she	it	we	they
my	your	his	her	its	our	their
my cat	your rabbit	his wife	her sister	its ball	our horse	their son

80.2 POSSESSIVE PRONOUNS

Possessive pronouns can also be used to explain who owns something. Unlike possessive determiners, they replace the noun they are showing possession of.

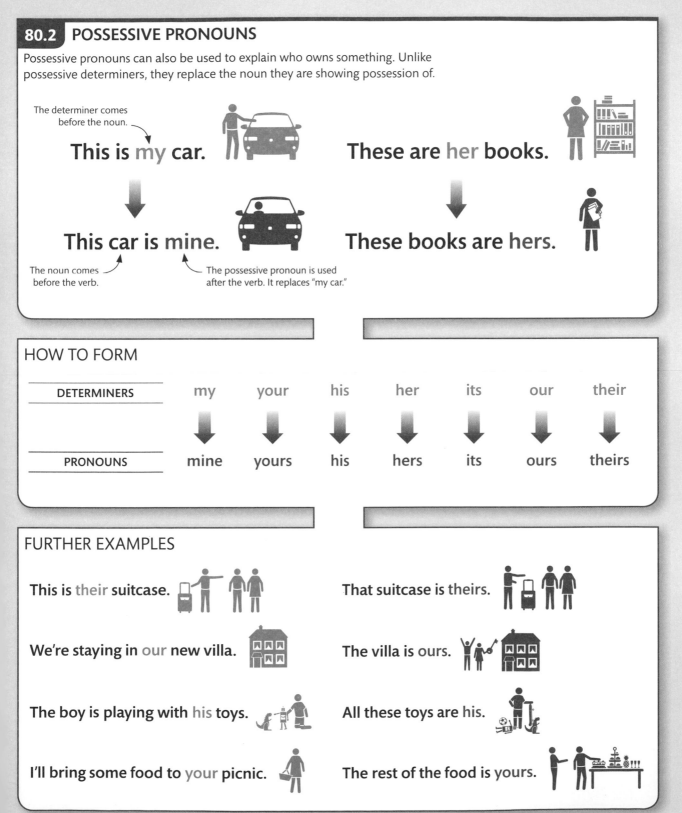

The determiner comes before the noun.

This is my car.

This car is mine.

The noun comes before the verb.

The possessive pronoun is used after the verb. It replaces "my car."

These are her books.

These books are hers.

HOW TO FORM

DETERMINERS	my	your	his	her	its	our	their
PRONOUNS	mine	yours	his	hers	its	ours	theirs

FURTHER EXAMPLES

This is their suitcase.

That suitcase is theirs.

We're staying in our new villa.

The villa is ours.

The boy is playing with his toys.

All these toys are his.

I'll bring some food to your picnic.

The rest of the food is yours.

80.3 APOSTROPHE WITH "S"

An apostrophe and the letter "s" are added to the end of a singular noun to show that what comes after the noun belongs to it.

This form is correct in English, but it is not normally used.

the mother of Lizzie

Lizzie's mother

This is a common way of talking about belonging.

An apostrophe with an "s" shows ownership.

FURTHER EXAMPLES

The "s" after the apostrophe is optional when the noun already ends in an "-s."

Tess' **dog**

Tia's **rabbit**

Dave's **grandmother**

If something belongs to more than one noun, "-'s" is only added to the last one.

Juan and Beth's **parrot**

The baby's **toy**

The dog's **ball**

⚠ COMMON MISTAKES APOSTROPHES

Apostrophes are often incorrectly added before the "s" when talking about years or decades.

I was born in the 1960s. ✓

The best decade was the 70s. ✓

I was born in the 1960's. ✗

The best decade was the 70's. ✗

This is neither possessive nor a contraction, so there is no need for an apostrophe.

80.4 APOSTROPHES AND PLURAL NOUNS

To show belonging with a plural noun that ends in "-s," just an apostrophe with no "s" is added.

Ginger is my parents' cat.

Plural nouns that end with "-s" use an apostrophe with no extra "s."

To show belonging with a plural noun that doesn't end in "-s," an apostrophe and an "s" are added.

Polly is our children's parrot.

This is formed in the same way as singular nouns, with an apostrophe and "s."

FURTHER EXAMPLES

My friends' dog is called Rex.

I'm looking after my cousins' rabbit.

That is his grandparents' house.

She cares about her students' grades.

These are the men's rooms.

It depends on the people's vote.

It is important not to confuse "its" with "it's." "Its" is a third person singular possessive determiner, and never has an apostrophe. "It's" is only ever a contraction of "it is."

The dog is playing with its ball. ✓

It's a shiny, red ball. ✓

This is a possessive so needs no apostrophe.

The dog is playing with it's ball. ✗

Its a shiny, red ball. ✗

This is a contraction of "it is," so should have an apostrophe before the "s."

80.5 "HAVE"

The verb "have" can be used to talk about what people own.

"Has" is used for the third person singular (he, she, or it).

I have **a large garage.**

She has **a yard.**

HOW TO FORM

SUBJECT	"HAVE"	OBJECT
I You We They	have	a large garage.
He She It	has	

These subject pronouns take "have."

These subject pronouns take "has."

80.6 "HAVE" NEGATIVES

Although "have" is irregular, its negative is formed in the usual way.
The negative form can also be contracted as with other verbs.

I have **a bathtub.**

I { do not / don't } have **a bathtub.**

"Do not" can be shortened to "don't."

"Does not" is used instead of "do not" for she, he, and it.

Jim has **a bathtub.**

Jim { does not / doesn't } have **a bathtub.**

"Does not" can be shortened to "doesn't."

"Have" is always used instead of "has" in the negative.

80.7 "HAVE" AND "HAVE GOT"

"Have got" is another way to say "have" when talking about possession. "Have" is appropriate in all situations, but "have got" is only used in spoken UK English.

I have **a new phone.**

"I've" cannot be used in this context.

"I have" can become "I've" when used with "got."

I've got **a new phone.**

"Got" doesn't change when the subject changes.

I don't have **a dishwasher.**

I haven't got **a dishwasher.**

"Have not" can become "haven't" when used with "got."

Do you have **your keys?**

The subject sits between "do" and "have" in questions.

Have you got **your keys?**

The subject sits between "have" and "got" in questions.

80.8 ANSWERING "HAVE" QUESTIONS

Short answers to "have" questions can be given using "do" and "don't."

"Do" is added to form a question.

Do you have **a microwave?**

"Do" goes in the positive answer.

Yes, I do.

No, I don't.

"Do not" or "don't" go in the negative answer.

Questions and answers using "have got" are formed differently. "Have got" is mostly heard in UK English.

"Have" or "has" moves to the start of the question.

Have you got **a microwave?**

"Got" does not move.

"Have" goes in the positive answer.

Yes, I have.

No, I haven't.

"Have not" or "haven't" go in the negative answer.

225

81 Defining relative clauses

A relative clause is a part of a sentence that gives more information about the subject. A defining, or restrictive, relative clause identifies the subject being talked about.

See also:
Non-defining relative clauses **82**
Other relative structures **83**

81.1 DEFINING RELATIVE CLAUSES

Defining relative clauses, also known as restrictive relative clauses, are used to describe exactly which person or thing the speaker is referring to. Without this information, the meaning of the sentence changes.

Here the defining clause gives essential information about people.

MAIN CLAUSE   DEFINING RELATIVE CLAUSE

She invited lots of friends who brought gifts.

Here the defining clause gives essential information about a thing.

MAIN CLAUSE   DEFINING RELATIVE CLAUSE

I'm looking for a job that I'll enjoy.

The defining clause can also go in the middle of the main clause.

MAIN CLAUSE   DEFINING RELATIVE CLAUSE   MAIN CLAUSE CONTINUED

The job that I heard about is interesting.

FURTHER EXAMPLES

I need a television that works!

Do you know anyone who knows how to fix a bike?

"That" can also be used for people.

He's the actor that we saw last week.

The book that I just read is excellent.

81.2 RELATIVE PRONOUNS

English uses different relative pronouns to talk about people and things.

PEOPLE

THINGS

who ⬊   ⬊ that ⬊   ⬊ which

81.3 SUBJECTS AND OBJECTS IN DEFINING RELATIVE CLAUSES

Relative clauses are made up of a subject, a verb, and usually an object. They usually start with a relative pronoun, which can be the subject or the object of the relative clause.

MAIN CLAUSE   RELATIVE CLAUSE

I'm writing about people who commit crimes.

"Who" is the subject of "commit."

MAIN CLAUSE   RELATIVE CLAUSE

I saw the car which the criminal stole.

"Which" is the object of "stole."

"The criminal" is the subject of "stole."

HOW TO FORM

If the relative pronoun is the subject of the relative clause, it must appear in the sentence.

SUBJECT OF MAIN CLAUSE	RELATIVE PRONOUN	REST OF RELATIVE CLAUSE	RETURN TO MAIN CLAUSE
The prisoner	who / that	escaped	**is very dangerous.**
The dog	which / that		

If the relative pronoun is the object of the relative clause, it can be left out. "Whom" is sometimes used when a person is the object, but this is very formal.

SUBJECT OF MAIN CLAUSE	RELATIVE PRONOUN	REST OF RELATIVE CLAUSE	RETURN TO MAIN CLAUSE
The woman	who / that / whom	you saw in the car	**is very dangerous.**
The weapon	which / that		

227

82 Non-defining relative clauses

Like defining relative clauses, non-defining relative clauses add extra information about something. However, this simply gives extra detail, rather than changing the sentence's meaning.

> **See also:**
> Quantity **75**
> Defining relative clauses **81**

82.1 NON-DEFINING RELATIVE CLAUSES

In non-defining relative clauses, also known as non-restrictive relative clauses, "who" is used to refer to people. "Whom" can be used if the person is the object of the relative clause, but this is very formal.

MAIN CLAUSE   NON-DEFINING RELATIVE CLAUSE

We spoke to Linda, who had recently been mugged.

"Who" refers to a person.

"Which" is used to refer to anything that is not a person. "That" is sometimes used instead of "which," but this is often considered wrong in non-defining relative clauses.

MAIN CLAUSE   NON-DEFINING RELATIVE CLAUSE   RETURN TO MAIN CLAUSE

Her necklace, which she'd just bought, was stolen.

"Which" refers to a thing.

FURTHER EXAMPLES

Jay, who I used to live with, came to stay with us for a few days.

"Whom" is only used in very formal situations.

The suspect, whom we had been following, was arrested.

All the burglars were arrested, which was a great relief.

The relative pronoun can refer to the entire previous clause.

Our new house, which is by the beach, is beautiful.

HOW TO FORM

Non-defining relative clauses can come in the middle of a sentence, or at the end.
If the relative clause comes in the middle, commas must go either side of it. If it
comes after the whole main clause, a comma must go at the end of the main clause.

MAIN CLAUSE	COMMA	NON-DEFINING RELATIVE CLAUSE
We spoke to Linda	**,**	**who had recently been mugged.**

A comma must go before the non-defining relative clause.

The non-defining relative clause comes at the end of the sentence.

MAIN CLAUSE	COMMA	NON-DEFINING RELATIVE CLAUSE	COMMA	REST OF MAIN CLAUSE
Her necklace	**,**	**which she'd just bought**	**,**	**was stolen.**

Commas go before and after the non-defining relative clause.

The non-defining relative clause comes between the subject and the main verb.

82.2 QUANTIFIERS WITH NON-DEFINING RELATIVE CLAUSES

In non-defining relative clauses, quantifiers can be used to say how
many people or things the relative clause refers to. In these structures,
"who" becomes "of whom," and "which" becomes "of which."

QUANTIFIER + OF + WHOM

I teach many students, all of whom are very talented.

QUANTIFIER + OF + WHICH

I teach many classes, some of which are very difficult.

FURTHER EXAMPLES

**My brother and sister, both of whom live
in Ireland, are coming to visit.**

**Lots of people, many of whom are
famous, will be at the event.**

**I have four essays due next week,
none of which are ready.**

**Tommy has three pets,
two of which are cats.**

83 Other relative structures

Relative words introduce phrases that describe a noun in the main part of the sentence. Different relative words are used to refer to different types of nouns.

See also:
Singular and plural nouns **69**
Possession **80**

83.1 "WHERE," "WHEN," AND "WHEREBY"

"Where" is the relative word used to refer to a place.

That is the place where the judge sits.
[The judge sits there.]

"When" is the relative word used to refer to a time.

He is looking forward to the day when he'll be released from prison.
[He's looking forward to the day of his release.]

"Whereby" is the relative word used to refer to a process.

A trial is the process whereby a person is found guilty or innocent of a crime.
[To be found guilty, you must go through a trial process.]

FURTHER EXAMPLES

This is the house where Shakespeare was born.

Dean is out at the moment. I'm not sure where he is.

I remember the day when you were born.

Next month is when the new students are starting.

They have an agreement whereby they share the company's profits.

There's a new system whereby students submit their work online.

83.2 "WHOSE"

"**Whose**" is the relative word used to show possession or belonging.

This is the lawyer whose client lied in court.

[This lawyer's client lied in court.]

FURTHER EXAMPLES

The UK is an example of a country whose traffic laws are very strict.

Smith & Smith, whose success rate is very high, is a respected law firm.

83.3 "WHAT"

"**What**" is the relative word used to mean "the thing which" or "the things which."

This house is just what we were looking for.

[This house is the thing which we were looking for.]

FURTHER EXAMPLES

I don't know what it is, but I'm excited to open it!

These paintings are what I've been spending all my time on.

⚠ COMMON MISTAKES WORD ORDER WITH RELATIVE STRUCTURES

If a relative structure uses a question word such as "where" or "what," the word order in the clause following this word should be left as normal and should not be formed like a question.

This is correct.

This is just what we were looking for. ✓

This is just what were we looking for. ✗

Do not invert the subject and verb.

84 Question words with "-ever"

Adding "-ever" to question words changes their meaning. These words can be adverbs or determiners in their own clauses, or they can join two clauses together.

See also:
Articles **63**   Singular and plural nouns **69**
Adverbs of manner **98**

84.1 QUESTION WORDS WITH "-EVER"

Words ending "-ever" are most commonly used to mean "it doesn't matter what," "I don't know," or to say that the options are unrestricted. They can be used as subjects and objects.

I'm still going to the game, whatever the weather's like.

[It doesn't matter what the weather is like. I'm still going.]

Here, "whichever" is an object.

We can take a taxi or walk, whichever you prefer.

[It doesn't matter to me which you choose, taxi or walking.]

Here, "whoever" is a subject.

Whoever invented the umbrella was a very clever person.

[I don't know who invented the umbrella, but they were very clever.]

We'll reschedule for whenever the sun comes out next.

[I don't know when it will be, but we'll reschedule for the next time it's sunny.]

I always check the forecast for wherever I'm going to be.

[I check the forecast for the place I am going to be, no matter where it is.]

I'm sure you'll arrive on time, however you decide to travel.

[No matter which mode of transportation you choose, I'm sure you'll be on time.]

Whatever he tells you, just ignore it.

Feel free to call in to see us whenever you're in town.

Whichever you choose, you'll have to spend a lot of money.

Wherever we end up going this summer, I know it'll be great.

Whoever did this painting is a very talented artist.

However he managed to break it, I'm not sure we'll be able to fix it.

84.2 "WHICHEVER" AND "WHATEVER" AS DETERMINERS

"Whichever" and "whatever" can come before nouns to show that the options are unspecified.

I'm sure you'll love whichever dog you choose.

[It doesn't matter which dog you choose, you'll love it.]

If you need help for whatever reason, just let me know.

[It doesn't matter what the reason is, let me know if you need help.]

84.3 OTHER USES OF "WHENEVER" AND "HOWEVER"

"**Whenever**" can also mean "every time that."

It always seems to rain whenever I go away.

[Any time I go away, it rains.]

"**However**" is often used before an adjective, as an adverb, to mean "to whatever extent."

If there's a chance of rain, however small, I'll take an umbrella.

[I'll take an umbrella, no matter how small the risk of rain.]

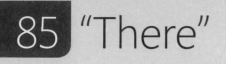

85 "There"

"There" can be used with a form of "be" to talk about the existence or presence of a person or thing. Sentences with "there" can be used in many different tenses.

See also:
Present perfect simple **11**   Future with "going to" **17**
Future with "will" **18**   Singular and plural nouns **69**

85.1 "THERE" IN THE PRESENT SIMPLE

"There is" is used to talk about singular or uncountable nouns, and "there are" is used to talk about plural nouns.

There is **a hospital in my town.**

There are **three hospitals in my town.**

FURTHER EXAMPLES

There is **a market every Saturday.**

There are **several schools and colleges.**

Uncountable noun.

There is **always traffic in the city.**

There are **some restaurants and bars.**

HOW TO FORM

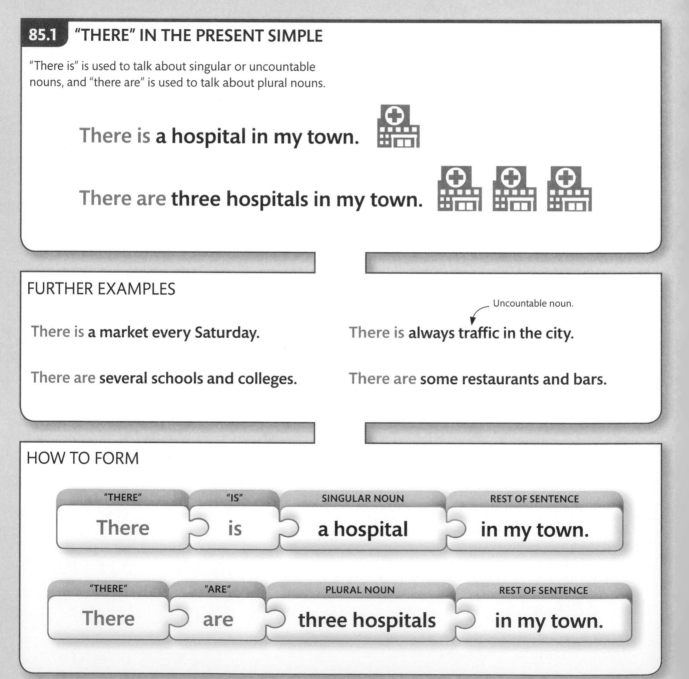

"THERE"	"IS"	SINGULAR NOUN	REST OF SENTENCE
There	is	a hospital	in my town.

"THERE"	"ARE"	PLURAL NOUN	REST OF SENTENCE
There	are	three hospitals	in my town.

85.2 "THERE" IN THE PAST SIMPLE

In the past simple, "there was" is used to talk about singular or uncountable nouns, and "there were" is used to talk about plural nouns.

There was **a party here last night.**

There were **150 people at the party!**

FURTHER EXAMPLES

There was **singing and dancing.**

There was **a clown to entertain the children.**

There was **a huge mess to clean afterwards.**

There were **balloons and streamers.**

There were **speeches after the meal.**

There were **waiters to refill the guests' drinks.**

HOW TO FORM

"THERE"	"WAS"	SINGULAR NOUN	REST OF SENTENCE
There	was	a party	here last night.

"THERE"	"WERE"	PLURAL NOUN	REST OF SENTENCE
There	were	150 people	at the party.

In the present perfect, "there has been" is used to talk about singular or uncountable nouns, and "there have been" is used to talk about plural nouns.

There has been **a decrease in client satisfaction.**

There have been **lots of complaints recently.**

"Been" doesn't change form.

FURTHER EXAMPLES

There has been **increased pressure on employees.**

There has been **a steady rise in unemployment.**

There has been **a decrease in petty crime.**

There has been **success in hiring graduates.**

There have been **many new jobs advertised.**

There have been **some thefts in the office.**

There have been **more training days for staff.**

There have been **big bonuses this year.**

HOW TO FORM

"THERE"	"HAS BEEN"	SINGULAR NOUN	REST OF SENTENCE
There	has been	a decrease	in client satisfaction.

"THERE"	"HAVE BEEN"	PLURAL NOUN	REST OF SENTENCE
There	have been	lots of complaints	recently.

"THERE" IN THE FUTURE

In the future with "will," "there will be" is used to talk about both singular and plural nouns.

There will be **a fire drill on Monday.**

There will be **fire wardens around to help.**

In the future with "going to," "there is going to be" is used to talk about singular nouns, and "there are going to be" is used to talk about plural nouns.

There is going to be **a big announcement.**

There are going to be **big changes!**

FURTHER EXAMPLES

There will be **a train strike next week.**

There will be **replacement bus services.**

There is going to be **a meeting at the office.**

There are going to be **severe delays.**

HOW TO FORM

"THERE"	"WILL BE"	SINGULAR / PLURAL NOUN	REST OF SENTENCE
There	will be	a fire drill	on Monday.

"THERE"	"IS GOING TO BE"	SINGULAR NOUN
There	is going to be	a big announcement.

"THERE"	"ARE GOING TO BE"	PLURAL NOUN
There	are going to be	big changes!

86 Introductory "it"

"It" is often used when a sentence has no clear subject, and is sometimes known as a dummy subject or empty subject.

See also:
Defining relative clauses **81**
Non-defining relative clauses **82**

86.1 "IT" AS A DUMMY SUBJECT

"It" is used to talk about the time, dates, distance, or the weather. In these sentences, "it" doesn't have a specific meaning, but it serves as the grammatical subject of the sentence.

"It" can be used to talk about the time.

What time is it? **It's 3 o'clock.**

"It" can be used to talk about distances.

How far is it to the beach? **It's 1 mile that way.**

"It" can be used to talk about the day, date, month, or year.

What day is it? **It's Tuesday.**

"It" can be used to talk about the weather.

What's the weather like today? **It's cloudy and raining.**

FURTHER EXAMPLES

It's 2 o'clock in the morning. Please stop singing!

It's the 21st century. I can't believe you still use that phone.

I'm going to walk to work. It's only two miles away.

I'm surprised that it's so sunny in the middle of January.

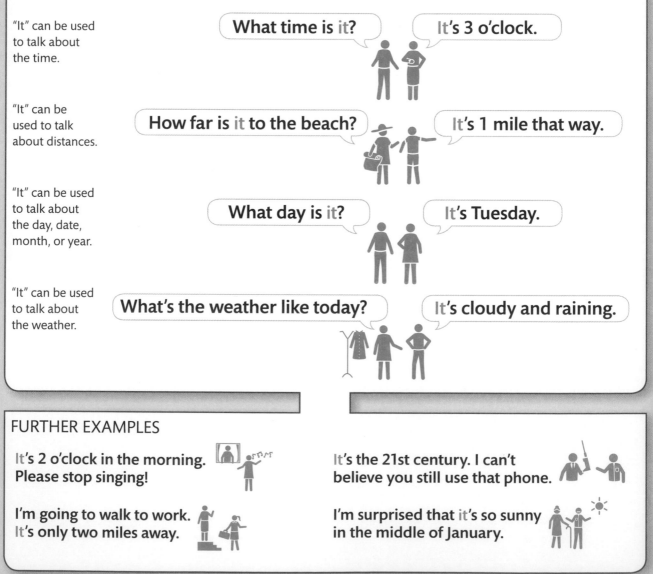

INTRODUCTORY "IT"

Certain set phrases beginning "it is" can be used at the start of a sentence. "It" is the subject of the sentence, and can be used to express a general truth or belief.

"IT" CLAUSE   INFINITIVE CLAUSE

It is easy to make mistakes in a new language.

Some "it" clauses are followed by a "to" infinitive.

"IT" CLAUSE   "THAT" CLAUSE

It is a shame that so many people give up.

Some "it" clauses are followed by "that" clauses.

FURTHER EXAMPLES INTRODUCTORY "IT"

It is important to be relaxed about making mistakes.

It is essential to give yourself time to study regularly.

It is difficult to remember facts if you don't write them down.

It's unlikely that you will be comfortable speaking aloud at first.

It's true that being able to speak a second language is useful.

It is often said that going to the country of the language helps.

"It" clauses, "what" clauses, or moving a noun to the front of a sentence can all be used to put emphasis on a certain word or phrase.

See also:
Types of verbs **49**   Defining relative clauses **81**
Non-defining relative clauses **82**

87.1 FOCUSING WITH "IT" CLAUSES

Part of a sentence can be emphasized by adding "it is" or "it was" before it, and "that" after it. This can correct a misunderstanding or emphasize something unexpected.

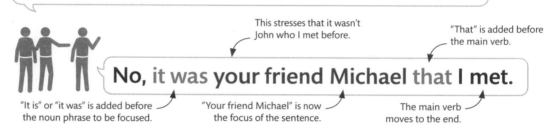

You've met my friend John before, haven't you?

This stresses that it wasn't John who I met before.

"That" is added before the main verb.

No, it was your friend Michael that I met.

"It is" or "it was" is added before the noun phrase to be focused.

"Your friend Michael" is now the focus of the sentence.

The main verb moves to the end.

FURTHER EXAMPLES

The second clause is a relative clause. It is most commonly introduced by "that," "which," or "who." "When" and "where" can also be used, but they're less formal.

It is the engine that I need to replace.

It was the doctor who I needed to call.

It was the cold weather which made me sick.

It was my colleague who prepared the food.

It was summertime when Zoe last saw her cousins.

It was in a bar where Olly first met his wife.

It was the price which changed my mind.

It was the toaster that set off the fire alarm.

87.2 FOCUSING WITH "WHAT" CLAUSES

Simple statements can be made more emphatic by adding "what" with the verb "be." This structure is often used with verbs expressing emotions, such as "love," "hate," "like," and "want."

Would you like to go to a movie?

This has more emphasis than "I really want to go to bed early."

No, thanks. What I really want is to go to bed early.

"What" is added to the start of the sentence.

The focused information is put outside the "what" clause.

FURTHER EXAMPLES

What **we hated** was the bad service.

What **I like here** is the weather.

What **they loved the most** were the museums.

What **she enjoys the most** is the music.

87.3 FOCUSING WITH A NOUN

If the subject of the sentence cannot be replaced with "what" (for example, people, places, or times) a general noun that has a similar meaning can be used.

I've been to many countries.
The place **I most enjoyed visiting** was Nepal.

I've read about some great people.
The woman **I respect the most** is Marie Curie.

I don't know why the show was canceled.
The reason **they gave** was not good enough.

I have lots of fun memories.
The evening **I remember most** is my first concert.

Inversion

Reversing the normal order of words, or inversion, can be used for emphasis or a sense of drama. It is common after certain types of adverbials.

See also:
Present simple **1**   Types of verbs **49**
Adverbs of frequency **102**

88.1 INVERSION AFTER NEGATIVE ADVERBIALS

In more formal or literary texts, inversion of a verb and its subject is used for emphasis after negative adverbial phrases like "not only," "not since," and "only when."

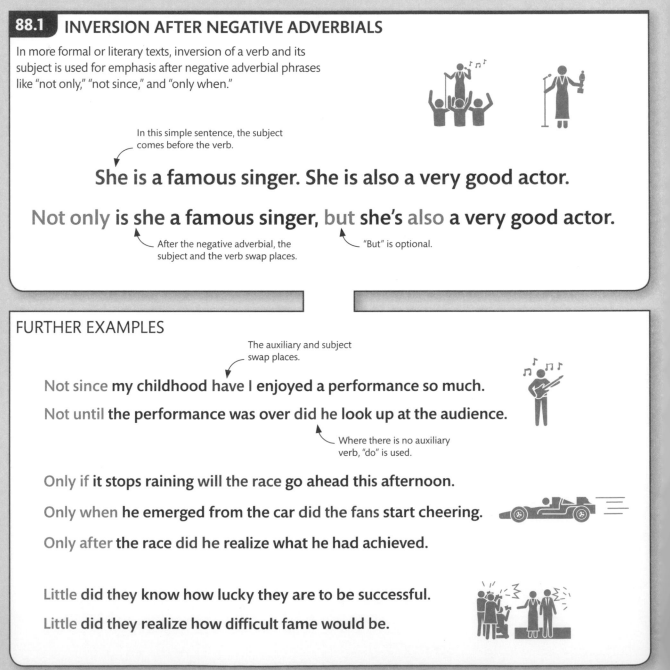

In this simple sentence, the subject comes before the verb.

She is a famous singer. She is also a very good actor.

Not only is she a famous singer, but she's also a very good actor.

After the negative adverbial, the subject and the verb swap places.

"But" is optional.

FURTHER EXAMPLES

The auxiliary and subject swap places.

Not since **my childhood have I enjoyed a performance so much.**

Not until **the performance was over did he look up at the audience.**

Where there is no auxiliary verb, "do" is used.

Only if **it stops raining will the race go ahead this afternoon.**

Only when **he emerged from the car did the fans start cheering.**

Only after **the race did he realize what he had achieved.**

Little **did they know how lucky they are to be successful.**

Little **did they realize how difficult fame would be.**

88.2 INVERSION AFTER TIME ADVERBIALS

Inversion can be used after time adverbials that are negative or restrictive, such as "no sooner" and "never before." This emphasizes the time at which something happens, or happened.

In this simple sentence, the subject comes before the verb.

Tina had just released an album when she starred in her first movie.

The subject ("Tina") and the auxiliary verb ("had") swap places.

No sooner had Tina released an album than she starred in her first movie.

FURTHER EXAMPLES

Hardly had she stepped out of the car when fans surrounded her.

Rarely do you meet a celebrity with such talent and style.

Never before had a song reached the top of the charts so quickly.

Only sometimes does it not snow during the ski season.

88.3 INVERSION AFTER "SO" AND "NEITHER"

In order to agree with a positive statement, "be" and its subject, or an auxiliary and its subject can be inverted after "so." For a negative statement, the same is done after "neither." For a sentence that doesn't have an auxiliary, "do" is used when it is inverted.

I've never been to China.

Neither have I.

I need to get some new clothes.

So do I.

When there is no auxiliary verb, "do" is used.

I'm excited for the party tonight.

So am I!

89 Ellipsis

Some words can be left out of a sentence to avoid repetition, or when the meaning can be understood without them. This is called ellipsis.

See also:
Question words **35**
Coordinating conjunctions **110**

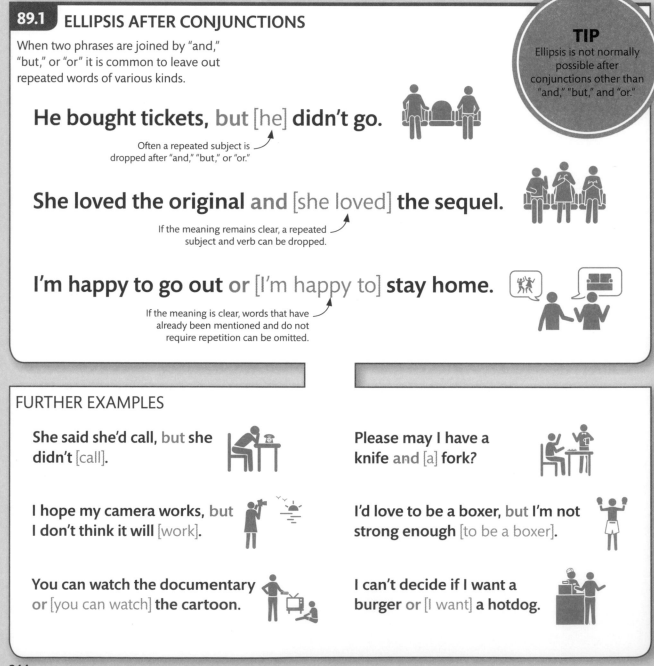

89.1 ELLIPSIS AFTER CONJUNCTIONS

When two phrases are joined by "and," "but," or "or" it is common to leave out repeated words of various kinds.

TIP
Ellipsis is not normally possible after conjunctions other than "and," "but," and "or."

He bought tickets, but [he] **didn't go.**

Often a repeated subject is dropped after "and," "but," or "or."

She loved the original and [she loved] **the sequel.**

If the meaning remains clear, a repeated subject and verb can be dropped.

I'm happy to go out or [I'm happy to] **stay home.**

If the meaning is clear, words that have already been mentioned and do not require repetition can be omitted.

FURTHER EXAMPLES

She said she'd call, but she didn't [call].

I hope my camera works, but I don't think it will [work].

You can watch the documentary or [you can watch] **the cartoon.**

Please may I have a knife and [a] **fork?**

I'd love to be a boxer, but I'm not strong enough [to be a boxer].

I can't decide if I want a burger or [I want] **a hotdog.**

89.2 CONVERSATIONAL ELLIPSIS

Words can also be left out of sentences if the meaning can be understood from the context. This kind of ellipsis does not have strict rules, and is very common in informal everyday speech, particularly when giving replies.

What time does the movie start?

Eight.

[It starts at eight o'clock.]

What kind of popcorn would you like?

Salted, please.

[I would like salted popcorn, please.]

What did you think of the film?

Complete nonsense.

[I thought the film was complete nonsense.]

89.3 QUESTION WORD CLAUSES

Clauses can be dropped after question words such as "who," "what," "where," and "how."

Somebody stole my watch, but I don't know who [stole it].

I want to buy my dad a present, but I'm not sure what [to buy him].

I want to go away, but I can't decide where [to go].

I need to fix my car, and I'm fairly certain I know how [to fix it].

90 Shortening infinitives

Phrases with infinitives can sometimes be reduced or shortened to prevent repetition. This helps language to sound more natural.

> **See also:**
> Infinitives and participles **51**

90.1 REDUCED INFINITIVES

Instead of repeating the whole infinitive clause, "to" can be used on its own if the meaning remains clear.

Let's see that new DJ tonight.

I don't really want to [see the new DJ].

If the main verb in the previous sentence or clause is "be," then the full infinitive "to be" must be used, rather than just "to."

She was really critical of the new album.

It's difficult not to be [critical of it]. The singing is awful!

FURTHER EXAMPLES

 He asked me if I wanted to cook tonight, but I'd prefer not to.

 All my friends are going to the basketball game, but I don't want to.

 I was going to bring an umbrella, but I decided not to.

 There are more flowers in the garden than there used to be.

 This packaging isn't recyclable, but it ought to be.

90.2 DROPPING THE ENTIRE INFINITIVE CLAUSE

The entire infinitive clause can be dropped, or "to" can be kept on its own after some verbs, such as "agree," "ask," "forget," "promise," "start," and "try."

Chris is going to come to the show. He { **promised** [to come]. / **promised to** [come]. }

The same structure can also be used after some nouns, such as: "chance," "plans," "promise," "idea," and "opportunity."

I haven't seen this band before. I'd love the { **chance** [to see them]. / **chance to** [see them]. }

The same structure can also be used after certain adjectives, such as "delighted," "afraid," "willing," and "determined."

I want to perform on stage, but I'm { **afraid** [to perform on stage]. / **afraid to** [perform on stage]. }

FURTHER EXAMPLES

We need to leave soon, but I'm not ready.

I would travel the world if I had the money.

I want to go out, but I haven't got any plans.

I would never do a bungee jump. I don't have the courage.

They told me I could join the team if I wanted to.
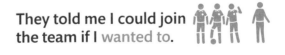

I'm going to pass my driving test. I'm determined to.

Remind me to lock the door, or I'll forget to.

Thanks for asking me to come to your wedding. I'd love to.

90.3 VERBS WITH COMPLEMENTS

The entire infinitive clause cannot be left out after verbs that have complement clauses
(phrases that complete their meaning), such as: "advise," "afford," "be able," "choose," "decide,"
"expect," "hate," "hope," "love," "need," and "prefer." "To" must be used after these.

We want to see a band tonight,
but we really can't afford to.

FURTHER EXAMPLES

I tried to get to the front of the
crowd, but I wasn't able to.

You could bring some snacks
along, but you don't need to.

I had piano lessons as a child,
but I didn't choose to.

I have never been to the opera,
but I would love to.

90.4 "WANT" AND "WOULD LIKE"

The "to" of the infinitive clause
is not usually dropped after
"want" or "would like."

He asked if I wanted to go,
and I said I would like to.

In "if" clauses, however, "to" can
be used on its own or the whole
infinitive can be dropped after
"want" or "would like."

You can come with us if you { want.
want to.

The "to" cannot be dropped in
a negative clause.

Don't go to the concert if you don't want to.

FURTHER EXAMPLES

We could play golf this
weekend, if you want.

I asked my friends to play,
but they didn't want to.

90.5 SHORTENING INFINITIVES

Sometimes "to" can be used instead
of repeating the whole infinitive.

> **Do you go to Spain
> every year?**

> **We** used to.

[We used to go to
Spain every year.]

After nouns and adjectives, sometimes
the whole infinitive can be left out.

> **Are you ready to leave?**

> **No, I'm** not ready **yet.**

[I'm not ready to leave yet.]

However the verbs "be" and "have" are not usually
omitted when they are used for possession.

> **She isn't paid much,
> but she** ought to be.

"She ought to" is wrong.

[She ought to be paid more.]

It's also not usually possible to leave out "to" after
"like," "love," "hate," "prefer," "want," and "choose."

> **Do you want to go
> to the festival?**

> **I'd** like to.

"I'd like" is wrong.

> **Do you want to
> cook tonight?**

> **I'd** prefer not to.

"I'd prefer not" is unlikely.

91 Substitution
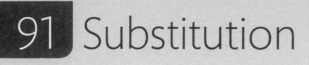

As well as ellipsis (leaving words out), repetition can be avoided by replacing some phrases with shorter ones. This is called substitution.

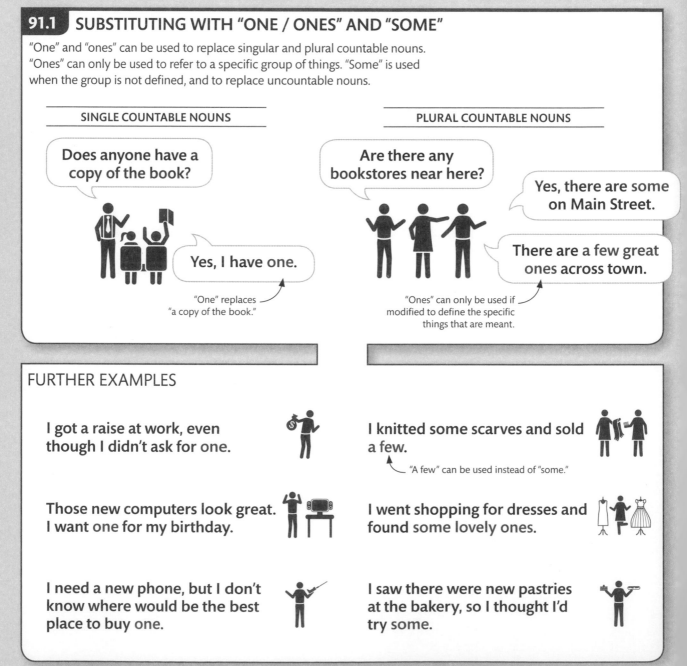

See also:
Countable and uncountable nouns **70**
The past simple **7**

91.1 SUBSTITUTING WITH "ONE / ONES" AND "SOME"

"One" and "ones" can be used to replace singular and plural countable nouns. "Ones" can only be used to refer to a specific group of things. "Some" is used when the group is not defined, and to replace uncountable nouns.

SINGLE COUNTABLE NOUNS

Does anyone have a copy of the book?

Yes, I have one.

"One" replaces "a copy of the book."

PLURAL COUNTABLE NOUNS

Are there any bookstores near here?

Yes, there are some on Main Street.

There are a few great ones across town.

"Ones" can only be used if modified to define the specific things that are meant.

FURTHER EXAMPLES

I got a raise at work, even though I didn't ask for one.

I knitted some scarves and sold a few.

"A few" can be used instead of "some."

Those new computers look great. I want one for my birthday.

I went shopping for dresses and found some lovely ones.

I need a new phone, but I don't know where would be the best place to buy one.

I saw there were new pastries at the bakery, so I thought I'd try some.

91.2 SUBSTITUTING WITH "DO"

Verbs and their complements can also be used with substitute words to avoid repetition. "Do" and "did" are often used to replace present and past simple tense verbs, for example.

Different forms of "do" replace "think."

There's water everywhere. Should I call a plumber?

Oh no! Yes, do.

"Do" prevents repetition of 'call a plumber'

I think this homework is really difficult.

I did too, so I asked for help.

I don't. It's easy.

FURTHER EXAMPLES

I need to brush my teeth more.

Yes, it's important that you do.

I thought the exam was really easy.

I didn't. I really struggled.

91.3 SUBSTITUTING WITH "SO" AND "NOT"

In positive clauses after verbs of thinking, "so" can be used to avoid repetition. "Not" or "not... so" are used in negative sentences.

Will she be signing copies of her book?

No, I don't think so.

I hope so!

I'm afraid not.

FURTHER EXAMPLES SUBSTITUTING NEGATIVES WITH "NOT... SO" AND "NOT"

It appears not.

It doesn't seem so.

"Not" or "not... so" are used with "appear," "seem," and "suppose."

I don't imagine so.

I hope not.

"Not... so" is used with "think," "believe," "expect," and "imagine."

"Not" is used with with "hope," "assume," and "be afraid" (when "afraid" means "sorry")

92 Adjectives

Adjectives are words that describe nouns. In English, they usually come before the noun that they are describing. There are several categories of adjective.

See also:
Singular and plural nouns **69**

92.1 USING ADJECTIVES

Adjectives in English are usually placed before the noun they describe. They do not change form to agree with the noun.

He is a busy man.

It is a busy town.

She is a busy woman.

Adjectives are the same for nouns that describe males or females.

These are busy streets.

Adjectives are the same for singular and plural nouns.

FURTHER EXAMPLES

This is a red shirt.

These are tall buildings.

It's a cold day.

She does great concerts.

92.2 OTHER WAYS TO USE ADJECTIVES

Sometimes, adjectives can be put after a verb such as "be" or "become."

The adjective can go at the end of the sentence after the verb "be."

The town is busy.

FURTHER EXAMPLES

That house is beautiful.

He is annoyed.

The noun can be replaced with a pronoun.

The cake is delicious.

She is very tired.

Natalie's dress is long.

92.3 TYPES OF FACT ADJECTIVES

Fact adjectives tell you a particular fact about the noun they are describing. There are many different categories of fact adjectives.

Size	The children saw an enormous dog.
Shape	It's a round ball.
Age	My great-grandmother is very old.
Color	Nicole just loves her red hat.
Nationality	I love eating French pastries.
Material	I've bought some leather shoes.

92.4 TYPES OF OPINION ADJECTIVES

Opinion adjectives describe what somebody thinks about something.
General opinion adjectives can describe lots of different things.
Specific opinion adjectives can only usually describe a certain type of thing.

| General opinion | I just bought a very nice guitar. |

"Nice" is a general opinion adjective. It can describe lots of different things.

| Specific opinion | Sylvester is such a friendly cat! |

"Friendly" is a specific opinion adjective. It usually only describes people or animals.

92.5 ADJECTIVE ORDER

When several adjectives are used together before a noun, they must go in a particular order. Opinion adjectives come before fact adjectives. General opinion adjectives always come before specific opinion adjectives, and the order of fact adjectives in a sentence depends on the type of fact that they describe.

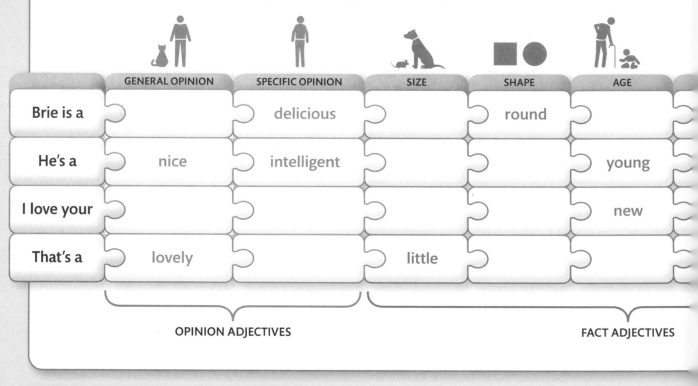

	GENERAL OPINION	SPECIFIC OPINION	SIZE	SHAPE	AGE
Brie is a		delicious		round	
He's a	nice	intelligent			young
I love your					new
That's a	lovely		little		

OPINION ADJECTIVES — FACT ADJECTIVES

92.6 ADJECTIVES WITH "-ING" AND "-ED"

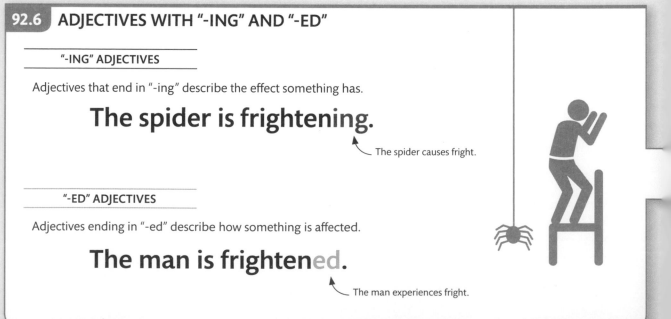

"-ING" ADJECTIVES

Adjectives that end in "-ing" describe the effect something has.

The spider is frightening.

The spider causes fright.

"-ED" ADJECTIVES

Adjectives ending in "-ed" describe how something is affected.

The man is frightened.

The man experiences fright.

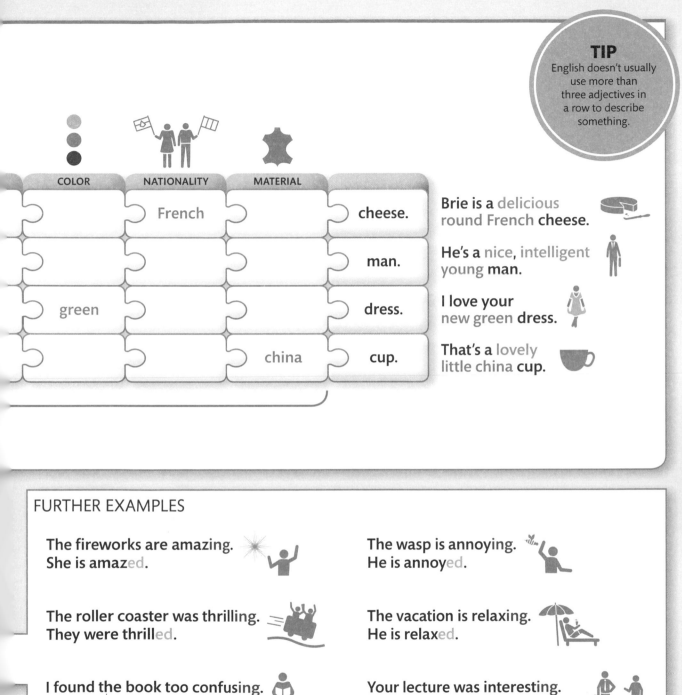

Gradable adjectives can be made weaker or stronger
by adverbs, whereas non-gradable adjectives describe
absolute qualities that cannot usually be graded.

See also:
Adjectives **92**
Adverbs of degree **100**

93.1 GRADABLE ADJECTIVES

Gradable adjectives can be
modified by adverbs to make
the adjective's original meaning
more or less powerful.

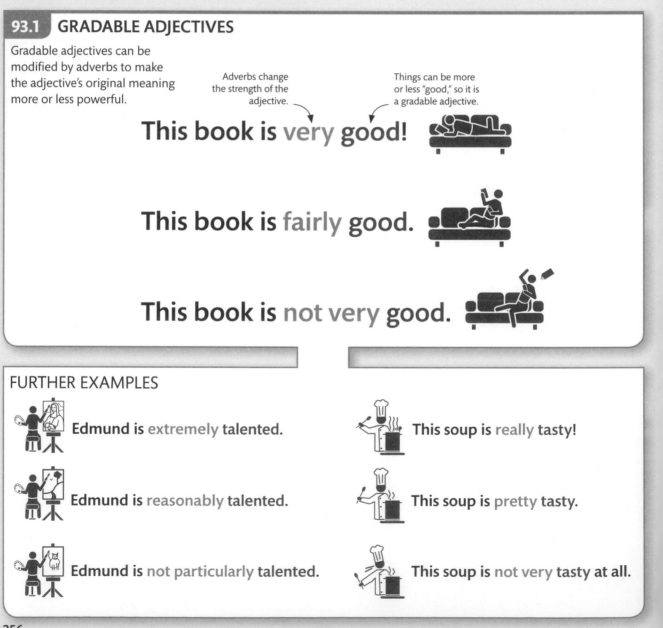

Adverbs change
the strength of the
adjective.

Things can be more
or less "good," so it is
a gradable adjective.

This book is very good!

This book is fairly good.

This book is not very good.

FURTHER EXAMPLES

Edmund is extremely talented.

Edmund is reasonably talented.

Edmund is not particularly talented.

This soup is really tasty!

This soup is pretty tasty.

This soup is not very tasty at all.

NON-GRADABLE ADJECTIVES

Non-gradable adjectives cannot usually be modified. These adjectives tend to fall into three categories: extreme, absolute, and classifying.

Non-gradable adjectives like "fantastic" cannot be modified by adverbs.

Her arguments were fantastic!

EXTREME ADJECTIVES

Extreme adjectives are stronger versions of gradable adjectives, such as "awful," "hilarious," "fantastic," or "terrifying."

The idea of "extremely" is is the meaning of "awful" already.

Her presentation was awful.

ABSOLUTE ADJECTIVES

Absolute adjectives cannot be graded because they describe fixed qualities or states, such as "unique," "perfect," or "impossible."

It is not possible for something to be more or less unique.

She has a unique presenting style.

CLASSIFYING ADJECTIVES

Classifying adjectives are used to say that something is of a specific type or class, such as "American," "nuclear," or "medical."

The audience was American.

FURTHER EXAMPLES

It's boiling in here. Can we open a window?

I'm terrified of spiders and snakes!

I am certain that he is the right person for the job.

Let's go for a walk. The weather outside is perfect.

94 Comparative adjectives

Comparative adjectives are used to compare two things. They can either be formed by adding the suffix "-er," or by putting "more" or "less" before the adjective.

See also:
Singular and plural nouns **69**
Adjectives **92**

94.1 COMPARATIVE ADJECTIVES

For most adjectives with one or two syllables, "-er" is added to make the comparative.

Ahmed is tall.
Ahmed is taller than Jonathan.

"-er" is added to make the comparative.

"Than" is used to introduce the thing that the subject is being compared to.

FURTHER EXAMPLES

Dean is stronger than Carlos.

A plane is faster than a train.

5°F is colder than 85°F.

Sanjay is younger than Tina.

Emma is older than Sharon.

My friends are quicker than me.

⚠ COMMON MISTAKES "THAN" WITH COMPARATIVES

"Then" and "than" can easily be confused because they sound similar, but it is never correct to use "then" to form a comparative.

Ahmed is taller than Jonathan. ✓

The correct word to use in comparatives is "than."

Ahmed is taller then Jonathan. ✗

"Then" sounds similar to "than," but it is not correct to use "then" after a comparative.

94.2 FORMING COMPARATIVES

There are different rules for forming comparatives depending on the ending of the simple form of the adjective.

ADJECTIVE	close	early	big
↓	↓	↓	↓
COMPARATIVE	**closer**	**earlier**	**bigger**

If the adjective ends in "-e," just an "-r" is added.

For some adjectives ending in "-y," the "-y" is removed and "-ier" added.

For single-syllable adjectives ending consonant-vowel-consonant, the final letter is doubled and "-er" added.

FURTHER EXAMPLES

An elephant is larger than **a rhino.**

My bedroom is tidier than **my sister's.**

Spain is hotter than **England.**

94.3 IRREGULAR COMPARATIVES

Some common adjectives have irregular comparatives.

TIP
In US English, "further" and "furthest" are used to describe figurative (not physical) distances.

ADJECTIVE	good	bad	far
↓	↓	↓	↓
COMPARATIVE	**better**	**worse**	**farther (US)** **further (UK)**

FURTHER EXAMPLES

The house is farther away than **the tree.**

Jill got a better grade than **John.**

London has worse weather than **Paris.**

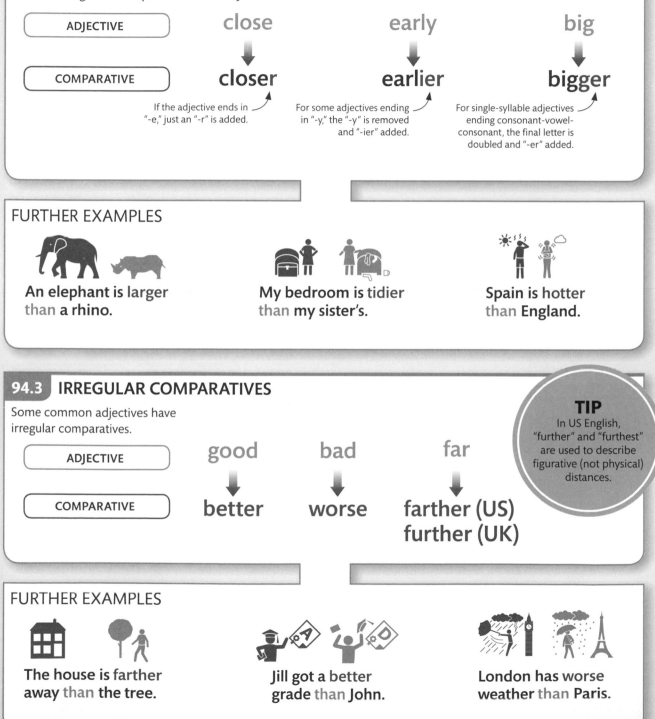

94.4 COMPARATIVES WITH LONG ADJECTIVES

For some two-syllable adjectives and adjectives with three syllables or more, "more" and "than" are used to make the comparative.

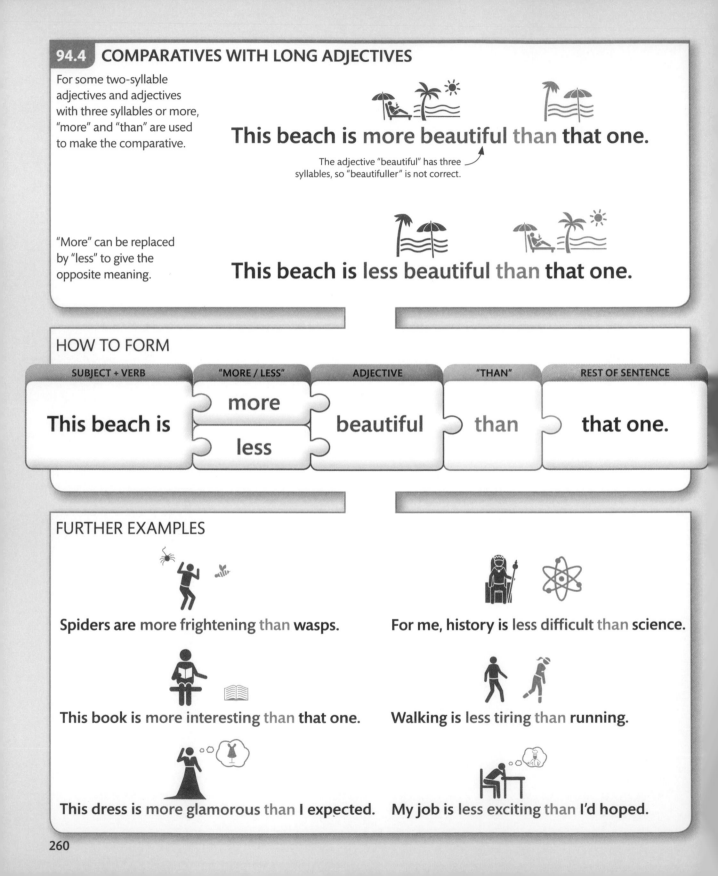

This beach is more beautiful than that one.

The adjective "beautiful" has three syllables, so "beautifuller" is not correct.

"More" can be replaced by "less" to give the opposite meaning.

This beach is less beautiful than that one.

HOW TO FORM

SUBJECT + VERB	"MORE / LESS"	ADJECTIVE	"THAN"	REST OF SENTENCE
This beach is	more / less	beautiful	than	that one.

FURTHER EXAMPLES

Spiders are more frightening than wasps.

For me, history is less difficult than science.

This book is more interesting than that one.

Walking is less tiring than running.

This dress is more glamorous than I expected.

My job is less exciting than I'd hoped.

TWO-FORM COMPARATIVES

Some two-syllable adjectives have two possible comparative forms. Either the comparative ending can be added, or "more" can be used before the adjective.

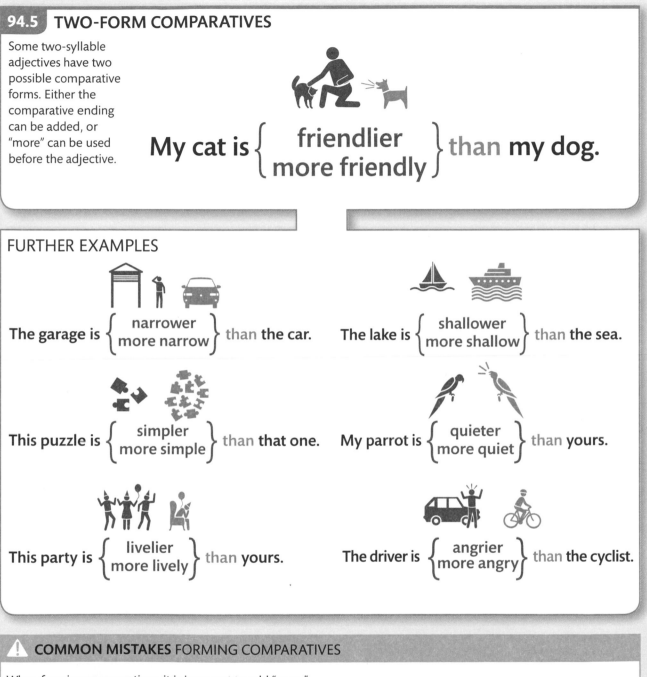

My cat is { friendlier / more friendly } than my dog.

FURTHER EXAMPLES

The garage is { narrower / more narrow } than the car.

The lake is { shallower / more shallow } than the sea.

This puzzle is { simpler / more simple } than that one.

My parrot is { quieter / more quiet } than yours.

This party is { livelier / more lively } than yours.

The driver is { angrier / more angry } than the cyclist.

⚠ **COMMON MISTAKES** FORMING COMPARATIVES

When forming comparatives, it is incorrect to add "more" before the adjective if it already has a comparative ending.

He's more friendly than her. ✓

He's friendlier than her. ✓

"Friendlier" and "more friendly" are correct, but "more friendlier" is not.

He's more friendlier than her. ✗

94.6 ADJECTIVES WITH MODIFIERS

Modifiers can go before comparatives
to make comparisons stronger or weaker.

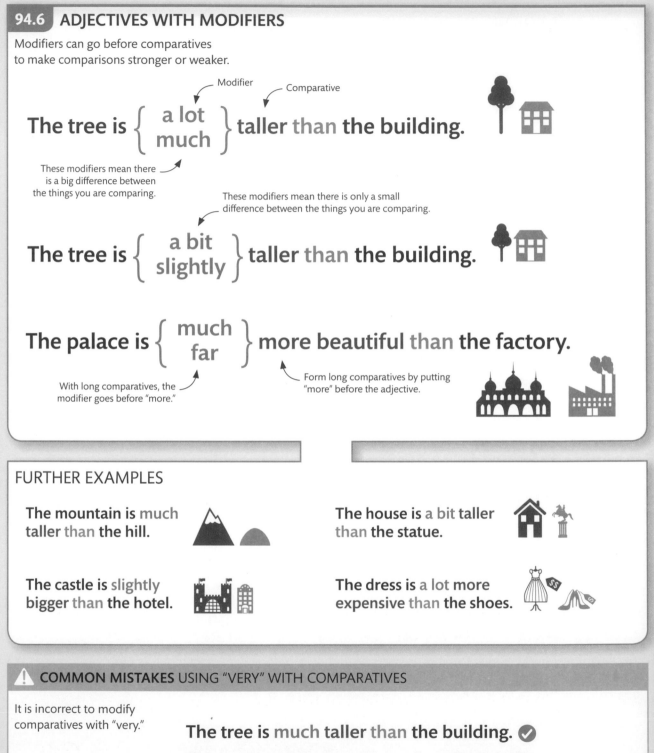

Modifier

Comparative

The tree is { a lot / much } **taller** than **the building.**

These modifiers mean there
is a big difference between
the things you are comparing.

These modifiers mean there is only a small
difference between the things you are comparing.

The tree is { a bit / slightly } **taller** than **the building.**

The palace is { much / far } **more beautiful** than **the factory.**

With long comparatives, the
modifier goes before "more."

Form long comparatives by putting
"more" before the adjective.

FURTHER EXAMPLES

The mountain is much **taller** than **the hill.**

The house is a bit taller than **the statue.**

The castle is slightly **bigger** than **the hotel.**

The dress is a lot more **expensive** than **the shoes.**

⚠ COMMON MISTAKES USING "VERY" WITH COMPARATIVES

It is incorrect to modify
comparatives with "very."

The tree is much **taller** than **the building.** ✓

The tree is very **taller** than **the building.** ✗

Two comparatives together

Two comparatives can be used together in a sentence to show the effect of an action. They are also used to show that something is changing.

See also:
Comparative adjectives **94**

95.1 COMPARATIVES SHOWING CAUSE AND EFFECT

Pairing two phrases that use comparative adjectives is a way of making comparisons that show cause and effect.

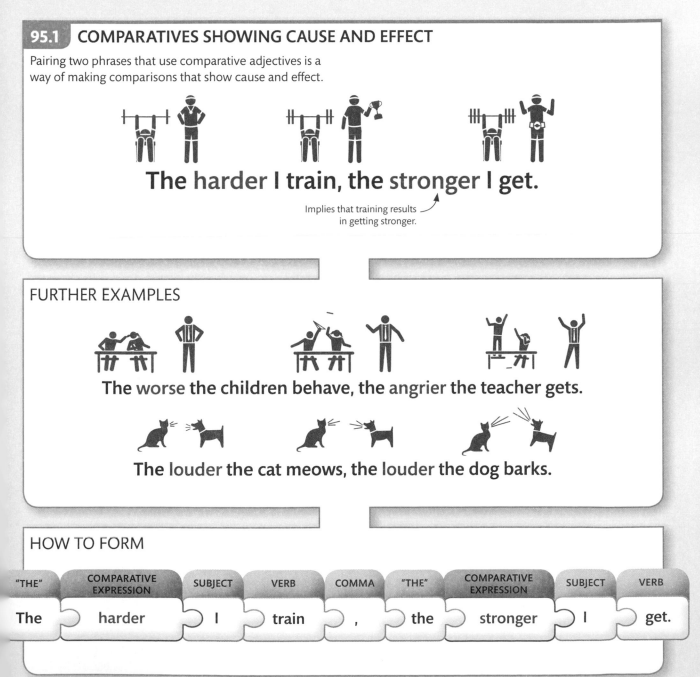

The harder I train, the stronger I get.

Implies that training results in getting stronger.

FURTHER EXAMPLES

The worse the children behave, the angrier the teacher gets.

The louder the cat meows, the louder the dog barks.

HOW TO FORM

"THE"	COMPARATIVE EXPRESSION	SUBJECT	VERB	COMMA	"THE"	COMPARATIVE EXPRESSION	SUBJECT	VERB
The	harder	I	train	,	the	stronger	I	get.

SHORTENING COMPARATIVE PHRASES

Double comparatives that end with "the better" are often shortened where the context makes the meaning obvious to the listener.

How do you like your tea?

The stronger the better.

The stronger [the tea is,] the better [it tastes].

These words are implied, or understood, and can be left out.

"The more the merrier" is a phrase that means when more people are at an event, the better it will be.

Can I bring my brother along?

Sure! The more the merrier.

This expression means people are welcome.

The more [people come,] the merrier [the party will be].

HOW TO FORM

"THE"	COMPARATIVE EXPRESSION	SUBJECT	VERB	"THE"	COMPARATIVE EXPRESSION	SUBJECT	VERB
The	stronger	the tea	is	the	better	it	tastes.

FURTHER EXAMPLES

What time do we need to leave?

The sooner the better.

Do we need to take a big suitcase?

Yes. The bigger the better.

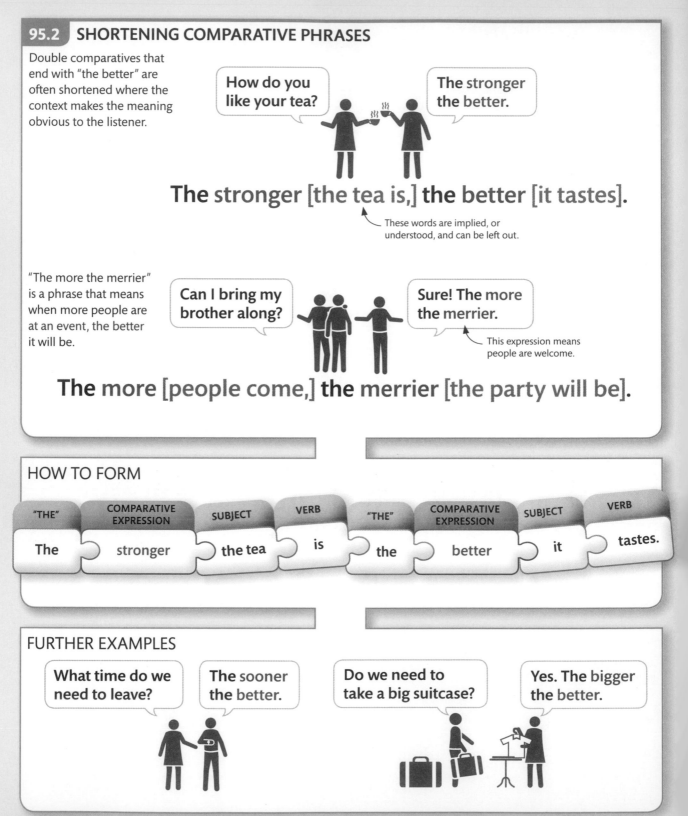

95.3 COMPARATIVES SHOWING CHANGE

A comparative can be repeated to show that something is changing. This expression emphasizes the change, and is often used to describe extremes.

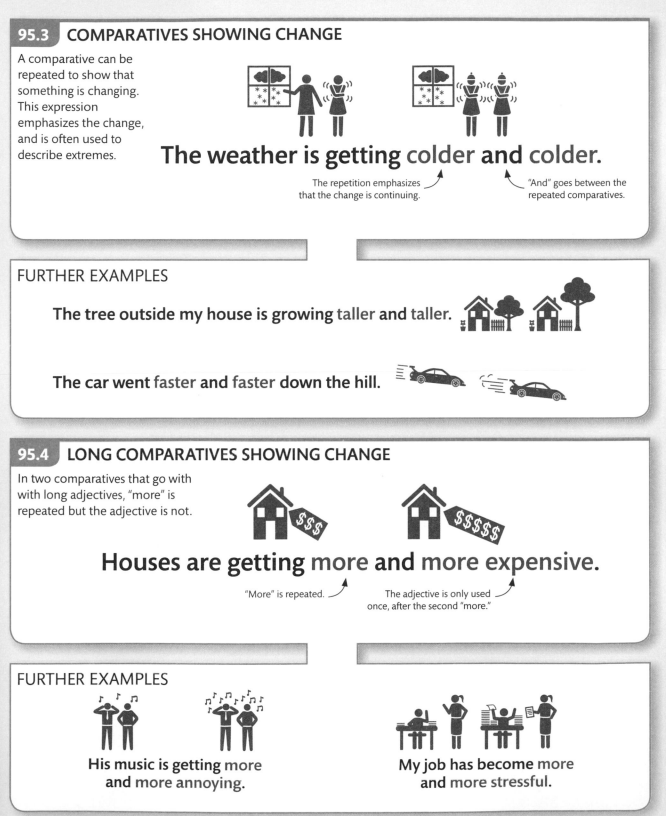

The weather is getting colored and colder.

The repetition emphasizes that the change is continuing.

"And" goes between the repeated comparatives.

FURTHER EXAMPLES

The tree outside my house is growing taller and taller.

The car went faster and faster down the hill.

95.4 LONG COMPARATIVES SHOWING CHANGE

In two comparatives that go with with long adjectives, "more" is repeated but the adjective is not.

Houses are getting more and more expensive.

"More" is repeated.

The adjective is only used once, after the second "more."

FURTHER EXAMPLES

His music is getting more and more annoying.

My job has become more and more stressful.

96 "As... as" comparisons

Comparisons using "as... as" constructions can be used to discuss degrees of similarity and difference. They can be modified with adverbs to make them stronger or weaker.

See also:
Adjectives **92**
Adverbs of degree **100**

96.1 "AS... AS" COMPARISONS

"As... as" comparisons are used with an adjective to compare things that are similar.

Lisa is as tall as Marc.

The adjective is in its normal form.

Penny is not $\left\{ \begin{array}{c} \text{as} \\ \text{so} \end{array} \right\}$ tall as Marc.

"Not" makes the sentence negative.

"So" is only used in negative comparisons.

HOW TO FORM

SUBJECT + VERB	"AS"	ADJECTIVE	"AS"	REST OF SENTENCE
Lisa is	as	tall	as	Marc.

FURTHER EXAMPLES

Will today be as hot as yesterday?

Your desk is as messy as mine.

The bus is not so crowded as the train.

Jenny is not as busy as Will.

96.2 "AS... AS" COMPARISONS WITH MODIFIERS

Modifiers can be added to "as... as" comparisons
to make them more detailed or to add emphasis.

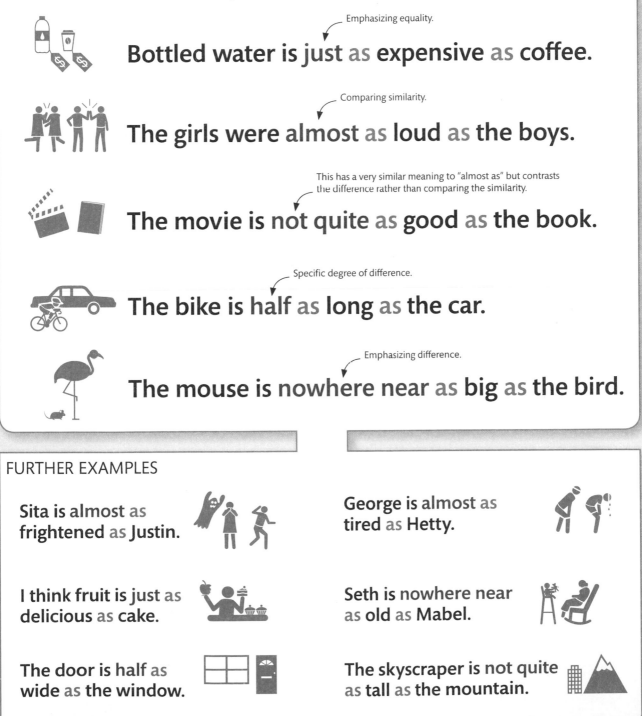

Emphasizing equality.

Bottled water is just as expensive as coffee.

Comparing similarity.

The girls were almost as loud as the boys.

This has a very similar meaning to "almost as" but contrasts
the difference rather than comparing the similarity.

The movie is not quite as good as the book.

Specific degree of difference.

The bike is half as long as the car.

Emphasizing difference.

The mouse is nowhere near as big as the bird.

FURTHER EXAMPLES

Sita is almost as frightened as Justin.

George is almost as tired as Hetty.

I think fruit is just as delicious as cake.

Seth is nowhere near as old as Mabel.

The door is half as wide as the window.

The skyscraper is not quite as tall as the mountain.

Superlative adjectives

Superlative adjectives, such as "the biggest" or "the smallest," are used to talk about extremes. Long adjectives take "most" and "least" to show an extreme.

See also:
Articles **63**   Adjectives **92**
Comparative adjectives **94**

97.1 SUPERLATIVE ADJECTIVES

For most adjectives with one or two syllables, "-est" is added to make the superlative.

The comparative describes the difference between two things.

Horses are faster than dogs, but cheetahs are the fastest land animals.

The definite article ("the") is always used before the superlative.

The superlative describes which thing is the most extreme.

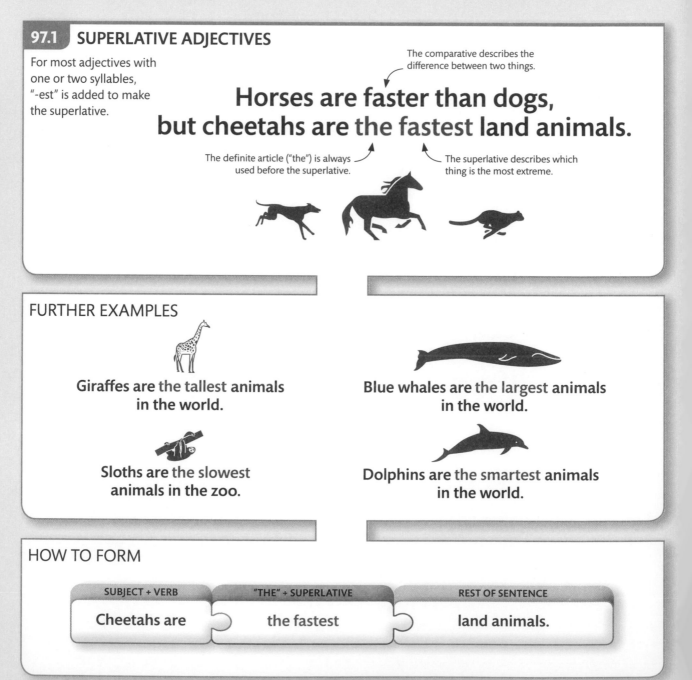

FURTHER EXAMPLES

Giraffes are the tallest animals in the world.

Blue whales are the largest animals in the world.

Sloths are the slowest animals in the zoo.

Dolphins are the smartest animals in the world.

HOW TO FORM

SUBJECT + VERB	"THE" + SUPERLATIVE	REST OF SENTENCE
Cheetahs are	the fastest	land animals.

FORMING SUPERLATIVES

There are different rules for forming superlatives depending
on the ending of the simple form of the adjective.

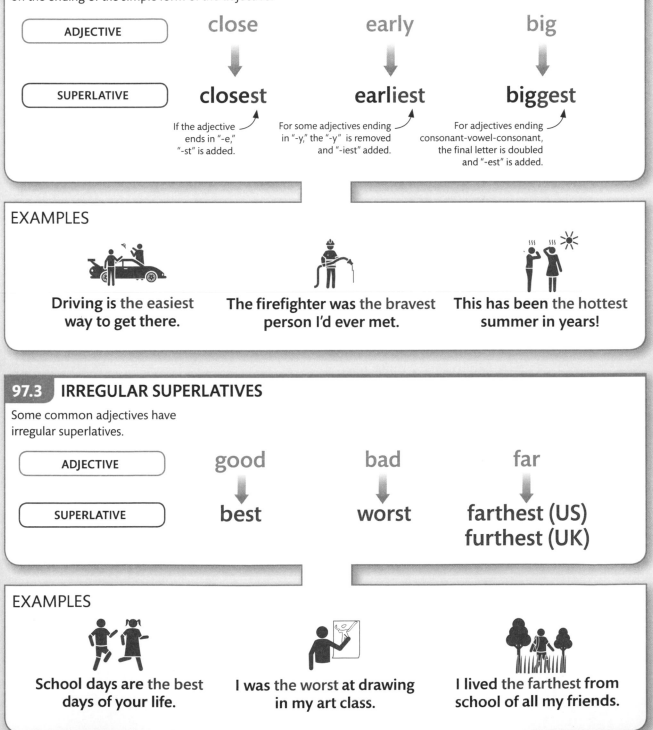

ADJECTIVE	close	early	big
SUPERLATIVE	**closest**	**earliest**	**biggest**

If the adjective ends in "-e," "-st" is added.

For some adjectives ending in "-y," the "-y" is removed and "-iest" added.

For adjectives ending consonant-vowel-consonant, the final letter is doubled and "-est" is added.

EXAMPLES

Driving is the easiest way to get there.

The firefighter was the bravest person I'd ever met.

This has been the hottest summer in years!

97.3　**IRREGULAR SUPERLATIVES**

Some common adjectives have
irregular superlatives.

ADJECTIVE	good	bad	far
SUPERLATIVE	**best**	**worst**	**farthest (US)** **furthest (UK)**

EXAMPLES

School days are the best days of your life.

I was the worst at drawing in my art class.

I lived the farthest from school of all my friends.

97.4 SUPERLATIVES WITH LONG ADJECTIVES

For some two-syllable adjectives and for adjectives of three syllables or more,
use "the most" or "the least" before the adjective to form the superlative.

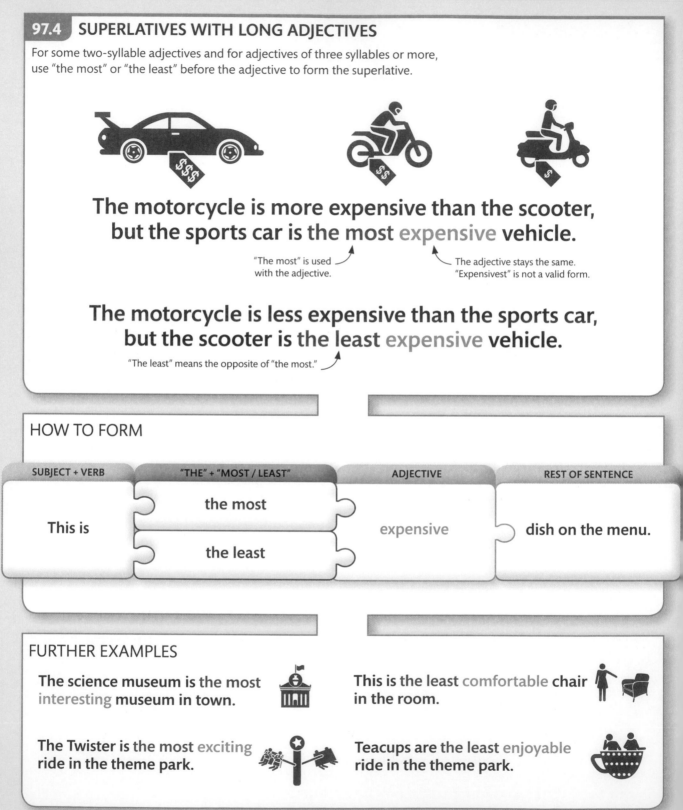

**The motorcycle is more expensive than the scooter,
but the sports car is the most expensive vehicle.**

"The most" is used
with the adjective.

The adjective stays the same.
"Expensivest" is not a valid form.

**The motorcycle is less expensive than the sports car,
but the scooter is the least expensive vehicle.**

"The least" means the opposite of "the most."

HOW TO FORM

SUBJECT + VERB	"THE" + "MOST / LEAST"	ADJECTIVE	REST OF SENTENCE
This is	the most / the least	expensive	dish on the menu.

FURTHER EXAMPLES

The science museum is the most interesting museum in town.

This is the least comfortable chair in the room.

The Twister is the most exciting ride in the theme park.

Teacups are the least enjoyable ride in the theme park.

⚠ COMMON MISTAKES FORMING SUPERLATIVES

When forming superlatives, it is incorrect to add "most" before the adjective if it already has a superlative ending.

"Best" is already a superlative adjective so "most" is unnecessary.

I am most best at running. ✗

I am the best at running. ✓

97.5 SUPERLATIVES WITH MODIFIERS

"Easily" or "by far" can make superlative adjectives more specific.
"One of" shows that the superlative belongs to a group of things.

The clock tower is { easily / by far } the tallest **building in the town.**

These modifiers make the superlative stronger.

"One of" makes the superlative part of a group.

With long superlatives the modifier goes before "the."

The clock tower is one of the most imposing buildings in the town.

If "one of" is used with superlatives, the noun must be in plural form.

FURTHER EXAMPLES

Sally is easily the tallest **person I know.**

Tim is easily the shortest **person I know.**

Physics is one of the most confusing **subjects I study.**

This hostel is by far the cheapest **place to stay.**

The Grand is by far the most expensive **place to stay.**

English is one of the least complicated **subjects I study.**

98 Adverbs of manner

Words such as "quietly" and "loudly" are adverbs. They describe and give more information about verbs, adjectives, phrases, and other adverbs.

> See also:
> Adjectives **92**
> Gradable and non-gradable adjectives **93**

98.1 ADVERBS OF MANNER

Adverbs of manner describe the way something is done. They usually come after the verb they describe.

"Quietly" describes how I speak.

I speak quietly.

He speaks loudly.

"Loudly" describes how he speaks.

Hello.

HELLO!

98.2 HOW TO FORM

Most adverbs of manner are formed by adding "-ly" to the adjective. If the adjective ends in "-y," the "-y" is left out and "-ily" is added to make the adverb.

bad

badly

careful

carefully

easy

easily

The "-y" is dropped. "-ily" is added.

FURTHER EXAMPLES

A tortoise moves slowly.

She sings beautifully.

My dad sneezes noisily.

Horses can run quickly.

I can play the piano badly.

My sister dresses stylishly.

IRREGULAR ADVERBS OF MANNER

Some adverbs aren't formed by
adding "-ly" to the adjective.

good

The adverb is
totally different
from the adjective.

↓

well

straight

The adverb
is the same as
the adjective.

↓

straight

early

Adjectives ending
"-ly" don't change
to become adverbs.

↓

early

FURTHER EXAMPLES

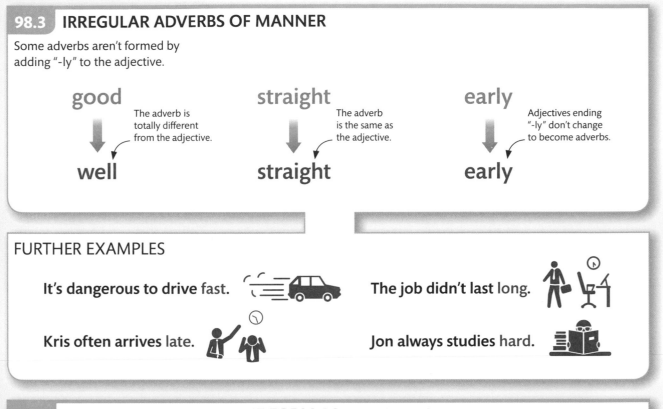

It's dangerous to drive fast.

The job didn't last long.

Kris often arrives late.

Jon always studies hard.

ADVERBS WITH THE SAME FORM AS ADJECTIVES

Some adjectives have more than one meaning. In these cases, the equivalent
adverb is often formed differently depending on the meaning of the adjective.

This means "small."

Chop the onion into fine pieces.

↓

Chop it finely.

The adverb is formed in the usual way by adding
"-ly" to the adjective. "Fine" is incorrect here.

This means "good."

I'm fine.

↓

I'm doing fine.

The adverb has the same form as the
adjective. "Finely" is incorrect here.

FURTHER EXAMPLES

It's free **for children.**

↓

Children are admitted free.

We advocate free **speech.**

↓

You can speak freely.

99 Comparative and superlative adverbs

Adverbs have comparative forms to compare or show differences. They also have superlative forms to talk about extremes.

See also:
Adjectives **92**   Comparative adjectives **94**
Superlative adjectives **97**   Adverbs of manner **98**

99.1 REGULAR COMPARATIVE AND SUPERLATIVE ADVERBS

Most **comparative** adverbs are formed using "more" or "less."

COMPARATIVE

Karen eats **more quickly than** Tim.

Tim eats **less quickly than** Sarah.

Most **superlative** adverbs are formed using "most" or "least."

SUPERLATIVE

Carmen cooks the **most frequently**.

Bob cooks the **least frequently**.

99.2 IRREGULAR COMPARATIVE AND SUPERLATIVE ADVERBS

"Well" and "badly" have the same comparative and superlative forms as their corresponding adjectives, "good" and "bad." They are both irregular.

ADJECTIVE	ADVERB	COMPARATIVE	SUPERLATIVE
good	well	better	best
bad	badly	worse	worst

99.3 SHORT COMPARATIVE AND SUPERLATIVE ADVERBS

For some shorter adverbs, the comparative or superlative adjective is sometimes used as the comparative or superlative adverb.

COMPARATIVE

My dog moves { slower / more slowly } than my cat.

Both are correct.

SUPERLATIVE

My tortoise moves the { slowest / most slowly } .

Both are correct.

FURTHER EXAMPLES

My sister always runs faster than me.

My sister can run fast, but our brother runs the fastest.

I got to work earlier than everyone else today.

I always arrive the earliest when I cycle, as I beat the traffic.

I'm training harder than my friend for the judo competition.

This is the hardest I've ever trained for a competition.

99.4 COMPARATIVE AND SUPERLATIVE ADVERBS

Adverbs that have the same form as an adjective can only become comparative and superlative adverbs by adding "-er" and "-est."

COMPARATIVE

My colleague always works later than me.

SUPERLATIVE

My boss always stays the latest.

100 Adverbs of degree

Adverbs of degree can be placed in front of adjectives and verbs to strengthen or weaken their original meaning. Some adverbs can only be paired with certain adjectives.

See also:
Adjectives **92**
Gradable and non-gradable adjectives **93**

100.1 GRADING ADVERBS

Adverbs that can be used with gradable adjectives are called grading adverbs. They can be used to make an adjective's meaning stronger or weaker.

TIP
Gradable adjectives are adjectives which can be made weaker or stronger by adverbs.

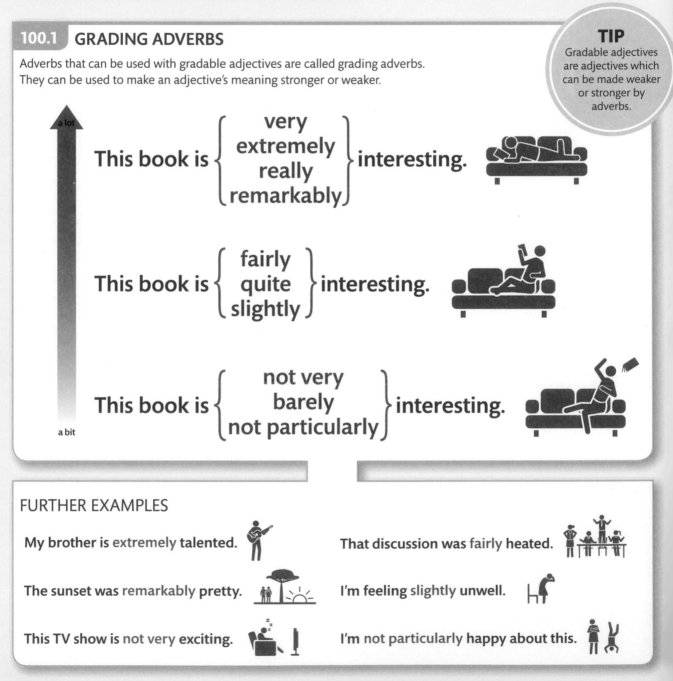

a lot

This book is { very / extremely / really / remarkably } interesting.

This book is { fairly / quite / slightly } interesting.

This book is { not very / barely / not particularly } interesting.

a bit

FURTHER EXAMPLES

My brother is **extremely talented.**

The sunset was **remarkably pretty.**

This TV show is **not very exciting.**

That discussion was **fairly heated.**

I'm feeling **slightly unwell.**

I'm **not particularly happy** about this.

NON-GRADING ADVERBS

Some adverbs can be used to qualify non-gradable adjectives. These are called "non-grading adverbs," and often mean "entirely" or "almost entirely." They cannot usually be used with gradable adjectives.

Her presentation was absolutely awful!

She has a totally unique presenting style.

She had a completely American audience.

COMMON NON-GRADING ADVERBS

absolutely

completely   utterly

wholly —— entirely —— totally

perfectly   entirely

thoroughly

nearly

essentially   practically

mostly —— almost entirely —— mainly

virtually   largely

almost

FURTHER EXAMPLES

The rain is utterly torrential.

Our trip was totally awesome.

My twin sons are entirely identical.

Your answers were perfectly correct.

This class is essentially pointless.

The weather's almost perfect.

This test is practically impossible.

I've virtually finished my work.

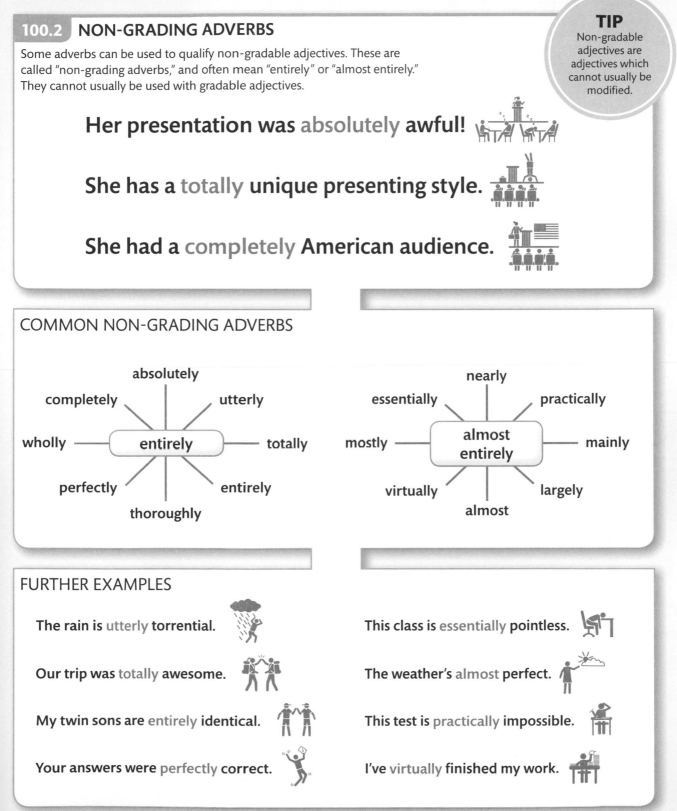

"REALLY," "FAIRLY," AND "PRETTY"

A few adverbs can be used with both gradable and non-gradable adjectives. They are "really" (meaning "very much"), and "pretty" and "fairly" (both meaning "quite a lot, but not very").

What you need is a really $\left\{\begin{array}{l}\text{good}\\\text{great}\end{array}\right\}$ idea.

Gradable

Non-gradable

You need to be fairly $\left\{\begin{array}{l}\text{confident}\\\text{certain}\end{array}\right\}$ it works.

Inventing a new product is pretty $\left\{\begin{array}{l}\text{difficult}\\\text{impossible}\end{array}\right\}$.

"QUITE"

"Quite" can be used with both gradable and non-gradable adjectives. In US English, it usually means "very." In UK English, it weakens gradable adjectives to mean "not very," but strengthens non-gradable adjectives to mean "very" or "completely."

Her invention is quite incredible.

[Her invention is absolutely fantastic.]

Her idea was quite good.

[Her idea was really good. (US)]
[Her idea was good, but not great. (UK)]

FURTHER EXAMPLES

I proposed to my husband. It was quite perfect.

I was quite upset when I lost my pet rabbit.

I find it quite necessary to shower after exercise.

It can be quite difficult to adjust when you move abroad.

Only grading adverbs can be used with gradable adjectives, and only non-grading adverbs can be used with non-gradable adjectives.

GRADING ADVERBS	NON-GRADING ADVERBS
This book is very good. ✓	The plot is very great. ✗
This book is absolutely good. ✗	The plot is absolutely great. ✓

100.5 USING ADVERBS OF DEGREE TO DESCRIBE VERBS

"Quite," "really," and "absolutely" can be used to modify verbs. These modifying words must go before the verb.

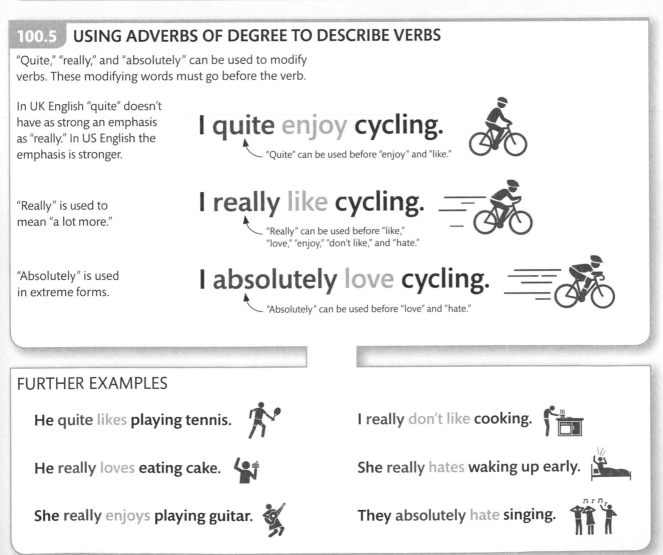

In UK English "quite" doesn't have as strong an emphasis as "really." In US English the emphasis is stronger.

I quite enjoy cycling.

"Quite" can be used before "enjoy" and "like."

"Really" is used to mean "a lot more."

I really like cycling.

"Really" can be used before "like," "love," "enjoy," "don't like," and "hate."

"Absolutely" is used in extreme forms.

I absolutely love cycling.

"Absolutely" can be used before "love" and "hate."

FURTHER EXAMPLES

He quite likes playing tennis.

He really loves eating cake.

She really enjoys playing guitar.

I really don't like cooking.

She really hates waking up early.

They absolutely hate singing.

101 Adverbs of time

Adverbs of time are used to give more precise information about exactly when something happens. They can also refer to a continuing event or action.

See also:
Present continuous **4**
Present perfect simple **11**

101.1 "JUST" AND "ABOUT TO"

These adverbs give more information about when or if an action happened.

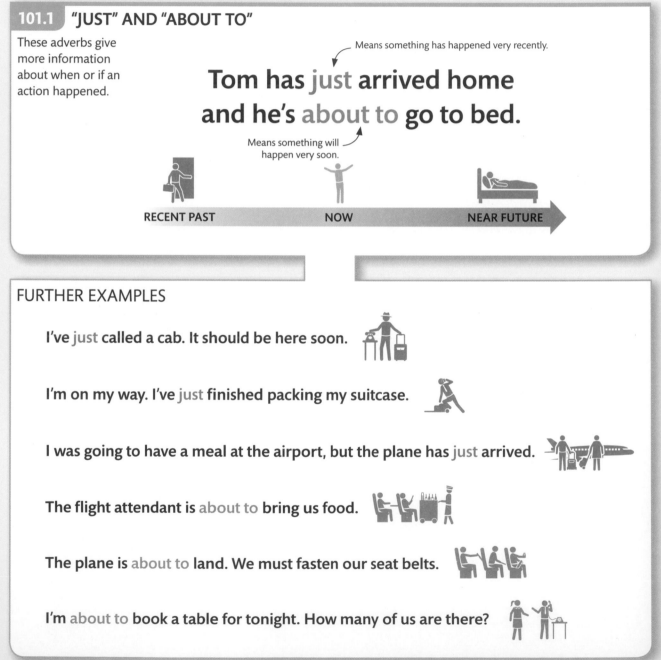

Means something has happened very recently.

Tom has just arrived home and he's about to go to bed.

Means something will happen very soon.

RECENT PAST   **NOW**   **NEAR FUTURE**

FURTHER EXAMPLES

I've just called a cab. It should be here soon.

I'm on my way. I've just finished packing my suitcase.

I was going to have a meal at the airport, but the plane has just arrived.

The flight attendant is about to bring us food.

The plane is about to land. We must fasten our seat belts.

I'm about to book a table for tonight. How many of us are there?

101.2 "ALREADY" AND "YET"

"Already" is used when something has happened, usually sooner than expected. **"Yet"** means "until now." It shows that something hasn't happened, but it will happen in the future.

Means something has happened.

The show has already started, but we haven't arrived yet.

Means "until now."

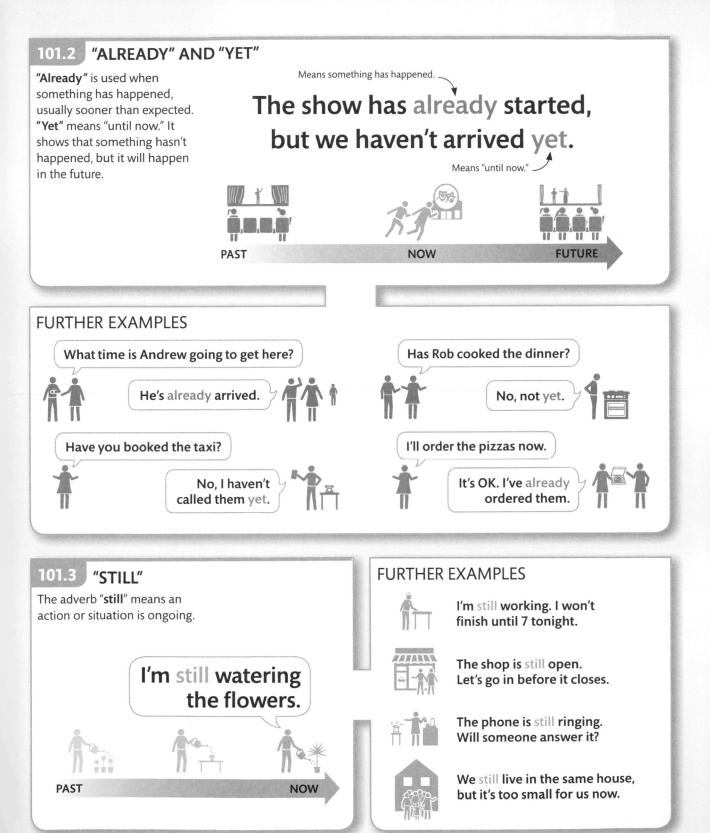

PAST

NOW

FUTURE

FURTHER EXAMPLES

What time is Andrew going to get here?

He's already arrived.

Have you booked the taxi?

No, I haven't called them yet.

Has Rob cooked the dinner?

No, not yet.

I'll order the pizzas now.

It's OK. I've already ordered them.

101.3 "STILL"

The adverb **"still"** means an action or situation is ongoing.

I'm still watering the flowers.

PAST

NOW

FURTHER EXAMPLES

I'm still working. I won't finish until 7 tonight.

The shop is still open. Let's go in before it closes.

The phone is still ringing. Will someone answer it?

We still live in the same house, but it's too small for us now.

102 Adverbs of frequency

Adverbs of frequency show how often something is done, from something done very frequently ("always") to something not done at all ("never").

See also:
Forming questions 34

102.1 ADVERBS OF FREQUENCY

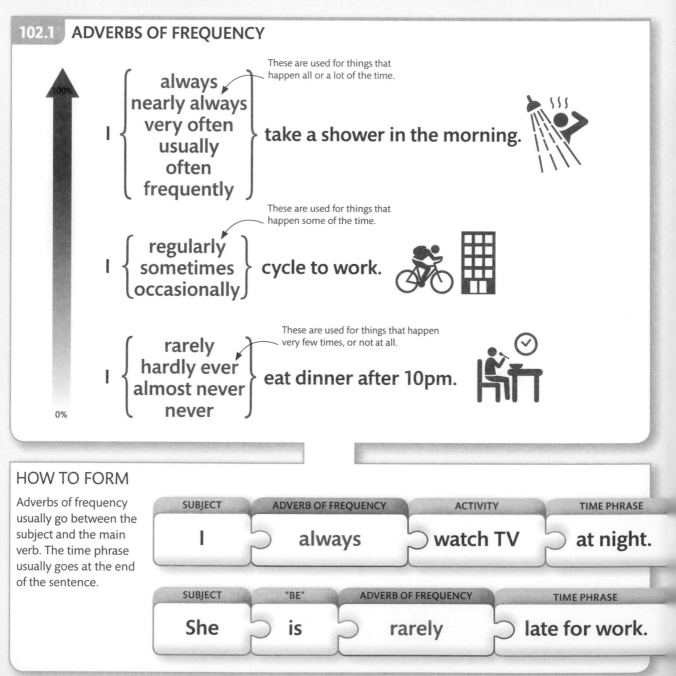

100%

These are used for things that happen all or a lot of the time.

I {
always
nearly always
very often
usually
often
frequently
} take a shower in the morning.

These are used for things that happen some of the time.

I {
regularly
sometimes
occasionally
} cycle to work.

These are used for things that happen very few times, or not at all.

I {
rarely
hardly ever
almost never
never
} eat dinner after 10pm.

0%

HOW TO FORM

Adverbs of frequency usually go between the subject and the main verb. The time phrase usually goes at the end of the sentence.

SUBJECT	ADVERB OF FREQUENCY	ACTIVITY	TIME PHRASE
I	always	watch TV	at night.

SUBJECT	"BE"	ADVERB OF FREQUENCY	TIME PHRASE
She	is	rarely	late for work.

102.2 ADVERBS AND EXPRESSIONS OF FREQUENCY

Frequency can also be described with more precise expressions.
Unlike adverbs of frequency, these must sit at the end of a phrase.

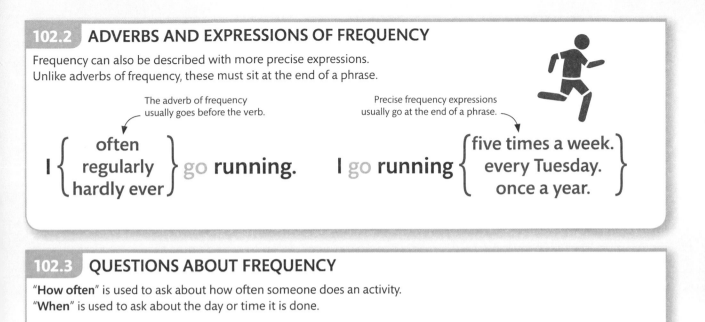

The adverb of frequency usually goes before the verb.

I { often / regularly / hardly ever } go running.

Precise frequency expressions usually go at the end of a phrase.

I go running { five times a week. / every Tuesday. / once a year. }

102.3 QUESTIONS ABOUT FREQUENCY

"**How often**" is used to ask about how often someone does an activity.
"**When**" is used to ask about the day or time it is done.

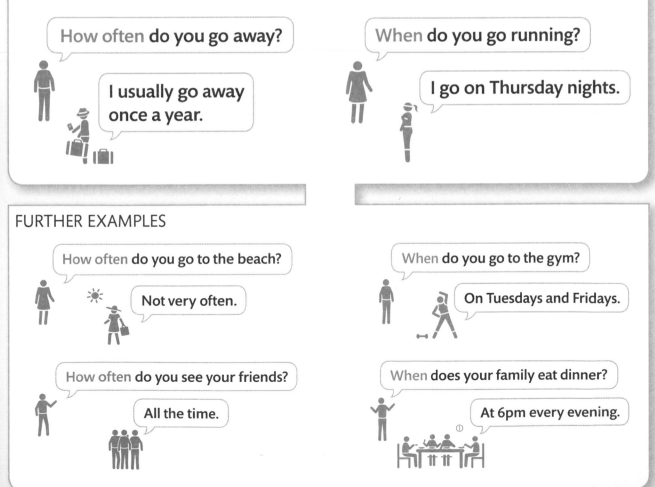

How often **do you go away?**

I usually go away once a year.

When **do you go running?**

I go on Thursday nights.

FURTHER EXAMPLES

How often **do you go to the beach?**

Not very often.

When **do you go to the gym?**

On Tuesdays and Fridays.

How often **do you see your friends?**

All the time.

When **does your family eat dinner?**

At 6pm every evening.

103 "So" and "such"

"So" and "such" are adverbs which can be used with certain words to add emphasis. They are similar in meaning, but they are used in different structures.

See also:
Adjectives **92**   Comparative adjectives **94**   Adverbs of manner **98**   Comparative and superlative adverbs **99**

103.1 "SO" AND "SUCH"

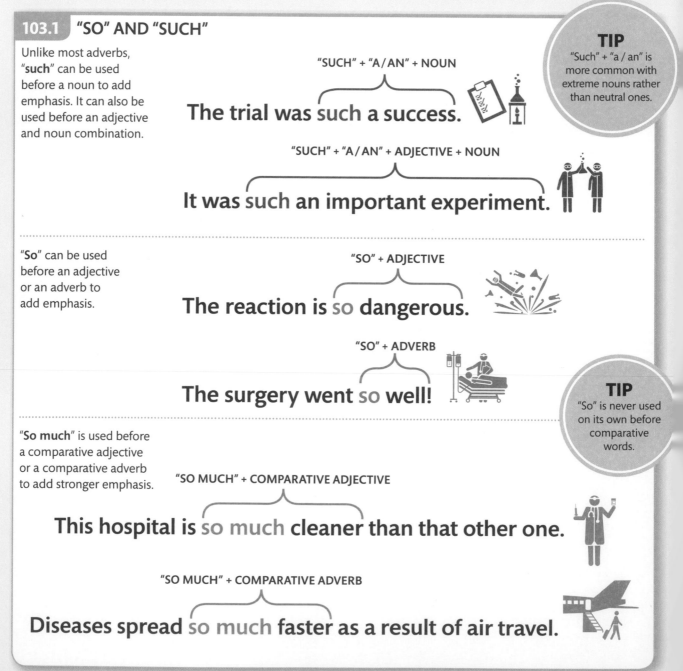

Unlike most adverbs, "**such**" can be used before a noun to add emphasis. It can also be used before an adjective and noun combination.

"SUCH" + "A/AN" + NOUN

The trial was such a success.

TIP
"Such" + "a / an" is more common with extreme nouns rather than neutral ones.

"SUCH" + "A/AN" + ADJECTIVE + NOUN

It was such an important experiment.

"**So**" can be used before an adjective or an adverb to add emphasis.

"SO" + ADJECTIVE

The reaction is so dangerous.

"SO" + ADVERB

The surgery went so well!

TIP
"So" is never used on its own before comparative words.

"**So much**" is used before a comparative adjective or a comparative adverb to add stronger emphasis.

"SO MUCH" + COMPARATIVE ADJECTIVE

This hospital is so much cleaner than that other one.

"SO MUCH" + COMPARATIVE ADVERB

Diseases spread so much faster as a result of air travel.

103.2 "SO" AND "SUCH" WITH "THAT"

"That" can be used with "so" and "such" to introduce a particular result caused by the fact being emphasized.

"SUCH" + "A / AN" + NOUN + "THAT"

The disease is **such a mystery** that it doesn't even have a name yet.

"SUCH" + "A / AN" + ADJECTIVE + NOUN + "THAT"

This is **such a strange injury** that it is hard to diagnose.

"SO" + ADJECTIVE + "THAT"

Medical research is **so expensive** that drugs are often costly.

"SO" + ADVERB + "THAT"

He recovered **so quickly** that he was able to go home the next day.

"SO MUCH" + COMPARATIVE ADJECTIVE + "THAT"

The new treatment was **so much more effective** that he felt better the same day.

"SO MUCH" + COMPARATIVE ADVERB + "THAT"

Hospitals are now being built **so much more quickly** that more people can be treated.

104 "Enough" and "too"

"Enough" is used when there is the correct degree or amount of something. "Too" is used when something is more than necessary or wanted.

See also:
Countable and uncountable nouns **70**
Adjectives **92**   Adverbs of manner **98**

104.1 ADJECTIVE / ADVERB + "ENOUGH"

"**Enough**" can be used after an adjective or adverb to show that it's the right degree.

ADJECTIVE + ENOUGH

This house is big enough for us.

ADVERB + ENOUGH

She isn't speaking loudly enough. I can't hear her.

FURTHER EXAMPLES

This food isn't hot enough to eat.

My bag is big enough for my books.

The traffic isn't moving quickly enough.

I didn't read the instructions carefully enough.

104.2 NOUN + "ENOUGH"

"**Enough**" and "**not enough**" can be used to talk about quantities of countable and uncountable nouns. "**Enough**" comes before the noun.

Do we have enough balloons?

Balloons are countable.

We only have two. That's not enough.

"Enough" can also be used without a noun.

Do we have enough food?

Food is uncountable.

We have these snacks. That'll be enough.

104.3 "TOO" + ADJECTIVE / ADVERB

"**Too**" can be used before an adjective or adverb to show that it's more than enough.

TOO + ADJECTIVE

That meal was too big. I'm so full.

TOO + ADVERB

This bus is going too slowly. I'm going to be late.

FURTHER EXAMPLES

"Far" and "much" can be used before "too" for emphasis.

In winter my house is far too cold.

Jo takes her job much too seriously.

My coat is too big for me.

Jessica talks far too quietly.

Don't go swimming in the lake. It's too dangerous.

I'm never on time for work. I always wake up too late.

104.4 "ENOUGH" AND "TOO" WITH AN INFINITIVE CLAUSE

In English, "**enough**" and "**too**" are used with infinitive clauses. They state whether something is to the right degree or extent for the infinitive clause to happen.

Is this mango ripe enough to eat?

Yes, it's ripe enough to eat.

No, it's not ripe enough to eat.

No, it's too ripe to eat.

105 Prepositions

Prepositions are words that are used to show relationships between different parts of a clause, for example relationships of time, place, or reason.

See also:
Infinitives and participles **51**   Verbs with prepositions **54**
Singular and plural nouns **69**   Personal pronouns **77**

105.1   SIMPLE PREPOSITIONS

Prepositions describe the relationship between two other words. They are usually part of a prepositional phrase, which is made up of a preposition followed by an object (a noun, pronoun, or noun phrase).

"By" describes where the park is in relation to the house.

There's a beautiful park by my house.

Chrissy goes to the gym on Wednesdays.

"On" helps to describe when Chrissy goes to the gym.

105.2   COMPLEX PREPOSITIONS

Some prepositions are made up of two words which act as a single unit. They behave the same way as one-word prepositions.

The bank is next to the library.

105.3   PARALLEL PREPOSITIONS

When the same preposition applies to more than one word in a list, the preposition only needs to be used once.

I sent presents to Al and [to] Ed.

When different words need different prepositions, each preposition must be used.

Look at and listen to the teacher.

105.4　PREPOSITIONS AND GERUNDS

If a verb comes immediately after a preposition, it has to be a gerund, which is the "-ing" form of a verb.

After graduating, I worked in a hospital.

Preposition　　　Gerund

FURTHER EXAMPLES

Instead of applying for a job, I went to college.

After seeing the job listing, I wrote a cover letter.

105.5　PREPOSITIONS AT THE END OF SENTENCES

Prepositions can come in many different places in a sentence, including at the end.

I'm listening to some music. ✓

I like having something to listen to. ✓

105.6　"TO"

"To" can cause confusion because it can be a preposition, but it is also used to form infinitives.

Here, "to" is part of the infinitive verb "to see." When used like this, it is not a preposition.

Here, "to" is part of the phrasal verb "look forward to," and is a preposition. Therefore, it must be followed by a noun, pronoun, or gerund.

I'm going to see my friends tonight.

I'm looking forward to seeing them.

Gerund

106 Prepositions of place

Prepositions of place are used to relate the position or location of one thing to another. Using a different preposition usually changes the meaning of a sentence.

See also:
Question words **35**
Prepositions **105**

106.1 "IN," "AT," AND "ON"

"In" is used to position something or someone inside a large area or in a three-dimensional space.

The Louvre is in Paris.

David is in his bedroom.

"In" positions David inside his bedroom.

"At" is used to talk about an exact point.

Turn left at the next corner.

Let's meet at the restaurant.

"On" is used to position something in line with, next to, on top of, or attached to something else.

I love traveling on trains.

There's a spider on the floor!

FURTHER EXAMPLES

They live in a hot country.

I will meet you at the beach.

I like that picture on the wall.

The dog is sleeping in his basket.

Jane is working at her desk.

The books are on the table.

106.2 PRECISE PREPOSITIONS OF PLACE

Some prepositions of place show the precise position or location of something in relation to something else. They can be used to answer a "where" question.

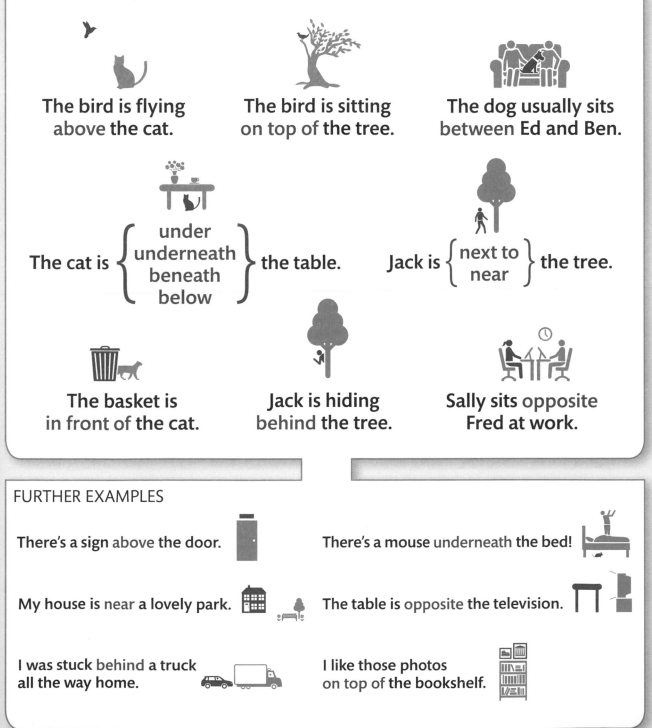

The bird is flying above **the cat.**

The bird is sitting on top of **the tree.**

The dog usually sits between **Ed and Ben.**

The cat is { under underneath beneath below } the table.

Jack is { next to near } the tree.

The basket is in front of **the cat.**

Jack is hiding behind **the tree.**

Sally sits opposite Fred at work.

FURTHER EXAMPLES

There's a sign above **the door.**

There's a mouse underneath **the bed!**

My house is near a lovely park.

The table is opposite **the television.**

I was stuck behind a truck all the way home.

I like those photos on top of **the bookshelf.**

107 Prepositions of time

Prepositions of time are often used to talk about schedules and routines. They give information about when something happens, and how long it lasts.

See also:
Present perfect continuous 12
Prepositions 105

107.1 "ON"

"**On**" is often used before days of the week to say when something happens.

"**-s**" can be added to the day of the week to show that the thing happens regularly on that day.

I work on Mondays.

In US English the preposition can be left out.

FURTHER EXAMPLES

The library is closed on Sundays.

I'm going shopping on Saturday.

I have orchestra practice on Fridays.

I'll visit my grandparents on Monday.

107.2 "AT"

"**At**" is usually used to express what time something happens.

I leave the house at 8am.

FURTHER EXAMPLES

They are meeting at 1 o'clock.

I have an appointment at 7 o'clock.

I have a yoga class at lunchtime.

I get the bus at half past 8.

107.3 "ON" AND "AT" WITH "THE WEEKEND"

When talking about the weekend, US English uses "on," whereas UK English uses "at."

"On the weekend" is more common in the US.

I watch TV { on at } the weekend.

"At the weekend" is more common in the UK.

107.4 "IN"

"In" has a similar meaning as "during" and is used before months, years, seasons, and general times of day, e.g. "morning" and "afternoon."

I go to the gym in the morning.

FURTHER EXAMPLES

I usually watch TV in the evening.

I was born in 1973.

She's going to Europe in June.

I enjoy gardening in summer.

107.5 "PAST" AND "TO"

"Past" and "to" are prepositions of time that are mainly used when telling the time.

"Past" means "after the hour."

It's twenty past seven.

"To" means "until the hour."

It's twenty to seven.

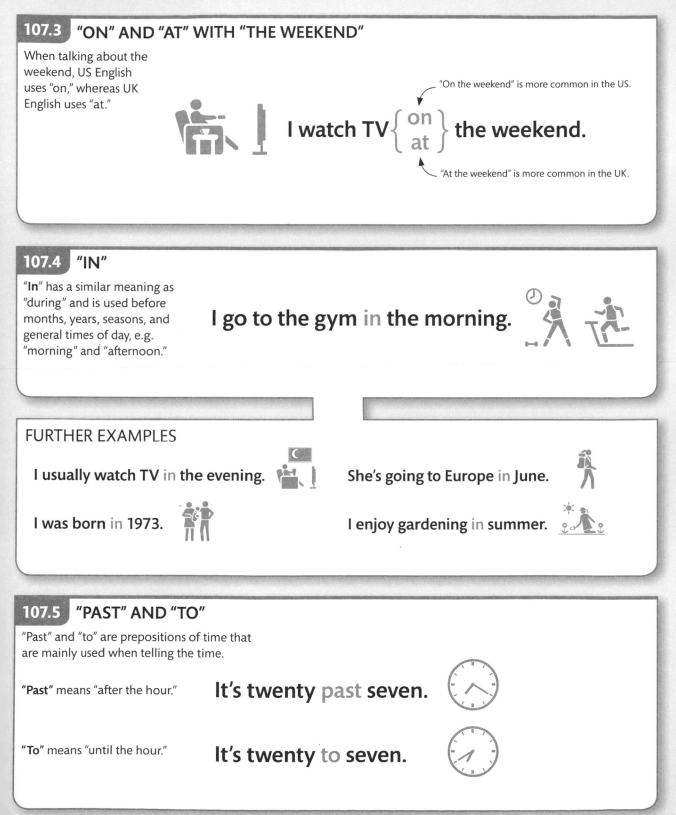

107.6 PREPOSITIONS SHOWING DURATION

"**From... to...**" or "**between... and...**" are used to say when an activity starts and finishes.

"From" is used to say the time something starts.

"To" is used to say the time something finishes.

"Between" is used to say the time something starts.

"And" is used to say the time something finishes.

I work from 9am to 5pm.

I work between 9am and 5pm.

9AM — 5PM

"**Until**" can be used to say when an ongoing situation finishes.

"UNTIL" + TIME OR DATE

I will be working until five o'clock.

9AM — 5PM

"**Since**" can be used to say when an ongoing situation started.

"SINCE" + TIME OR DATE

I have been working since 9am.

9AM — NOW

"**For**" can be used to express how long something has been happening.

"FOR" + QUANTITY OF TIME

I have been working for six hours.

6 HOURS AGO — NOW

"**During**" can be used to express when something was happening, rather than how long it went on for.

I relaxed during my break.

BREAK — NOW

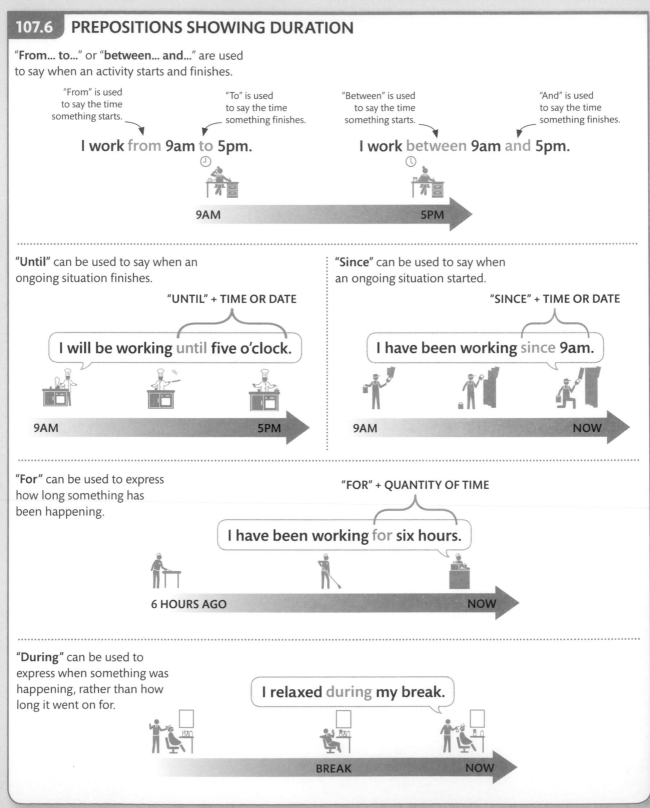

⚠ **COMMON MISTAKES** TENSES WITH "SINCE"

"**Since**" is usually used with perfect tenses with reference to the past. It is not used with the present simple.

The present perfect continuous is often used with since.

Tim has been working here since last year. ✓

Tim works here since last year. ✗

Since can't be used with the present simple.

107.7 OTHER PREPOSITIONS OF TIME

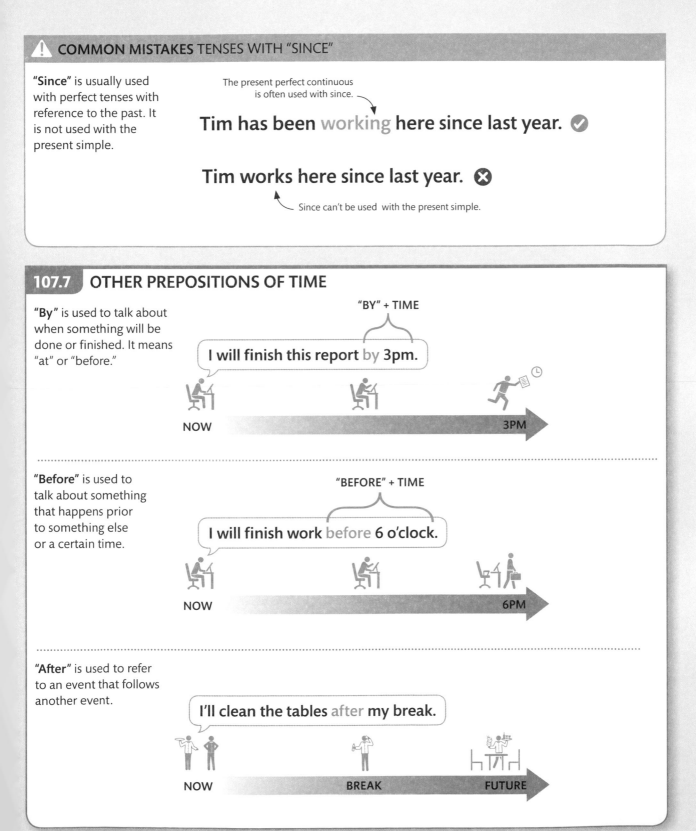

"**By**" is used to talk about when something will be done or finished. It means "at" or "before."

"BY" + TIME

I will finish this report by 3pm.

NOW   3PM

"**Before**" is used to talk about something that happens prior to something else or a certain time.

"BEFORE" + TIME

I will finish work before 6 o'clock.

NOW   6PM

"**After**" is used to refer to an event that follows another event.

I'll clean the tables after my break.

NOW   BREAK   FUTURE

108 Other prepositions

Prepositions can be used to express relationships other than place and time, such as origin, ownership, and absence.

See also:
The passive 24 Verb patterns with prepositions 54 Prepositions 105

108.1 "BY"

"**By**" has several common uses in English.

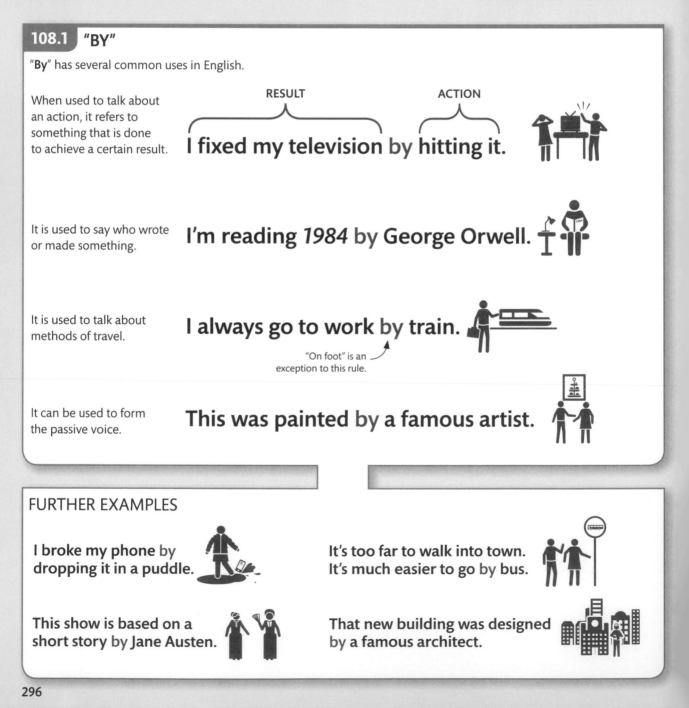

When used to talk about an action, it refers to something that is done to achieve a certain result.

RESULT   ACTION

I fixed my television by hitting it.

It is used to say who wrote or made something.

I'm reading *1984* by George Orwell.

It is used to talk about methods of travel.

I always go to work by train.

"On foot" is an exception to this rule.

It can be used to form the passive voice.

This was painted by a famous artist.

FURTHER EXAMPLES

I broke my phone by dropping it in a puddle.

It's too far to walk into town. It's much easier to go by bus.

This show is based on a short story by Jane Austen.

That new building was designed by a famous architect.

108.2 "WITH" AND "WITHOUT"

"**With**" has several common uses in English.

It can mean "accompanied by."

I went to a restaurant with my wife.

It is used to talk about possession.

I want a job with a good salary.

It is used to talk about the thing used to perform an action.

I cut this apple with a knife.

"**Without**" is used to talk about the absence of something.

Vera came to the party without a gift.

FURTHER EXAMPLES

I need to move somewhere with better phone reception.

Christina paid for the dress with her credit card.

I need to hire someone with excellent computer skills.

Wait! Don't leave without me!

108.3 "ABOUT"

"**About**" is mainly used to mean "on the subject of."

I'm watching a documentary about Ancient Greece.

FURTHER EXAMPLES

I'm going to call the bank about their bad service.

I'm sorry, but I have no idea what you're talking about.

109 Dependent prepositions

Some words must be followed by a specific preposition, called a dependent preposition. These words can be adjectives, verbs, or nouns.

See also:
Types of verbs **49**   Singular and plural nouns **69**
Adjectives **92**   Prepositions **105**

109.1 ADJECTIVES WITH DEPENDENT PREPOSITIONS

Some adjectives are always followed by the same preposition when used in a sentence.

ADJECTIVE + PREPOSITION

It was good of my friend to offer to babysit last night.

Some adjectives can take one of a choice of prepositions in the same sentence without changing their meaning.

"Surprised" can be followed by either "at" or "by" without a change in meaning.

You seemed surprised { at / by } their behavior.

FURTHER EXAMPLES

The babysitter was angry about looking after naughty children.

The children are impressed by practical jokes.

My parents are annoyed with me for not cleaning my room.

Janine is tired of watching children's shows on TV.

My friends are getting ready for their new baby.

She is excited about going hiking in the mountains.

109.2 VERBS WITH DEPENDENT PREPOSITIONS

Some verbs are followed by a specific preposition before an object. Different verbs are followed by different prepositions.

VERB + PREPOSITION

The head chef used to shout at the staff to encourage them to work harder.

FURTHER EXAMPLES

The café was counting on the new menu to impress its customers.

The café advertised for another chef to join the team.

The head chef spoke to the manager about hiring more kitchen staff.

What do you think about leaving early on Fridays?

109.3 VERBS WITH "TO" OR "FOR"

Some verbs can take either "to" or "for," depending on the context. "To" is usually used when there is a transfer of something, whereas "for" is used when someone benefits from something.

He sold the house to the family.

[The family bought the house.]

He sold the house for the family.

[He sold the house on behalf of the family.]

NOUNS WITH DEPENDENT PREPOSITIONS

Some nouns are always followed by the
same preposition when used in a sentence.

NOUN + PREPOSITION

I always keep a photograph of my family on my desk.

Some nouns can take one of a choice of prepositions
in the same sentence without changing their meaning.

"Advantages" can be followed
by either "in" or "to" without a
change in meaning.

There are advantages { in to } moving away to study.

FURTHER EXAMPLES

It is important to have a positive attitude toward studying.

The cause of traffic jams is often bad town planning.

I've been working hard to find a solution to this problem.

There has been a steady increase in students passing their exams.

The demand for public buses increases every year.

Take your time planning a response to the essay question.

WORDS WITH DIFFERENT DEPENDENT PREPOSITIONS

Some adjectives, verbs, and nouns can be followed by a choice of prepositions. The meaning of the phrase is dependent on which preposition the adjective, verb, or noun is paired with.

I'm anxious for **my vacation to start.**
[I'm excited for my vacation.]

I'm anxious about **being late for my flight.**
[I'm worried I'm going to miss my flight.]

He talked to **the teacher.**
[He had a conversation with the teacher.]

He talked about **the teacher.**
[He had a conversation with someone else, discussing the teacher.]

I have a good relationship with **my parents.**
[The relationship between me and my parents is good.]

The relationship between **family members is important.**
[It's important that family members have a good relationship.]

FURTHER EXAMPLES

I'm upset about **how badly my exams went.**

I'm upset with **myself for failing my exams.**

The charity needs to appeal for **more volunteers.**

The campaigns appeal to **students.**

Pests are a serious problem for **farmers.**

Farmers have a serious problem with **pests.**

110 Coordinating conjunctions

Coordinating conjunctions are words that link words, phrases, or clauses of equal importance. There are special rules for using commas with coordinating conjunctions.

See also:
Defining relative clauses **81**
Ellipsis **89**

110.1 USING "AND" TO JOIN SENTENCES

"**And**" is used to join two sentences together in order to avoid repeating words that appear in both, and to link ideas.

"There's" is the same as "There is."

There's a library. There's a restaurant.

There's a library and a restaurant.

The second "there's" can be dropped when joining sentences using "and."

FURTHER EXAMPLES

Jazmin's sister lives and works in Paris.

I bought a dress and some shoes for the party tonight.

My father and brother are both engineers.

My sister called earlier, and she told me she's pregnant!

Simon plays video games and watches TV every night.

I feel sick, I ate two sandwiches and a large slice of cake for lunch.

110.2 USING A COMMA INSTEAD OF "AND"

For lists of more than two items, a comma can replace "and."

This comma is replacing "and" in the list.

Another comma is used before the "and."

There's a library, a store, and a café.

The "and" is kept between the final two nouns.

110.3 "OR"

"**Or**" is most often used to list two or more choices or alternatives.

"Or" is used if there is a choice.

Do you want to go to Germany or France?

"**Or**" can also be used to talk about the consequences (usually negative) of an action.

"Or" is used to show that missing the train is a consequence of being late.

Don't be late, or you will miss the train.

FURTHER EXAMPLES

Should we go out or should we stay at home instead?

I can't decide whether to get a dog or a cat.

Should we paint the kitchen blue or green?

Be careful when cooking, or you might burn yourself.

110.4 "NOR"

"**Nor**" shows that two or more things are not true or do not happen. After "nor," use a positive form of the verb, and invert the verb as for a question.

I've never eaten lobster, nor do I want to.

The subject comes after the verb.

TIP
"Nor" is uncommon in informal English.

FURTHER EXAMPLES

He can't play the guitar, nor can he sing.

Fiona didn't turn up to dinner, nor did she answer my calls.

My television doesn't work, nor does my stereo.

110.5 "BUT"

"**But**" is used to join a positive statement to a negative statement, or to show a contrast between two clauses.

There's a hotel. There isn't a store.

There's a hotel, but there isn't a store.

FURTHER EXAMPLES

My daughter likes to eat apples, but she doesn't like pears.

I went to the supermarket, but I forgot my purse.

My friend does tap dancing, but she doesn't do ballet.

I wanted to be an architect, but I didn't pass my exams.

I'm on a diet, but I find it hard to avoid chocolate.

My friends invited me out tonight, but I don't feel well enough to go.

110.6 "YET"

"**Yet**" has a similar meaning to "but." It is used when something happens in spite of something else, or when something is true, even though it seems to contradict something else.

It's a warm day, yet Raymond's wearing a coat.

FURTHER EXAMPLES

George lives in the countryside, yet he works in a nearby city.

There was a school near my house, yet I went to one on the other side of town.

I've asked him to be quiet and yet he continues to talk during lessons.

110.7 "SO"

When "**so**" is a conjunction, it is used to show that something happens as a consequence of something else.

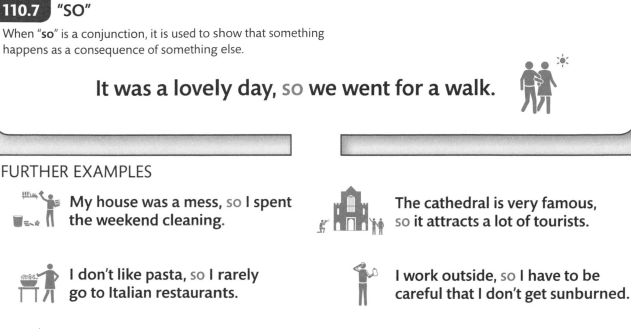

It was a lovely day, so we went for a walk.

FURTHER EXAMPLES

 My house was a mess, so I spent the weekend cleaning.

The cathedral is very famous, so it attracts a lot of tourists.

I don't like pasta, so I rarely go to Italian restaurants.

I work outside, so I have to be careful that I don't get sunburned.

Stephen moved to London, so he speaks English quite well now.

I ate before I came out, so I will only have a coffee.

110.8 USING COMMAS WITH COORDINATING CONJUNCTIONS

If a coordinating conjunction is joining two main clauses, a comma usually goes before the conjunction.

 It was raining, and there was lightning.

If a coordinating conjunction is joining two items, there is no need for a comma.

I'm going to wear jeans and a shirt.

If "and" or "or" is joining three or more items, a comma is usually added between each item and before the conjunction.

I need eggs, flour, and milk.

Would you like tea, coffee, or juice?

Subordinating conjunctions

Subordinating conjunctions are used to connect words, phrases, and clauses of unequal importance. They're used to say why, where, or when something happens.

See also:
Present simple **1**   Modal verbs **56**
Defining relative clauses **81**

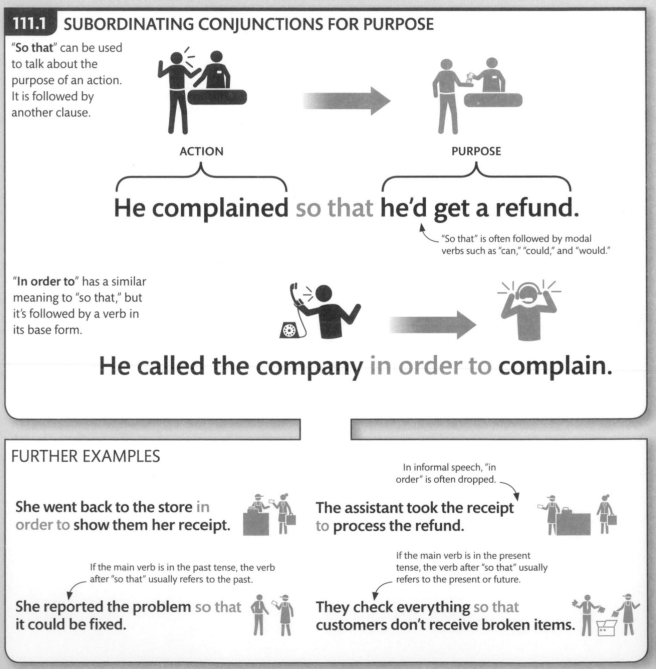

111.1 SUBORDINATING CONJUNCTIONS FOR PURPOSE

"**So that**" can be used to talk about the purpose of an action. It is followed by another clause.

ACTION   PURPOSE

He complained so that he'd get a refund.

"So that" is often followed by modal verbs such as "can," "could," and "would."

"**In order to**" has a similar meaning to "so that," but it's followed by a verb in its base form.

He called the company in order to complain.

FURTHER EXAMPLES

She went back to the store in order to **show them her receipt.**

In informal speech, "in order" is often dropped.

The assistant took the receipt to **process the refund.**

If the main verb is in the past tense, the verb after "so that" usually refers to the past.

She reported the problem so that **it could be fixed.**

If the main verb is in the present tense, the verb after "so that" usually refers to the present or future.

They check everything so that **customers don't receive broken items.**

111.2 CAUSE AND REASON

"**Because**" is used to talk about why something happens or the reasons behind a decision.

RESULT → REASON

He got a refund because he complained.

This is the main clause.

"Because" is used before giving the reason.

This is the reason.

FURTHER EXAMPLES

It's a noisy town because there are lots of cars.

My village is quiet because there are only a few families here.

I decided to move to the country because it's beautiful.

111.3 CONTRAST AND CONCESSION

"**Although**" is used to talk about something that is unexpectedly true. "**Even though**" means the same thing as "although," and it's more common in speech.

{ Although / Even though } I got up early, I was late to work.

FURTHER EXAMPLES

Although I've done it before, I found the run very difficult.

Even though I have two cousins, I've never met them.

I'm going to the beach this weekend, even though I can't swim.

111.4 "WHEN"

English uses **"when"** as a conjunction to talk about events or actions in the future that must happen before another event or action can take place. These phrases are called subordinate time clauses and are usually used with the present simple.

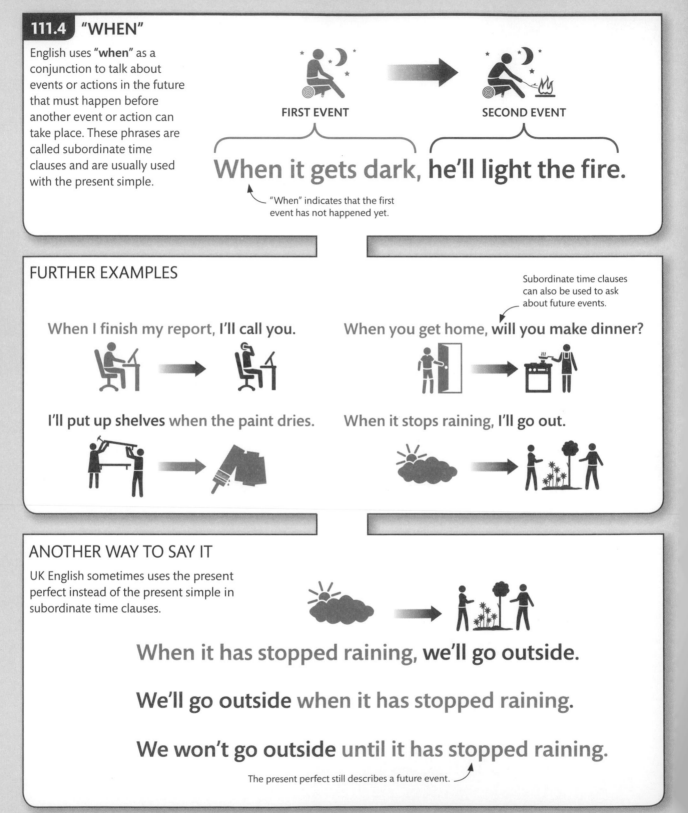

FIRST EVENT

SECOND EVENT

When it gets dark, he'll light the fire.

"When" indicates that the first event has not happened yet.

FURTHER EXAMPLES

Subordinate time clauses can also be used to ask about future events.

When I finish my report, **I'll call you.**

When you get home, **will you make dinner?**

I'll put up shelves when the paint dries.

When it stops raining, **I'll go out.**

ANOTHER WAY TO SAY IT

UK English sometimes uses the present perfect instead of the present simple in subordinate time clauses.

When it has stopped raining, **we'll go outside.**

We'll go outside when it has stopped raining.

We won't go outside until it has stopped raining.

The present perfect still describes a future event.

111.5 "AS SOON AS"

"As soon as" has a similar meaning to "when," but it implies that the second event will take place immediately once the first event is complete.

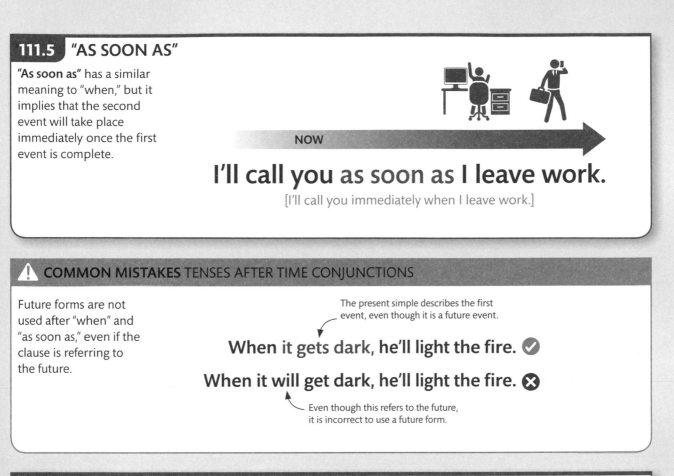

NOW

I'll call you as soon as I leave work.

[I'll call you immediately when I leave work.]

⚠ COMMON MISTAKES TENSES AFTER TIME CONJUNCTIONS

Future forms are not used after "when" and "as soon as," even if the clause is referring to the future.

The present simple describes the first event, even though it is a future event.

When it gets dark, he'll light the fire. ✓

When it will get dark, he'll light the fire. ✗

Even though this refers to the future, it is incorrect to use a future form.

111.6 "WHILE"

"While" is used to connect two clauses that are happening at the same time.

I watered the plants while my husband mowed the lawn.

FURTHER EXAMPLES

 I chopped the vegetables while Ted washed the potatoes.

 I didn't get any sleep while the owl was hooting outside.

 I read the newspaper while I waited for the kettle to boil.

309

Some words can be used to show a relationship between two sentences, or parts of a sentence. This can be cause, effect, emphasis, contrast, or comparison.

See also:
Coordinating conjunctions **110**
Subordinating conjunctions **111**

112.1 FORMAL LINKING WORDS

Some linking words are used most often in formal writing and speaking situations.

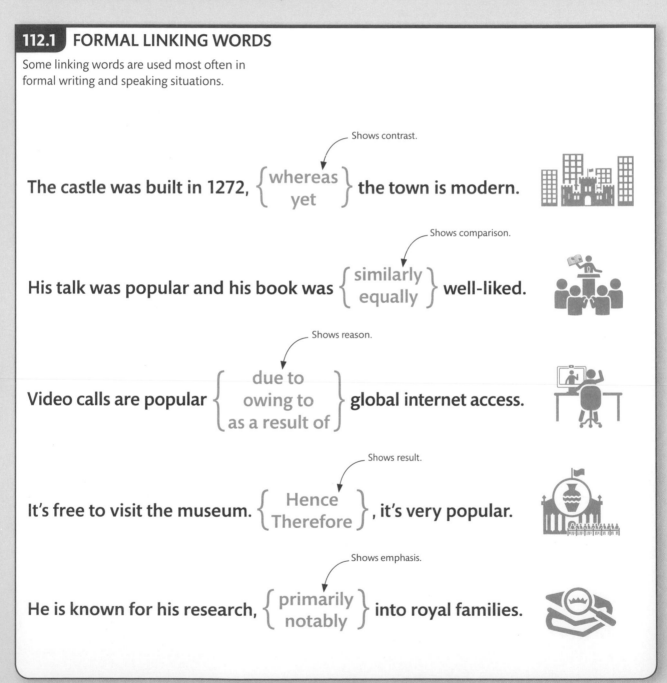

Shows contrast.

The castle was built in 1272, { whereas / yet } the town is modern.

Shows comparison.

His talk was popular and his book was { similarly / equally } well-liked.

Shows reason.

Video calls are popular { due to / owing to / as a result of } global internet access.

Shows result.

It's free to visit the museum. { Hence / Therefore }, it's very popular.

Shows emphasis.

He is known for his research, { primarily / notably } into royal families.

112.2 INFORMAL LINKING WORDS

Some linking words are mostly used in informal writing and speech.

TIP
Stress can be added to the linking word to emphasize the relationship between words when speaking.

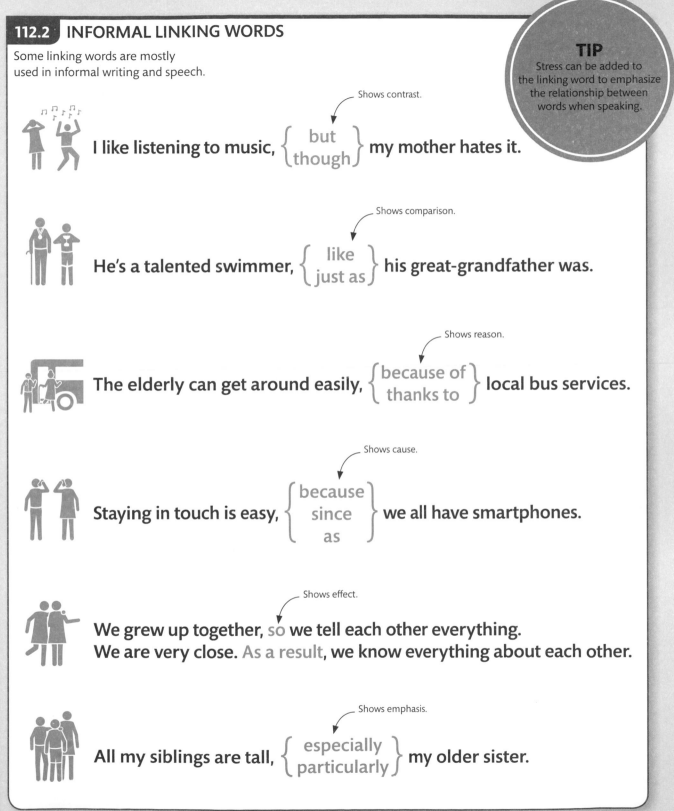

Shows contrast.

I like listening to music, { but / though } my mother hates it.

Shows comparison.

He's a talented swimmer, { like / just as } his great-grandfather was.

Shows reason.

The elderly can get around easily, { because of / thanks to } local bus services.

Shows cause.

Staying in touch is easy, { because / since / as } we all have smartphones.

Shows effect.

We grew up together, so we tell each other everything.
We are very close. As a result, we know everything about each other.

Shows emphasis.

All my siblings are tall, { especially / particularly } my older sister.

113.1 CONJUNCTIONS

Coordinating conjunctions join together two words, phrases, or clauses of equal importance.

Coordinating conjunction

I like roses and sunflowers.

I like gardening, but I hate mowing the lawn.

A comma is used before a conjunction to link two main clauses with different subjects. The comma shows where one main clause ends and another begins.

Subject of first main clause.

Flora tried to water her flowers, but the hose burst.

The second main clause has a different subject.

A comma is placed before the conjunction.

113.2 USES OF CONJUNCTIONS

Conjunctions can be used to describe a variety of relationships between two words, phrases, or clauses.

condition

if
in case
unless
as long as
so long as
even if

time

after
until
when
before
while
as soon as

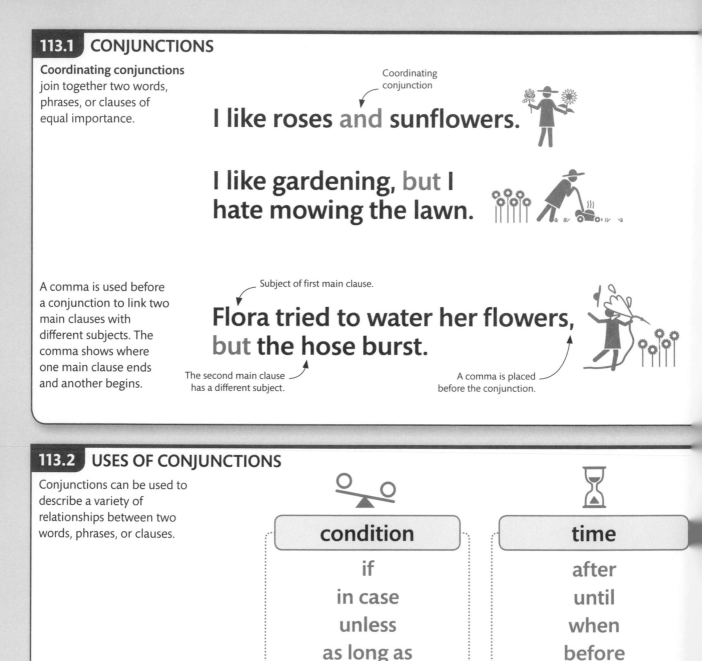

Conjunctions are linking words that describe the relationship between two parts of a sentence. They can be coordinating or subordinating.

See also:
"Either / neither / both" 68
Linking words R25

Subordinating conjunctions join together two words, phrases, or clauses of unequal importance. A subordinate clause adds more information about the main clause.

MAIN CLAUSE

She had to cut the tree down **because** it was too tall.

Subordinating conjunction

SUBORDINATE CLAUSE

SUBORDINATE CLAUSE   MAIN CLAUSE

Before she started, she put on gloves.

The subordinate clause can also go at the start of a sentence.

contrast	cause	reason
although	as	in order to
but	because	in order that
however	since	so
even though		so that
whereas		since
yet		

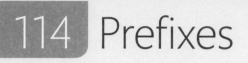

114 Prefixes

Prefixes are small groups of letters which can be
added to the start of many words to give them
different meanings.

See also:
Types of verbs **49**
Singular and plural nouns **69**   Adjectives **92**

114.1 PREFIXES

Prefixes attach to the start of a word to change its meaning. Prefixes
usually give the same change in meaning to each word they attach to.

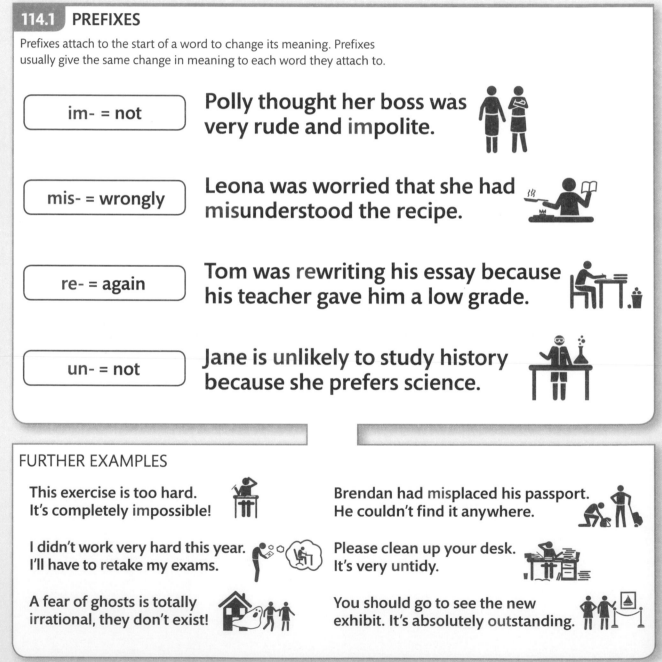

im- = not

**Polly thought her boss was
very rude and impolite.**

mis- = wrongly

**Leona was worried that she had
misunderstood the recipe.**

re- = again

**Tom was rewriting his essay because
his teacher gave him a low grade.**

un- = not

**Jane is unlikely to study history
because she prefers science.**

FURTHER EXAMPLES

**This exercise is too hard.
It's completely impossible!**

**Brendan had misplaced his passport.
He couldn't find it anywhere.**

**I didn't work very hard this year.
I'll have to retake my exams.**

**Please clean up your desk.
It's very untidy.**

**A fear of ghosts is totally
irrational, they don't exist!**

**You should go to see the new
exhibit. It's absolutely outstanding.**

114.2 USING PREFIXES

Some words can take more than one kind of prefix to give different meanings.

The fish is cooked perfectly. It's delicious!

The fish is undercooked. It tastes terrible.

The fish is overcooked. It's totally burned.

114.3 COMMON PREFIXES

PREFIX	MEANING	SAMPLE SENTENCE
anti-	against	It's always safer to use an antibacterial handwash.
co-	together	Erika loves her job because her coworkers are so nice.
dis-	not	My parents disapprove of my career decisions.
ex-	former	Clara is an ex-soldier. She used to be in the army.
im-, in-, ir-	not	Unfortunately, most of my answers were incorrect.
inter-	between, among	Matteo's band had become an international success.
mid-	middle	Jo's essay got a low grade because it finished mid-sentence.
mis-	wrongly	I think the referee misjudged the situation.
non-	not	I don't like this book at all. The plot is complete nonsense.
out-	better than others	Yue's work is fantastic. She's outperforming everyone.
over-	too much	It's okay to work hard, but make sure you don't overdo it.
post-	after	New mothers should receive good postnatal care.
pre-	before	The experiment will go ahead at a prearranged time.
re-	again	If you don't get into the school, you could reapply next year.
self-	oneself	Ronda can be a little bit too self-confident sometimes.
sub-	under	Mark's work this year has been substandard.
super-, sur-	above, over	There's a small surcharge if you want to use a credit card.
un-	reverse, cancel, not	Stacy couldn't find the right key to unlock the safe.
under-	beneath, below	I think the waiter has undercharged us for this meal.

115 Suffixes

Suffixes are small groups of letters which can be added to the end of many words to give them different meanings.

See also:
Types of verbs **49**
Singular and plural nouns **69**   Adjectives **92**

115.1 SUFFIXES

Suffixes attach to the end of a word to change its meaning. Suffixes usually give the same change in meaning to each word they attach to.

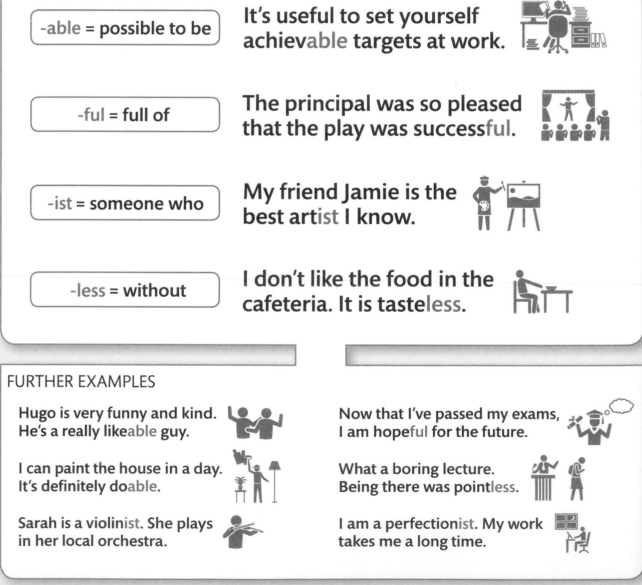

-able = possible to be

It's useful to set yourself achievable targets at work.

-ful = full of

The principal was so pleased that the play was successful.

-ist = someone who

My friend Jamie is the best artist I know.

-less = without

I don't like the food in the cafeteria. It is tasteless.

FURTHER EXAMPLES

Hugo is very funny and kind. He's a really likeable guy.

I can paint the house in a day. It's definitely doable.

Sarah is a violinist. She plays in her local orchestra.

Now that I've passed my exams, I am hopeful for the future.

What a boring lecture. Being there was pointless.

I am a perfectionist. My work takes me a long time.

115.2 USING SUFFIXES

Some words can take more than one kind of suffix to give different meanings.

The best jokes are in good taste.

That joke was hilarious. It was very tasteful.

That joke was offensive. It was very tasteless.

115.3 COMMON SUFFIXES

SUFFIX	MEANING	SAMPLE SENTENCE
-able, -ible	able to be	It is perfectly acceptable to submit your essays online.
-al, -ial	having characteristics of	The verdict was based entirely on circumstantial evidence.
-ance, -ence	state of	Male lions fight each other to assert their dominance.
-ate	become	You need to activate your credit card before you can use it.
-dom	place or state of being	Older children can be given a greater amount of freedom.
-en	become	They are planning to widen the roads to reduce congestion.
-er, -or	person who performs an action	Shakespeare is probably the most famous English writer.
-ful	full of	The computer is one of the most useful inventions ever.
-ic, -tic, -ical	having characteristics of	Running is a great form of physical exercise.
-ism	an action, state, or system	Surrealism was a major art movement of the 20th century.
-ist, -ian	someone who plays or does	A pianist is somebody who can play the piano.
-ity, -ty	quality of	Equality is the belief that everybody should be equal.
-ize	make	I'm trying to maximize our profits by selling more stock.
-less	without	The possibilities of technology are limitless.
-ment	condition of, act of	Buying property can be a very good investment.
-ness	state of	Lots of people today are interested in health and fitness.
-ous	having qualities of	The inland taipan is the most venomous snake in the world.
-sion, -tion	state of being or act of	All essays should end with a good conclusion.
-y	characterized by	The weather's terrible today. It's very cloudy outside.

115.4 SUFFIXES CHANGING WORD CLASS

Certain suffixes are only used for specific types of words. The suffix
of a word can sometimes show what part of speech the word is.

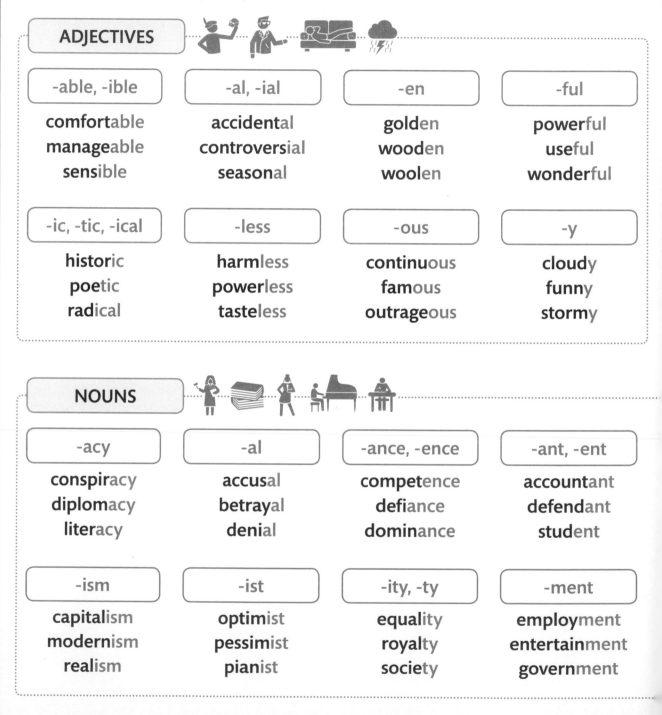

ADJECTIVES

-able, -ible
- comfortable
- manageable
- sensible

-al, -ial
- accidental
- controversial
- seasonal

-en
- golden
- wooden
- woolen

-ful
- powerful
- useful
- wonderful

-ic, -tic, -ical
- historic
- poetic
- radical

-less
- harmless
- powerless
- tasteless

-ous
- continuous
- famous
- outrageous

-y
- cloudy
- funny
- stormy

NOUNS

-acy
- conspiracy
- diplomacy
- literacy

-al
- accusal
- betrayal
- denial

-ance, -ence
- competence
- defiance
- dominance

-ant, -ent
- accountant
- defendant
- student

-ism
- capitalism
- modernism
- realism

-ist
- optimist
- pessimist
- pianist

-ity, -ty
- equality
- royalty
- society

-ment
- employment
- entertainment
- government

VERBS

-ate
activate
debate
inflate

-en
brighten
sweeten
widen

-ify
classify
mystify
simplify

-ize
energize
immunize
minimize

-dom
freedom
kingdom
wisdom

-er, -or
generator
singer
writer

-ness
happiness
sadness
sickness

-sion, -tion
appreciation
collision
infection

115.5 SUFFIX SPELLING RULES

If the suffix starts with a vowel, and the root ends with a stressed final syllable ending consonant-vowel-consonant, the last letter of the root is doubled before adding the suffix.

occur
⬇
occurrence

If the suffix starts with a vowel and the root ends with an "-e," the final "-e" is dropped from the root before adding the suffix. Roots ending "-ge" or "-ce" are an exception.

Root ends with "-ge."

debate
⬇
debatable

manage
⬇
manageable

The "e" stays in the word.

If the root ends consonant plus "-y," the "y" changes to an "i" before any suffix is added. The exception is "-ing."

plenty
⬇
plentiful

apply
⬇
applying

"-y" doesn't change before "-ing."

If the root ends vowel plus "-y," the final "-y" does not change.

Root ends vowel plus "-y."

employ
⬇
employable

The "-y" does not change to an "i."

319

In English, there are several phrases which sound or look similar, but have different meanings. It is important not to get these confused.

> **See also:**
> Present simple **1** Present continuous **4**
> "Used to" and "would" **15**

116.1 "GET USED TO" AND "BE USED TO"

To "**get used to** (doing) something" describes the process of adapting to new or different situations until they become familiar or normal.

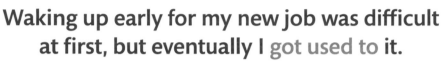

Waking up early for my new job was difficult at first, but eventually I got used to it.

To "**be used to** (doing) something" means that something has been done for long enough that it is normal and familiar.

I've lived in the city for years, so I am used to the bad pollution.

TIP
These phrases should not be confused with "used to" (without "be" or "get"), which is used when talking about a regular past action.

FURTHER EXAMPLES

 When I travel, I get used to different customs very quickly.
[I find it easy to adapt to different customs when I travel.]

I got used to the cold weather within a couple of weeks.
[I adapted to the cold weather within two weeks.]

I am used to spicy food as I've always eaten it.
[I am accustomed to eating spicy food.]

 We were used to the old teacher, so it was a shame when she left.
[We were accustomed to our previous teacher, but then she left.]

116.2 "HAVE / GET SOMETHING DONE"

"Have" and "get" can be used with a noun and the past participle to talk about something someone does for someone else. "Get" is less formal than "have."

Did you get your computer updated?

[Did somebody update your computer for you?]

Yes, the company has the computers updated regularly.

[Yes, somebody regularly updates them for the company.]

FURTHER EXAMPLES

The structure is used with "should" to give advice.

You should get your connection checked.

[I think you should arrange for someone to check your connection.]

Will you get the oven fixed soon?

[Will somebody fix the oven for you soon?]

I need to get my hair cut.

[I need someone to cut my hair.]

They haven't had the locks changed yet.

[They haven't arranged for somebody to change the locks for them.]

The store has its produce checked daily.

[Somebody checks the store's produce each day.]

Most people have burglar alarms installed.

[Most people have someone fit them a burglar alarm.]

HOW TO FORM

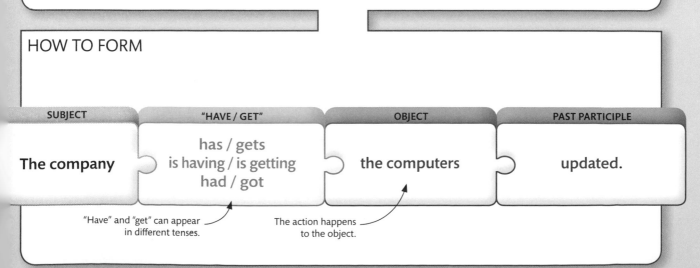

SUBJECT	"HAVE / GET"	OBJECT	PAST PARTICIPLE
The company	has / gets is having / is getting had / got	the computers	updated.

"Have" and "get" can appear in different tenses.

The action happens to the object.

There are a number of words and phrases in English which help to explain the order of events. They can also be used to organize text and make it easier to understand.

See also:
More linking words **112**
Making conversation **120**

117.1 SEQUENCING PHRASES

Certain words and phrases indicate at what point in a sequence something happens.

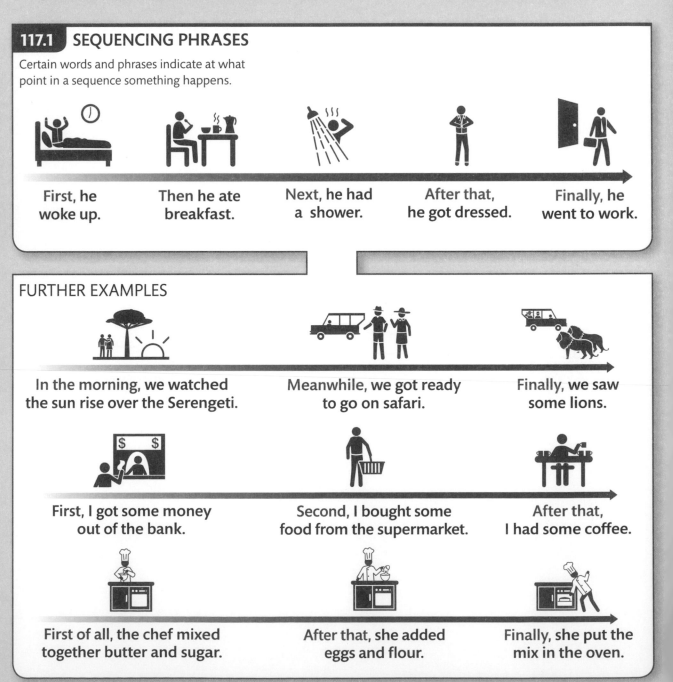

First, he woke up.

Then he ate breakfast.

Next, he had a shower.

After that, he got dressed.

Finally, he went to work.

FURTHER EXAMPLES

In the morning, we watched the sun rise over the Serengeti.

Meanwhile, we got ready to go on safari.

Finally, we saw some lions.

First, I got some money out of the bank.

Second, I bought some food from the supermarket.

After that, I had some coffee.

First of all, the chef mixed together butter and sugar.

After that, she added eggs and flour.

Finally, she put the mix in the oven.

117.2 FORMAL ORGANIZING PHRASES

Some discourse markers show what is coming next. They help organize paragraphs and longer passages of formal text.

TIP
These organizing words often go at the beginning of a clause or sentence.

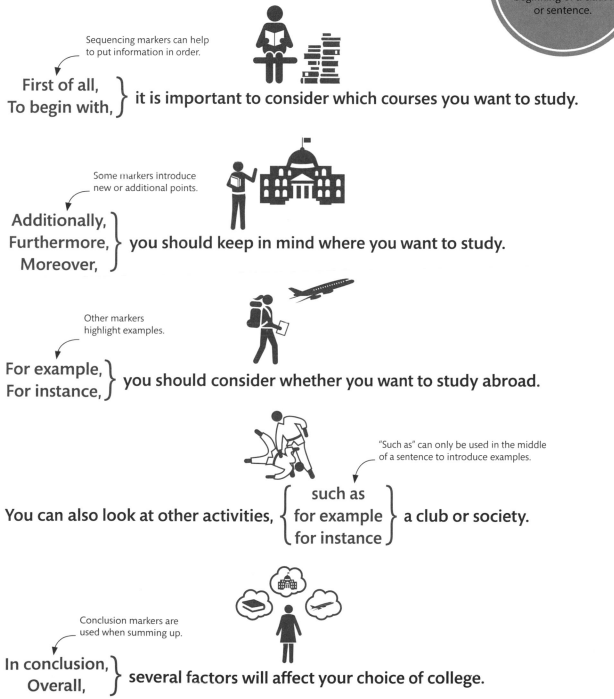

Sequencing markers can help to put information in order.

First of all,
To begin with, } it is important to consider which courses you want to study.

Some markers introduce new or additional points.

Additionally,
Furthermore,
Moreover, } you should keep in mind where you want to study.

Other markers highlight examples.

For example,
For instance, } you should consider whether you want to study abroad.

"Such as" can only be used in the middle of a sentence to introduce examples.

You can also look at other activities, { such as / for example / for instance } a club or society.

Conclusion markers are used when summing up.

In conclusion,
Overall, } several factors will affect your choice of college.

118 Correcting and changing the subject

Set words and phrases can be used to correct someone, disagree, change the subject, or concede a point. They often come at the beginning of the sentence.

See also:
More linking words **112** Deciding and hedging **119** Making conversation **120**

118.1 CORRECTING AND DISAGREEING

Certain words can be used to show you disagree with someone or to correct a misunderstanding.

TIP
These phrases can appear impolite if spoken with heavy emphasis.

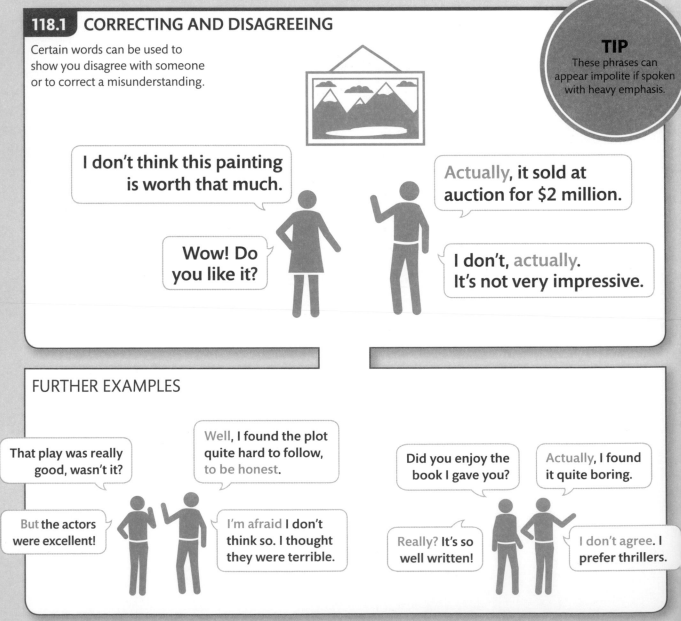

I don't think this painting is worth that much.

Wow! Do you like it?

Actually, it sold at auction for $2 million.

I don't, actually. It's not very impressive.

FURTHER EXAMPLES

That play was really good, wasn't it?

Well, I found the plot quite hard to follow, to be honest.

But the actors were excellent!

I'm afraid I don't think so. I thought they were terrible.

Did you enjoy the book I gave you?

Actually, I found it quite boring.

Really? It's so well written!

I don't agree. I prefer thrillers.

118.2 CHANGING SUBJECT

"By the way" shows a change of subject.

I think this gallery is fantastic. Oh, by the way, did you read the article about this exhibit in *The Times*?

"As I was saying" returns to a previous subject after a change of subject or an interruption.

As I was saying, **this is a fantastic exhibit. I really like the range of artwork.**

"Anyway" returns to a subject after an interruption or a change in subject. It can also end a subject or a conversation.

Anyway, **I should say goodbye. I want to visit the gallery shop before it closes.**

118.3 CONCEDING A POINT

Certain words can be used to agree to, or concede, a point, particularly after first doubting it to be true.

FURTHER EXAMPLES

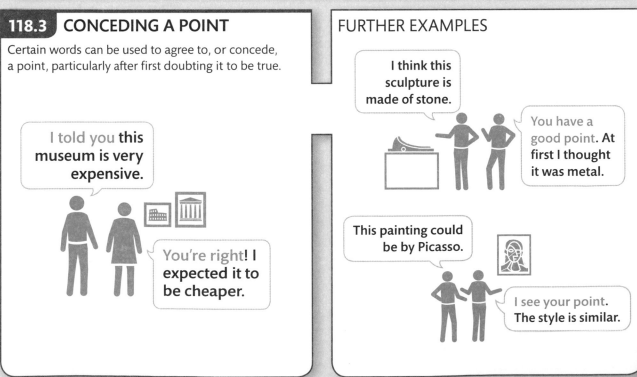

I told you **this museum is very expensive.**

You're right! I **expected it to be cheaper.**

I think this sculpture is made of stone.

You have a good point. **At first I thought it was metal.**

This painting could be by Picasso.

I see your point. **The style is similar.**

119 Deciding and hedging

English uses a number of words and phrases to discuss
the different sides of an argument or to make sentences
sound less definite.

See also:
Infinitives and participles **51**   More linking
words **112**   Making conversation **120**

119.1 DISCUSSING ARGUMENTS

There are specific words and phrases which are used to
discuss or compare the good and bad sides of an argument.

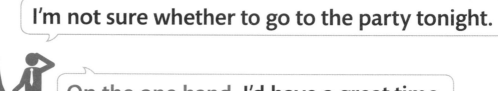

I'm not sure whether to go to the party tonight.

On the one hand, **I'd have a great time.**
On the other hand, **I have work to do.**

FURTHER EXAMPLES

Although **my friends will be at the party, I don't want to stay up late.**

I could go to the party. Alternatively **I could stay in and study.**

Of course, **there is going to be good music and lots of food.**

I don't want to study Art. However, **my teacher thinks I'm good at it.**

Despite **my reservations, I think I'll go to the party anyway.**

119.2　HEDGING

Hedging words and phrases can be added to a sentence
to make its meaning less definite, direct, or strong.

Polls $\left\{ \begin{array}{l} \text{suggest} \\ \text{indicate} \end{array} \right\}$ **that locals dislike the new statue.**

└─ Hedging verbs.

It is $\left\{ \begin{array}{l} \text{arguably} \\ \text{potentially} \end{array} \right\}$ **the strangest statue around.**

└─ Hedging adverbs.

$\left. \begin{array}{l} \text{To a certain degree,} \\ \text{To some extent,} \end{array} \right\}$ **locals feel their views are being ignored.**

└─ Hedging phrases.

119.3　"SEEM" AND "APPEAR"

"Seem" and "appear" are words used to distance oneself from a
statement. This is useful when it is not certain if the statement is true.

The prisoners $\left\{ \begin{array}{l} \text{seem} \\ \text{appear} \end{array} \right\}$ **to have vanished.**

└─ "Seem" and "appear" are often followed
by another verb in the infinitive.

It $\left\{ \begin{array}{l} \text{seems} \\ \text{appears} \end{array} \right\}$ **that the prison cell was left unguarded.**

└─ "It seems" or "It appears" can be
followed by a "that" clause.

It would $\left\{ \begin{array}{l} \text{seem} \\ \text{appear} \end{array} \right\}$ **that a file was used to break the bars.**

└─ "Would" adds even more
distance or uncertainty.

120 Making conversation

Many words and phrases are used in English to ease the flow of conversation. These techniques are often called organizing, backchanneling, or stalling.

See also:
More linking words **112**
Hedging **119**

120.1 INFORMAL ORGANIZING WORDS

A number of general words can be used to move from one topic to another in conversational English.

"Right" gets attention before saying something important.

Right, let's get started...

"OK" acknowledges that the other speaker has been heard.

... OK, and are you happy with your choice?

"So" indicates that a conclusion is being reached.

... So, I think we agree overall.

120.2 BACKCHANNELING

When listening to another speaker, it's common to use words to show you agree and are paying attention. This is known as backchanneling.

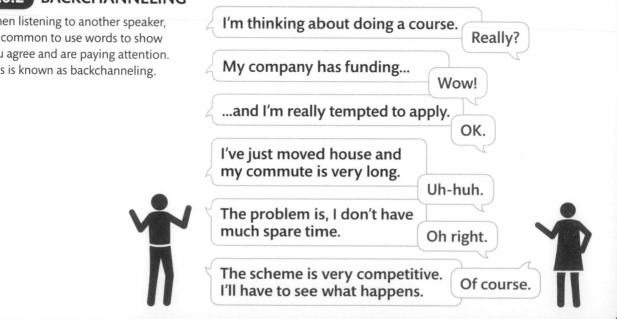

I'm thinking about doing a course.

Really?

My company has funding...

Wow!

...and I'm really tempted to apply.

OK.

I've just moved house and my commute is very long.

Uh-huh.

The problem is, I don't have much spare time.

Oh right.

The scheme is very competitive. I'll have to see what happens.

Of course.

120.3 STALLING TECHNIQUES

If extra time is needed to think about a difficult question before answering it, a response can be started with a stalling phrase to indicate that the question is being considered.

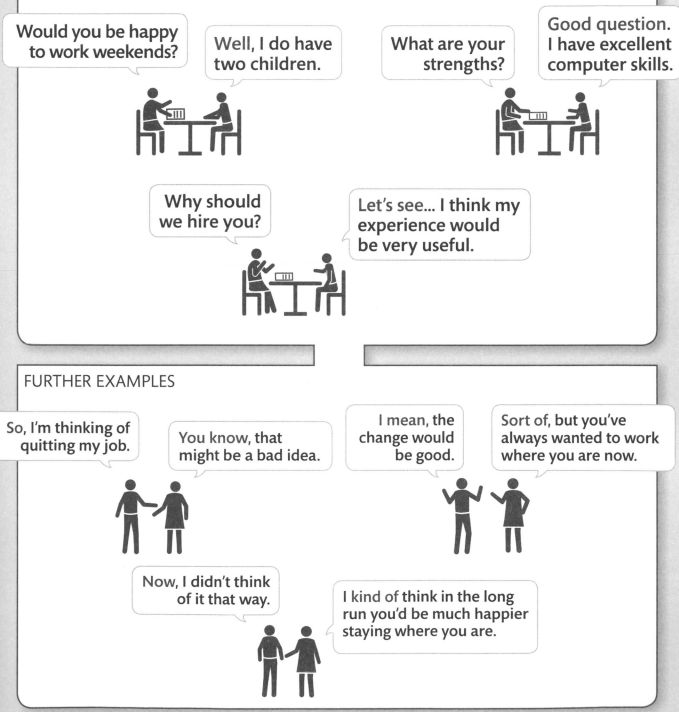

Would you be happy to work weekends?

Well, I do have two children.

What are your strengths?

Good question. I have excellent computer skills.

Why should we hire you?

Let's see... I think my experience would be very useful.

FURTHER EXAMPLES

So, I'm thinking of quitting my job.

You know, that might be a bad idea.

I mean, the change would be good.

Sort of, but you've always wanted to work where you are now.

Now, I didn't think of it that way.

I kind of think in the long run you'd be much happier staying where you are.

R Reference

PARTS OF SPEECH

The different types of words that make up sentences are called parts of speech. Only nouns and verbs are essential elements of a sentence, but other parts of speech, such as adjectives and adverbs, can make a sentence more descriptive.

PART OF SPEECH	DEFINITION	EXAMPLES
noun	a name, object, concept or person	**cat**, **Evie**, **girl**, **house**, **water**, **happiness**
adjective	describes a noun or pronoun	**big**, **funny**, **light**, **red**, **young**
verb	shows an action or a state of being	**be**, **go**, **read**, **speak**, **swim**, **walk**
adverb	describes verbs, adjectives, and other adverbs, giving information on how, where, when, or how much	**briskly**, **easily**, **happily**, **here**, **loudly**, **quite**, **rather**, **soon**, **together**, **very**
pronoun	takes the place of a noun	**he**, **she**, **you**, **we**, **them**, **it**
preposition	describes the relationship between a noun or pronoun and another word in the sentence	**about**, **above**, **from**, **in**
conjunction	a joining word, used to link words, phrases, or clauses	**and**, **because**, **but**, **while**, **yet**
interjection	an exclamation or remark	**ah**, **hey**, **hi**, **hmm**, **wow**, **yes**
article	used with a noun to specify whether the noun is a particular person or thing, or something general	**a**, **an**, **the**
determiner	precedes a noun and puts the noun in context	**all**, **her**, **my**, **their**, **your**

R2 **THE ALPHABET**

The English alphabet has 26 letters. "A," "E," "I," "O," and "U" are vowels, and the rest are consonants.

Aa Bb Cc Dd Ee Ff Gg Hh Ii Jj Kk Ll Mm Nn Oo Pp Qq Rr Ss Tt Uu Vv Ww Xx Yy Zz

PUNCTUATION MARK	NAME	USE
.	period (US) full stop (UK)	• marks the end of a complete statement • marks the end of an abbreviated word
...	ellipsis	• marks where text has been omitted or a sentence is unfinished
,	comma	• follows an introductory word, phrase, or clause • can separate a non-essential part of a sentence • can be used with a conjunction to join two main clauses • separates words or phrases in a list • represents omitted words to avoid repetition in a sentence • can be used between an introduction to speech and direct speech
;	semi-colon	• separates two main clauses that are closely related • separates items in a complex list
:	colon	• connects a main clause to a clause, phrase, or word that is an explanation of the main clause, or that emphasizes a point in the main clause • introduces a list after a complete statement • introduces quoted text
'	apostrophe	• marks missing letters • indicates possession
-	hyphen	• links two words in compound modifiers and some compound nouns • can be used in fractions and in numbers from twenty-one to ninety-nine • can join certain prefixes to other words
" "	inverted commas	• can be used before and after direct speech and quoted text • pick out a word or phrase in a sentence • can be used around titles of short works
?	question mark	• marks the end of a sentence that is a question
!	exclamation mark	• marks the end of a sentence that expresses strong emotions • can be used at the end of an interruption to add emphasis
()	parentheses (US) brackets (UK)	• can be used around non-essential information in a sentence • can be used around information that provides clarification
—	dash	• can be used in pairs around interruptions • marks a range of numbers (5–6 hours) • indicates start and end of a route (Paris–Dover rally)
•	bullet point	• indicates a point in a list
/	slash	• can be used to show an alternative instead of using the word "or"

PRESENT TENSES

The present simple is used to make simple statements of fact, to talk about things that happen repeatedly, and to describe things that are always true.

SUBJECT	VERB	REST OF SENTENCE
I / You / We / They	play	tennis every day.
He / She	plays	

The present continuous is used to talk about ongoing actions that are happening in or around the present moment. It is formed with "be" and a present participle.

SUBJECT	"BE"	PRESENT PARTICIPLE	REST OF SENTENCE
I	am		
He / She	is	wearing	jeans today.
You / We / They	are		

R5 **THE IMPERATIVE**

Imperatives are used to give commands or to make requests. They are formed using the base form of the verb.

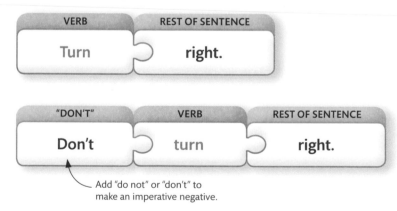

VERB	REST OF SENTENCE
Turn	right.

"DON'T"	VERB	REST OF SENTENCE
Don't	turn	right.

Add "do not" or "don't" to make an imperative negative.

R6   PAST TENSES

The past simple describes single, completed actions in the past.
It is the most commonly used past tense in English.

SUBJECT	VERB	REST OF SENTENCE
I / You / He She / We / They	washed	the car on Tuesday.

The past continuous is used in English to talk about actions or events that were ongoing
at some time in the past. It is formed with "was" or "were" and a present participle.

SUBJECT	"BE"	PRESENT PARTICIPLE	REST OF SENTENCE
I / He / She	was	having	lunch with a friend.
You / We / They	were		

R7   PRESENT PERFECT TENSES

The present perfect simple is used to talk about events in the past that still have
an effect on the present moment. It is formed with "have" and a past participle.

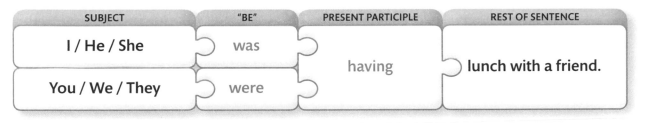

SUBJECT	"HAVE / HAS"	PAST PARTICIPLE	REST OF SENTENCE
I / You / We / They	have	arrived	in London.
He / She	has		

The present perfect continuous describes an activity that took place over a period of time
in the recent past. The activity might just have stopped or might still be happening.

SUBJECT	"HAVE / HAS"	"BEEN"	PRESENT PARTICIPLE	REST OF SENTENCE
I / You / We / They	have	been	working	all day.
He / She	has			

R8   PAST PERFECT TENSES

The past perfect simple is used to talk about a completed action that
took place before another completed action in the past.

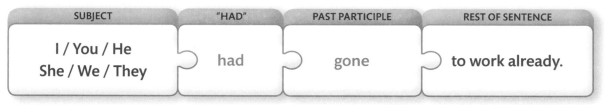

SUBJECT	"HAD"	PAST PARTICIPLE	REST OF SENTENCE
I / You / He She / We / They	had	gone	to work already.

The past perfect continuous describes a repeated action or ongoing activity
that was taking place before another completed event in the past.

SUBJECT	"HAD BEEN"	PRESENT PARTICIPLE	REST OF SENTENCE
I / You / He She / We / They	had been	studying	English for two years.

R9   "USED TO" AND "WOULD"

"Used to" is used with the base form of a verb to talk about past habits or past
states. **"Would"** can also be used in this way, but only to talk about past habits.

SUBJECT	"USED TO / WOULD"	BASE FORM	REST OF SENTENCE
I / You / He She / We / They	used to / would	play	tennis every day.

R10   FUTURE FORMS

The future with "going to" is used to talk about decisions that have already been made,
or to make predictions when there is evidence in the present moment to support them.

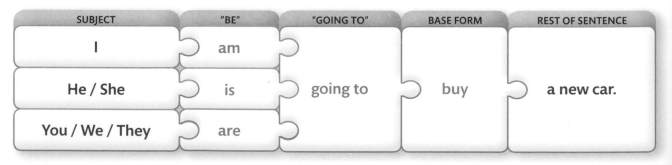

SUBJECT	"BE"	"GOING TO"	BASE FORM	REST OF SENTENCE
I	am			
He / She	is	going to	buy	a new car.
You / We / They	are			

The future with "will" is used to talk about decisions made at the time of speaking, to make predictions not supported by evidence, to offer to do something, or to make promises.

SUBJECT	"WILL"	BASE FORM	REST OF SENTENCE
I / You / He She / We / They	will	love	the new movie.

The future continuous uses "will" or "going to" and "be" with a present participle to describe an event or situation that will be in progress at some point in the future.

SUBJECT	"WILL BE"	PRESENT PARTICIPLE	REST OF SENTENCE
I / You / He She / We / They	will be	running	a bistro.

R11 FUTURE PERFECT

The future perfect is used to talk about an event that will overlap with, or finish before, another event or point in the future.

SUBJECT	"WILL HAVE"	PAST PARTICIPLE	REST OF SENTENCE
I / You / He She / We / They	will have	finished	the project tomorrow.

The future perfect continuous is used to predict the length of an activity. This tense looks back from that imagined time in the future.

SUBJECT	"WILL HAVE BEEN"	PRESENT PARTICIPLE	REST OF SENTENCE
I / You / He She / We / They	will have been	working	here for a year.

TENSE	POSITIVE STATEMENT	NEGATIVE STATEMENT
Present simple with "be"	I am interested in politics.	I am **not** interested in politics.
Present simple with other verbs	I play tennis every day.	I **do not** play tennis every day.
Present continuous	He is wearing jeans today.	He is **not** wearing jeans today.
Past simple with "be"	She was at the lecture yesterday.	She was **not** at the lecture yesterday.
Past simple with other verbs	We cooked enough food last night.	We did **not** cook enough food last night.
Past continuous	It was raining this morning.	It was **not** raining this morning.
Present perfect simple	I have seen the new movie.	I have **not** seen the new movie.
Present perfect continuous	I have been waiting for a long time.	I have **not** been waiting for a long time.
Past perfect simple	Sam had cooked dinner for me.	Sam had **not** cooked dinner for me.
Past perfect continuous	Fey had been looking for a new job.	Fey had **not** been looking for a new job.
Future with "going to"	It is going to be sunny tomorrow.	It is **not** going to be sunny tomorrow.
Future with "will"	They will be here before 5pm.	They will **not** be here before 5pm.
Future continuous	Tania will be arriving soon.	Tania will **not** be arriving soon.
Future perfect simple	The play will have finished by 7pm.	The play will **not** have finished by 7pm.
Future perfect continuous	I will have been working for a long time.	I will **not** have been working for a long time.

MODAL VERB	POSITIVE STATEMENT	NEGATIVE STATEMENT
"Can"	I can play the piano.	I **cannot** play the piano.
"Could"	I could sing when I was younger.	I could **not** sing when I was younger.
"Should"	We should buy a new house.	We should **not** buy a new house.
"Might"	He might come to the party tonight.	He might **not** come to the party tonight.
"Must"	You must write in pencil.	You must **not** write in pencil.

PRONOUN	"BE"	"WILL"	"WOULD"	"HAVE"	"HAD"
I	I am ➡ **I'm**	I will ➡ **I'll**	I would ➡ **I'd**	I have ➡ **I've**	I had ➡ **I'd**
you	you are ➡ **you're**	you will ➡ **you'll**	you would ➡ **you'd**	you have ➡ **you've**	you had ➡ **you'd**
he	he is ➡ **he's**	he will ➡ **he'll**	he would ➡ **he'd**	he has ➡ **he's**	he had ➡ **he'd**
she	she is ➡ **she's**	she will ➡ **she'll**	she would ➡ **she'd**	she has ➡ **she's**	she had ➡ **she'd**
it	it is ➡ **it's**	it will ➡ **it'll**	it would ➡ **it'd**	it has ➡ **it's**	it had ➡ **it'd**
we	we are ➡ **we're**	we will ➡ **we'll**	we would ➡ **we'd**	we have ➡ **we've**	we had ➡ **we'd**
they	they are ➡ **they're**	they will ➡ **they'll**	they would ➡ **they'd**	they have ➡ **they've**	they had ➡ **they'd**
that	that is ➡ **that's**	that will ➡ **that'll**	that would ➡ **that'd**	that has ➡ **that's**	that had ➡ **that'd**
who	who is ➡ **who's**	who will ➡ **who'll**	who would ➡ **who'd**	who has ➡ **who's**	who had ➡ **who'd**

VERB AND "NOT"	CONTRACTION
is not	**isn't**
are not	**aren't**
was not	**wasn't**
were not	**weren't**
have not	**haven't**
has not	**hasn't**
had not	**hadn't**
will not	**won't**
would not	**wouldn't**
do not	**don't**
does not	**doesn't**
did not	**didn't**
cannot	**can't**
could not	**couldn't**
should not	**shouldn't**
might not	**mightn't**
must not	**mustn't**

MODAL VERB AND "HAVE"	CONTRACTION
would have	**would've**
should have	**should've**
could have	**could've**
might have	**might've**
must have	**must've**

⚠ COMMON MISTAKES CONTRACTIONS

These contractions are often spelled incorrectly because they look and sound very similar to other words. Contracted forms always use an apostrophe.

You are
⬇
You're ✅
Your ❌

They are
⬇
They're ✅
Their ❌
There ❌

Prepositions are words that are used to create or show relationships between different parts of a clause, for example time, place, or reason. They can only be followed by a noun, pronoun, noun phrase, or gerund.

PREPOSITION	SAMPLE SENTENCE
about	Today's lecture is **about** the Cold War.
above	The balloon flew **above** the city.
after	We can go to the park **after** lunch.
against	I'm **against** building new houses here.
among	The document is **among** these papers.
at	Let's meet **at** the bus stop later.
because of	I'm late **because of** the trains delays.
before	Could you get here **before** lunchtime?
behind	The park is **behind** that hedge.
below	He lives in the apartment **below** mine.
beneath	Potatoes grow **beneath** the ground.
between	I live **between** Vancouver and Calgary.
between... and	They'll arrive **between** 7pm **and** 8pm.
by	Please pay **by** the end of the month.
despite	The café is busy **despite** the high prices.
during	Turn off your phone **during** the show.
due to	**Due to** the rain, the game was canceled.
except (for)	Everyone had arrived **except for** Liam.
following	**Following** losses, the store closed down.
for	I haven't been back to Delhi **for** years.
from	Our new colleague is **from** Lithuania.
from ... to	I work **from** 9am **to** 5pm.
in	There's plenty of food **in** the cupboard.

PREPOSITION	SAMPLE SENTENCE
in front of	Don't stand **in front of** the television!
instead of	Can we have pizza **instead of** pasta?
like	This tastes **like** butter, but it has less fat.
near	We live quite **near** the airport.
next to	The supermarket is **next to** the bank.
on	I have piano lessons **on** Tuesdays.
on top of	Put the vase **on top of** the bookcase.
out of	Don't let the cat **out of** her box yet.
over	Lots of planes fly **over** my village.
past	It's ten **past** nine. You're late!
regarding	Let's talk **regarding** your new job.
since	I haven't been to Las Vegas **since** 2007.
thanks to	**Thanks to** your efforts, we won a prize.
through	Shall we walk **through** the park?
throughout	I laughed **throughout** the whole movie.
to	When are you going **to** Canada?
toward	The child just ran **toward** his mother.
unlike	It's **unlike** Karen to be so rude.
until	We'll be in Portugal **until** Friday.
under(neath)	I think the ball's **under(neath)** the bush.
with	Will you come **with** us to the concert?
within	I ran the marathon **within** four hours.
without	I've come out **without** my phone.

R15 ADJECTIVES AND PREPOSITIONS

Some adjectives have to be followed by a specific preposition.

ADJECTIVE	PREPOSITION	SAMPLE SENTENCE
afraid	of	It's surprising how many adults are **afraid of** the dark.
ashamed	of	You should be **ashamed of** that remark. It was very hurtful.
bored	with	If you're **bored with** that book, read a different one instead.
close	to	I'm very **close to** my cousins because we're all similar ages.
crazy	about	All the children at the school are **crazy about** the same TV show.
different	from (UK) / than (US)	He's always been **different from / than** other boys of his age.
excited	about	Max was very **excited about** his first football game.
famous	for	She was mainly **famous for** her career in politics.
good / bad	at	I've always been very **good at** geography, but **bad at** history.
good / bad	for	Too much sugar is **bad for** us and should be avoided.
good / bad	of	It was very **good of** you to look after the children for me.
guilty	of	The vandal was found **guilty of** criminal damage.
impressed	by	I've always been **impressed by** your ability to forgive people.
interested	in	More and more students are **interested in** media studies.
jealous	of	Older children are often **jealous of** their younger brothers or sisters.
keen	on	My parents aren't very **keen on** classical music.
nervous	of	I've been **nervous of** dogs since one bit me when I was a child.
pleased	at / with	Most of the voters were **pleased at / with** the result of the election.
proud	of	The coach felt very **proud of** his team when they lifted the trophy.
responsible	for	I'm **responsible for** ensuring that everything runs smoothly.
similar	to	Don't you think she looks very **similar to** her cousin?
surprised	at / by	We were all **surprised at / by** the news of your resignation.
suitable	for	The village roads aren't **suitable for** heavy trucks.
tired	of	We're **tired of** city life and would like to move to the country.
wrong	with	Can you tell me what's **wrong with** my answer?

Some nouns have to be followed by a specific preposition.

NOUN	PREPOSITION	SAMPLE SENTENCE
advantage	in	The **advantage in** going last is that you know the target time.
aim	of	The **aim of** this lesson is to understand algebra.
amazement	at	I gasped in **amazement at** the price tag!
anger	at	Sally felt a flash of **anger at** the suggestion that she hadn't tried.
apology	for	The referee gave a public **apology for** his bad decision.
belief	in	We share a strong **belief in** the goodness of people.
cause	of	Political disagreement is the **cause of** many family arguments.
danger	of / in	The **danger in / of** trying to please everyone is that you please no one.
demand	for	There is always an increased **demand for** ice cream in hot weather.
difficulty	in	If you experience any **difficulty in** breathing, call the doctor.
excitement	about / at	There was great **excitement about / at** the treasure they had found.
fear	of	Many people experience a **fear of** flying at some point.
hope	of	The **hope of** a cure for cancer is growing all the time now.
interest	in	Several teachers have expressed an **interest in** the new course.
lack	of	The building project will not go ahead because of a **lack of** money.
photograph	of	Have you seen this **photograph of** my grandmother's wedding?
point	in	There's no **point in** arguing; we won't change our minds.
possibility	of	With this grade, there is the **possibility of** postgraduate study.
problem	with	There was a **problem with** the delivery of the package.
reason	for	The customer gave poor quality as the **reason for** her complaint.
response	to	We had a terrific **response to** our survey about salaries.
solution	to	I can offer you a simple **solution to** this problem.
success	in / at	He said that his **success in / at** the sport was down to his training.
surprise	at	There was huge **surprise at** the result of the election.
way	of	The best **way of** removing stains is with warm, soapy water.

VERBS AND PREPOSITIONS

Some verbs have to be followed by a specific preposition.

VERB	PREPOSITION	SAMPLE SENTENCE
accuse (someone)	of	The security guard **accused the girl of** shoplifting.
apologize	for	I'd like to **apologize for** that last comment.
appeal	to	The magazine really needs to **appeal to** teenagers.
apply	for	Are you going to **apply for** that job in the newspaper?
approve	of	Matt doesn't **approve of** his daughter's new boyfriend.
ask (someone)	about	Can you **ask someone about** the time of the next train?
believe	in	This company doesn't **believe in** asking you to work overtime.
belong	to	Does this coat **belong to** you?
blame (someone)	for	Don't **blame me for** being late.
compare (someone)	to / with	We shouldn't **compare the new teacher to / with** Mr. Hockly.
concentrate	on	I'm finding it difficult to **concentrate on** this homework.
congratulate (someone)	on	Let me be the first to **congratulate you on** your new baby.
count	on	We're **counting on** everyone's support for this new venture.
criticize (someone)	for	The politician was **criticized for** his extravagant lifestyle.
deal	with	This training will help you to **deal with** difficult members of the public.
decide	against	We've **decided against** floor-to-ceiling closets.
decide	on	We've **decided on** pale blue for the bedroom. It looks great.
happen	to	Accidents always seem to **happen to** Paul. He's very unlucky.
insist	on	The club **insists on** its members dressing up.
remind (someone)	of	Doesn't Ellie **remind you of** her mother? She's so like her.
shout	at	There's no point in **shouting at** the dog. He's deaf!
stop (someone)	from	The yellow band is there to **stop people from** tripping over the step.
succeed	in	Fran **succeeded in** passing her driving test on the third try.
think	about	Take time to **think about** the proposal. There's no rush.
worry	about	It's natural to **worry about** your children when they're out.

R18 VERBS WITH GERUNDS OR INFINITIVES

Some verbs are followed by an infinitive or a gerund. Some can be followed by either without changing their meaning.

VERBS FOLLOWED BY AN INFINITIVE			
advise	compel	hope	promise
afford	dare	instruct	refuse
agree	decide	intend	remind
aim	demand	invite	seem
allow	deserve	learn	teach
appear	enable	manage	tell
arrange	expect	offer	tend
ask	encourage	order	threaten
beg	fail	persuade	wait
cause	forbid	plan	want
choose	guarantee	prepare	warn
claim	help	pretend	wish

VERBS FOLLOWED BY A GERUND			
admit	discuss	involve	recommend
avoid	dislike	justify	resent
appreciate	enjoy	keep	risk
complete	fancy	mind	see someone
consider	feel like	miss	spend time / money
delay	finish	practice	suggest
deny	imagine	prevent	understand

VERBS FOLLOWED BY AN INFINITIVE OR A GERUND (NO CHANGE IN MEANING)			
begin	cease	like	prefer
can't bear	continue	love	propose
can't stand	hate	need	start

State verbs describe states, such as emotions, possession, senses, or thoughts. They are not usually used in continuous tenses.

MEANING	STATE VERB	SAMPLE SENTENCE
feeling / wanting	**like / love**	I **like / love** Italian ice cream.
	need	We really **need** to spend more time together as a family.
	prefer	Most people **prefer** summer to winter.
	want	The band **wants** to become famous and make money.
thinking	**believe**	I **believe** your story, but it is rather unlikely.
	doubt	Lots of people **doubt** that he can do the job properly.
	know	Do you **know** where we parked the car?
	mean	What do you **mean** when you say you aren't ready?
	think	What do you **think** about the proposed policy?
	understand	Could you speak more slowly? I don't **understand** you.
being / existing	**appear / seem**	It **appears / seems** that the house has already been sold.
	exist	Strange creatures **exist** at the bottom of the sea.
possessing	**belong**	Excuse me, that book **belongs** to me.
	have / own	My neighbor **has / owns** three classic cars.
	include	Did you **include** Lucy in the guest list?
sensing	**feel**	Does your leg **feel** better today?
	hear	I can **hear** you, but I'm not sure what you're saying.
	hurt	My arm really **hurts**. I think I should go to see the doctor.
	see	Can you **see** the blackbird in the bush over there?
having a quality	**feel**	This rug **feels** so soft. It would be lovely to walk on.
	smell	Something **smells** delicious. Is it the soup?
	sound	That **sounds** like thunder, or is it just fireworks?
	taste	This milk **tastes** a bit sour. I think it's gone bad.

Some phrasal verbs can be separated by the object of the verb. In these cases, the verb goes first, then the object, then the particle. This separation is usually optional. However, if the object of a separable phrasal verb is a pronoun, then the phrasal verb must be separated by the pronoun.

PHRASAL VERB	DEFINITION	SAMPLE SENTENCE
bring up	look after a child until he / she is an adult	Samira's grandparents **brought** her **up**.
bring up	mention something	You should **bring** any problems **up** with your manager.
carry out	perform an action	If you give me instructions, I'll **carry** them **out**.
clean up	clean something thoroughly	Can you help me **clean** the kitchen **up** please?
do up	restore / decorate something	We've bought an old house and we're going to **do** it **up**.
fill in / out	write information in a form	Could you just **fill** this short form **in / out** for me, sir?
fill up	make something completely full	I'm just going to the gas station to **fill** the car **up**.
get back	find / get something after it has been lost / taken	The police **got** my car **back** after it had been stolen.
give up	stop doing something	Smoking is really bad for you. You should **give** it **up**.
hand out	distribute something	Be quiet! I'm about to **hand** the exam papers **out**.
leave out	not include something / someone	I can't believe that they **left** you **out** of the team!
let out	release something / someone	The school's going to **let** the children **out** early today.
look up	find information, e.g. in a dictionary	When does the show start? Can you **look** it **up** for me?
make up	invent something	I didn't believe Dave's story. I think he **made** it **up**.
pick up	take hold of something and lift it	**Pick** that paper bag **up**!
pull down	demolish / destroy something	They're going to **pull** all those old apartments **down**.
put off	delay doing something	I'm going to **put** the party **off** until Dad feels better.
set up	arrange / organize something	We're helping to **set** the music festival **up**.
take up	start a new hobby	I never thought I'd **take** birdwatching **up**, but I love it!
throw away	get rid of something	We never **throw** any food **away**.
turn down	refuse / reject something / someone	It was a great job offer but I **turned** it **down**.
turn on	start an electrical device	Quick! **Turn** the TV **on**. The final is about to start.
wake up	make someone stop sleeping	Will you **wake** me **up** at 8am if I oversleep?
write down	write something on paper	Could you **write** your email address **down** for me?

R21 INSEPARABLE PHRASAL VERBS

Some phrasal verbs cannot be separated. Their object always comes after them, even if it is a pronoun.

PHRASAL VERB	DEFINITION	SAMPLE SENTENCE
check in / into	announce your arrival	Guests may **check into** the hotel from 4pm.
come across	find by chance	I **came across** some old photographs while cleaning up.
cut back on	reduce / decrease something	The government wants to **cut back on** spending.
deal with	handle / manage someone or something	We learned how to **deal with** difficult customers.
do without	manage without something	We can **do without** a vacation this year.
get along / on with	have a good relationship	I find it easy to **get along / on with** people.
get on / off	walk / climb on or off a bus, train, plane, etc.	Please take care when you **get off** the plane.
get out of	leave a car / taxi, etc.	Be careful when you **get out of** the car.
get over	recover (from an illness)	It took me a long time to **get over** the last cold I had.
get through	finish something successfully	The trial was very stressful, but we **got through** it.
go over	check or examine something	Remember to **go over** your answers carefully.
go with	match, suit	Does this scarf **go with** my jacket?
hear from	get news from somebody	Have you **heard from** your cousins recently?
keep up with	keep the same pace as others	Slow down! I can't **keep up with** you!
look after	take care of someone	Marie **looks after** her younger sister after school.
look for	try to find, search	Peter is going to **look for** a job when he leaves school.
look forward to	be excited about something in the future	My children are **looking forward to** the holidays.
look into	examine something carefully	The police are **looking into** the case.
look up to	respect and admire someone	Lots of young people **look up to** sports stars.
run into	meet someone by chance	I **ran into** Dave earlier. I hadn't seen him for ages.
run out of	not have any left	We've **run out of** food. Let's go to the store.
stand for	mean, represent	What do the initials UNICEF **stand for**?
take after	be similar to an older relative	Sally's so stubborn. She really **takes after** her mother.
turn into	become something else	You can sleep here. The sofa **turns into** a bed.

R22 COMMONLY CONFUSED WORDS

Some words in English sound the same or very similar,
but mean different things. It is essential to spell the words
correctly to achieve the correct meaning in a sentence.

accept / except
I accept your apology.
Everyone was on the list except for me.

adverse / averse
She was feeling unwell due to the adverse effects
of her medication.
He was lazy and averse to playing sport.

aisle / isle
The bride walked down the aisle.
They visited an isle near the coast of Scotland.

aloud / allowed
She read the book aloud.
He was allowed to choose which book to read.

amoral / immoral
Her amoral attitude meant that she didn't care if
her actions were wrong.
He was fired from the firm for immoral conduct.

appraise / apprise
The manager needed to appraise the employee's skills.
The laywer apprised the defendant of his rights.

assent / ascent
He nodded his assent.
They watched the ascent of the balloon.

aural / oral
The aural test required her to listen.
The dentist performed an oral examination.

bare / bear
The trees were stripped bare.
The large bear roamed the woods.

break / brake
The chocolate was easy to break apart.
The car didn't brake fast enough.

broach / brooch
He decided to broach the subject for discussion.
She wore a pretty brooch.

cereal / serial
He ate a bowl of cereal for breakfast.
She found the serial number on her computer.

complement / compliment
The colors complement each other well.
He paid her a compliment by telling her she was pretty.

cue / queue
The actor waited for his cue before walking on stage.
The checkout queue was very long.

desert / dessert
The desert is extremely hot and dry.
She decided to have cake for dessert.

draught / draft
There was a draught coming from under the door.
He had written a draft of the letter.

pore / pour
I could see every pore on his nose.
She helped pour the drinks at the party.

principle / principal
The man believed in strong principles.
He was given the role of the principal character.

stationary / stationery
The aircraft landed and remained stationary.
She looked in the stationery cupboard for a pen.

R23 SPELLING RULES

All present participles and gerunds are formed by adding "-ing" to the base form of the verb. The spelling of some base forms changes slightly before adding "-ing."

BASE FORM	RULE	GERUND
choose	Remove the silent "-e" before adding "-ing."	choosing
tie	Change "-ie" to "y" before adding "-ing."	tying
forget	Double last letter if word ends with stressed syllable of consonant-vowel-consonant.	forgetting

Regular past participles are made with the base form of the verb plus "-ed." The spelling of some of these base forms changes slightly before adding "-ed."

BASE FORM	RULE	PAST PARTICIPLE
like	Last letter is "-e," so just add "-d"	liked
cry	Change consonant plus "-y" to "-ied."	cried
drop	Double last letter if word ends with stressed syllable of consonant-vowel-consonant.	dropped

R24 IRREGULAR PLURALS

Most plurals in English are formed by adding "-s" to the end of the singular noun.
However, some plurals are irregular, either taking a different ending, or not changing at all.

SINGULAR	PLURAL	SINGULAR	PLURAL
aircraft	aircraft	man	men
analysis	analyses	medium	media
appendix	appendices	mouse	mice
axis	axes	ox	oxen
bureau	bureaux	person	people
cactus	cacti	phenomenon	phenomena
child	children	scarf	scarves
crisis	crises	series	series
deer	deer	sheep	sheep
fish	fish	species	species
foot	feet	tooth	teeth
formula	formulae	vertebra	vertebrae
fungus	fungi	wife	wives
leaf	leaves	wolf	wolves
loaf	loaves	woman	women

Linking words are used to link two or more words, phrases or clauses together.
They are usually conjunctions, but can also be adverbial phrases.

LINKING WORD	USE	SAMPLE SENTENCE
although / even though	adds a contrast	The show went ahead, **even though** it was raining.
anyway	contrasts with something just said	I knew the climb would be hard, but I did it **anyway**.
and / both... and	links two similar words, phrases, or clauses	I can speak **(both)** French **and** English.
as	gives a reason for an action	The experiment failed **as** the sample was too old.
as long as	adds a condition	You can go out **as long as** you come home by 11pm.
as well as	adds further information	Mint is used in savory dishes **as well as** sweet ones.
because	gives a reason for an action	I was late again **because** the train was delayed.
but	links two contrasting words, phrases, or clauses	He's quite heavy **but** he's very fast on his feet.
consequently	gives a result of a previous action	The vote was close. **Consequently**, there was a recount.
furthermore	adds supporting information	I love this cream. **Furthermore**, it's great for dry skin.
however	adds contrasting information	I'd love to come. **However**, I'm away that weekend.
if	adds a condition	These plants will grow better **if** you water them daily.
in addition	adds information	I go to the gym a lot. **In addition**, I run 20km a week.
in order to	gives a purpose for an action	We moved here **in order to** be closer to work.
moreover	adds supporting information	It's quicker to travel by plane. **Moreover**, it's cheaper.
neither... nor	links two things that are not true or possible	These instructions are **neither** helpful **nor** legible.
or / either... or	links two alternatives	We can **(either)** go to the cinema **or** have a meal.
since	gives a reason for an action	**Since** dessert is included, we might as well have one.
so	gives a reason for an action	It was raining, **so** we stayed indoors.
so that	gives a purpose for an action	I'm saving money **so that** I can buy a house.
therefore	gives a result of an action	It's a very clear night. **Therefore**, you can see the stars.
unless	adds a condition	You won't be able to travel **unless** you have a visa.
whereas	adds a contrast	My mother likes tea, **whereas** my father prefers coffee.
yet	adds a contrast	Dean is a good musician, **yet** he can't read music.

English has lots of words to talk about when things happen. They usually act as prepositions, conjunctions, or adverbs.

TIME WORD	USE	SAMPLE SENTENCE
about to	shows an event will happen very soon	The train on platform 6 is **about to** leave.
after	shows an event in the main clause follows another event	Wash your hands **after** you've been gardening.
already	shows an event has happened before another event or a particular time	Don't worry, I've **already** ordered some food.
as	indicates an event happens at the same time as another event	It started raining **as** we were leaving the house.
as soon as	indicates an event (in the main clause) happens straight after another event	Please call us **as soon as** you arrive in New York.
before	shows an event (in the main clause) precedes another event	I was a teacher **before** I became a politician.
by the time	shows an event precedes or happens at the same time as an event in the main clause	**By the time** we arrived, the game had started.
eventually	shows an event happened after a long time	It was a long wait, but **eventually** our exam results arrived.
finally	indicates an event at the end of a list / sequence, or that happened after a long time	I'd like to thank my family, my team, and **finally** my fans.
in the end	shows an event happened after a long time	Joe took the exam three times, but **in the end** he passed.
just	shows an event happened very recently	Quick! I've **just** seen something really amazing!
later	indicates an event after the time of speaking or the time that is being talked about	I can't take you to the mall now. We'll go there **later**.
meanwhile	indicates an event happens at the same time as another event	The show started at 8. **Meanwhile**, we went for dinner.
next	indicates an event in a sequence	Stir the melted chocolate. **Next**, pour it into the cake pan.
once	indicates an event starts to happen (in the main clause) after another one	**Once** you've cleaned the stove, wipe all the handles.
since	shows an event continuing from a past time to the present	I haven't seen you **since** we were in school!
still	shows an event at the time of speaking started in the past and is continuing	Are they **still** repairing the main road?
then	indicates an event in a sequence, or one event that happens after another	We went to the cinema, **then** we went out for a meal.
until	shows an event continues up to the time of another event	I won't stop saving **until** I've bought a new car.
when	shows an event happens at the same time as or after another event	Could you call me **when** all the salespeople have arrived?
while	indicates an event happens at the same time as another event	Please don't interrupt me **while** I'm trying to concentrate.
yet	shows an expected event has not happened, or asks whether it has happened	Have you finished the sales report **yet**?

Glossary

absolute adjective
A word that describes a quality which cannot be changed or modified, e.g. **unique**.

abstract noun
A word that refers to a quality rather than a thing or person, e.g. **beauty**, **hope**.

action verb (dynamic verb)
A type of verb that describes an action, e.g. **run**, and can be used in the simple and **continuous** tenses.
see also **state verb**

active voice
Indicates that the person or thing who is doing the action is the **subject** of the **verb**.
see also **passive voice**

adjective
A word that describes a **noun** or **pronoun**, e.g. **quick**.

adverb
A word that describes a **verb**, **adjective**, or another adverb, e.g. **quickly**.

adverb of degree
An adverb that tells you "how much," e.g. **extremely**.

adverb of frequency
An adverb that tells you "how often," e.g. **usually**.

adverb of manner
An adverb that tells you "how," e.g. **badly**.

adverbial
A phrase that is used as an adverb, e.g. **on the table** (expressing place), **tomorrow evening** (expressing time).

agent
The person or thing that does the action. The **subject** of the verb in an **active** clause, but not in a **passive** clause.

agreement
When the **verb** form is correct for the **subject**, e.g. He is = **singular** subject + singular verb.

apostrophe
The punctuation mark that shows either belonging, e.g. **John's cat**, or a contraction e.g. **I'm happy**.

article
The words **a**, **an**, and **the**, which show whether something is general or specific.
see also **zero article**

auxiliary verb
A verb which is used with another verb, e.g. to form **tenses**, most commonly **be**, **do**, and **have**.
see also **main verb**

backchanneling
The words and noises that a listener makes to show they are listening, e.g. **Really?**

backshift
In **reported speech**, when the **verb** moves back one tense into the past, e.g. **present simple** to **past simple**.

base form (bare infinitive)
The most basic form of a **verb**, e.g. **be**, **run**, **write**.
see also **infinitive**

cardinal number
The numbers used for counting, e.g. **one**, **two**.
see also **ordinal number**

classifying adjective
An adjective that describes the type of the **noun** that it defines, e.g. in **medical student**, "medical" describes the type of student.

clause
A group of words that contains a **verb**.

closed question
A question that can be answered with "yes" or "no," e.g. **Are you English?**
see also **open question**

collective noun
A **singular** noun that refers to a group of people or things, e.g. **family**, **team**.

comparative adjective
An adjective that compares one thing or group of things with another, e.g. **better**.
see also **superlative adjective**

complement
The word or phrase that comes after **verbs** such as **be**, **become**, **seem**, **appear**, e.g. "happy" in She's happy.
see also **linking verb**

complex preposition
A preposition that contains two or more words, e.g. **next to**, **because of**.

compound noun
A noun that contains two or more words, e.g. **post office**.

compound tense
A **tense** which uses an **auxiliary verb**, e.g. the **present perfect**: **has done**.

concrete noun
A noun that refers to something you can touch, see, hear, smell, or taste, e.g. **table**, **teacher**.

conditional
The verb structure used when one event or situation depends on another event or situation happening first.

conjunction
A word that links two words or groups of words, e.g. **and**, **because**, **if**.

consonant
Most letters / sounds in English, but not **a**, **e**, **i**, **o**, **u**. **y** can operate as a consonant or a **vowel**.

continuous (progressive)
Continuous **tenses** express actions that are in progress at a specific time, e.g. **I'm writing**.

contraction
Two words that are joined with an **apostrophe** to form one word, e.g. **we're**.

conversational ellipsis
When words are left out in **informal** conversation, e.g. **[Do you] Want a cup of coffee?**

coordinating conjunction
A word that links two **clauses** of equal importance, e.g. **and**, **but**, **or**.
see also **subordinating conjunction**

countable
A **noun** that can be counted, e.g. **one book**, **two books**.
see also **uncountable**

defining relative clause
A clause that starts with a **relative pronoun** (such as **who** or **which**). It gives information that defines something in the **main clause**.
see also **non-defining relative clause**

definite article
The word **the**, which specifies which noun that follows it, e.g. **the house in the woods**.
see also **indefinite article**

demonstrative determiner / pronoun
Words that specify a **noun** as closer to (**this**, **these**) or more distant from (**that**, **those**) the speaker, e.g. **This watch is cheaper than that one in the window.**

dependent preposition
A preposition that always follows a particular **verb**, **noun**, or **adjective**, e.g. **afraid of**.

determiner
A word that comes before a **noun** and identifies it, e.g. **the book**, **this book**.

direct object
The person or thing affected by the action of the **verb**, e.g. "him" in **We followed him**. see also **indirect object**

direct question
A question without an introductory phrase, e.g. **What time is it?**

direct speech
The words that are actually said to make a statement or question, e.g. **It's raining.**

discourse marker
A word or phrase that is used in conversation to direct the discussion or add comment, e.g. **Well, Right.**

double object verb
A verb that has two objects, e.g. "me" and "the phone" in **Give me the phone.**

dummy subject
The word "it" used without referring to a noun, e.g. **It's five o'clock.**

-ed adjective
An adjective that describes how somthing is affected, e.g. **bored, excited**. see also **-ing adjective**

ellipsis
When words or phrases are left out of a clause, usually because they don't need to be repeated, e.g. **He got up and [he] had a shower.**

emphasis
When a word is said more loudly because it is more important. see also **stress**

extreme adjective
An adjective that has a stronger meaning than a **gradable adjective** with a similar meaning, e.g. **freezing** is the extreme adjective for **cold**.

first conditional
A sentence with "if" that describes a possible future situation that depends on another situation, e.g. **If it rains, I'll stay here.**

focus
Part of a **sentence** that is moved to the beginning because it is more important.

formal
Formal language is used in situations where you don't know the people very well, or when you want to keep social distance. see also **informal**

future continuous
A **tense** that is formed with **will be** and the **present participle**. It expresses an action that will be in progress at a point in the future.

future perfect
A **tense** that is formed with **will have** and the **past participle**, e.g. **will have done**. It expresses an action that will be complete at a point in the future.

future perfect continuous
A **tense** that is formed with **will have been** and the **present participle**, e.g. **will have been doing**. It expresses an ongoing action that will be complete at a point in the future.

gerund (verbal noun)
The **-ing** form of a **verb**, when it is used as a noun, e.g. **No smoking.**

gradable adjective
An adjective that can be used with **adverbs of degree** (such as **very**) and can be used in the **comparative** form. see also **non-gradable adjective**

grading adverb
An **adverb of degree** that can be used with **gradable adjectives**. see also **non-grading adverb**

hedging
Words or phrases that make a speaker seem less certain or direct, e.g. **apparently, I think.**

imperative
An order to someone, e.g. **Stop!** The imperative is often a **verb** on its own in its **base form**.

indefinite article
The words **a** and **an**, which come before **nouns** when it doesn't matter which noun is being referred to, or if it is being mentioned for the first time, e.g. **Can I borrow a pen?** see also **definite article**

indefinite pronoun
A pronoun that does not refer to a specific person or thing, e.g. **someone, nothing.**

indirect object
The person or thing that is affected by the action of a **transitive verb**, but is not the direct object, e.g. "the dog" in **I gave the ball to the dog.** see also **direct object**

indirect question
A question that begins with a polite phrase, e.g. **Can you tell me what time it is?**

infinitive
The **base form** of a **verb**, often with the infinitive marker "to," e.g. **to go, to run.**

infinitive clause
A clause whose verb is in the **infinitive** form, e.g. **It's important to complete the form in full.**

informal
Informal language is used in situations where you know the people well and feel relaxed. see also **formal**

-ing adjective
An adjective that describes the effect something has, e.g. **boring, exciting.** see also **-ed adjective**

inseparable phrasal verb
A **phrasal verb** that is always used with the **particle**, e.g. **I take after my mother.** see also **separable phrasal verb**

intransitive verb
A verb that does not take a **direct object**. see also **transitive verb**

introductory "it"
"It is" used at the start of a **sentence** to refer to a general idea, e.g. **It is difficult to ski.**

inversion
When positions of two parts of a **clause** swap around, e.g. the **subject** and the **verb** in questions.

irregular
A word that behaves differently from most words like it, e.g. **men** is an irregular **plural noun**. see also **regular**

linking verb
A verb that links two parts of a **clause** (the **subject** and **complement**) rather than describing an action, such as **be, seem, become**, e.g. **She is really angry.**

main clause
A **clause** that could form a complete **sentence** on its own. see also **subordinate clause**

main verb
The verb in a group of verbs that carries the meaning, e.g. "ride" in **I can ride a bike.**

modal verb
A type of **auxiliary verb** that is used with a **main verb** to show ideas like ability and permission.

modifier
A word that adds information to another word, e.g. "really" in **really interesting.**

negative
A **clause** that contains a word like **not** or **never**.

negative adverbial
A phrase that acts as an *adverb* and has a negative meaning, e.g. **not only**, **not until**.

non-defining relative clause
A clause that starts with a *relative pronoun* (such as **who** or **which**). It gives non-essential information about the *main clause*.
see also *defining relative clause*

non-gradable adjective
An adjective that cannot be used in the *comparative* form and can only be used with certain *adverbs of degree* (such as **absolutely**).
see also *gradable adjective*

non-grading adverb
An *adverb of degree* that can be used with *non-gradable adjectives*.

noun
A word that refers to a person, place, or thing.

noun phrase
A *noun*, *pronoun*, or a number of words that are linked to a noun, e.g. **the blue house**.

object
A *noun* or *pronoun* that follows a *verb* or a *preposition*.

object pronoun
A pronoun that usually follows a *verb* or a *preposition*, e.g. **me**, **them**.

object question
A question where the question word is the *object*, e.g. "What" in **What did you say?**

open question
A question that cannot be answered with "yes" or "no" and starts with a question word (such as **when** or **who**).
see also *closed question*

ordinal number
The numbers used for ordering, e.g. **first**, **second**.
see also *cardinal number*

participle
The form of a *verb* used to make *compound tenses*.
see also *past participle* and *present participle*

particle
A word that follows a *verb* to form a *phrasal verb*.

passive voice
Indicates that the person or thing affected by the action is the *subject* of the *verb*.
see also *active voice*

past continuous
A *tense* that is formed with **was** or **were** and the *present participle*, e.g. **was doing**. It expresses an ongoing action in the past.

past participle
The *participle* form of a *verb* that is used to make *perfect tenses* and the passive, e.g. **walked**, **done**, **eaten**.

past perfect
A *tense* that is formed with **had** and the *past participle*, e.g. **had done**. It expresses a completed action that happened before another action or state in the past.

past perfect continuous
A *tense* that is formed with **had been** and the *present participle*, e.g. **had been doing**. It expresses an ongoing action that happened before another action or state in the past.

past simple
A *tense* that consists only of the past form of a *verb*, e.g. **walked**, **said**, **ate**. It expresses a completed action in the past.

perfect
Perfect *tenses* express a link between two times, e.g. the *present perfect* links the past with the present.

person
The form of a *pronoun* that shows who is speaking (**I**, **we**),

who is being spoken to (**you**) or who or what is being mentioned (**he**, **she**, **it**, **they**). *Verbs* also reflect person, e.g. **am** is the first person singular form of **be**.

personal pronoun
A word that refers to people or things that have already been mentioned, e.g. **he**, **they**.

phrasal verb
A combination of *verb* + *particle* that is always used together and has a different meaning from the verb on its own, e.g. **make up** meaning "invent."

plural
The form of a word used when there is more than one of something, e.g. **books**, **they**.
see also *singular*

positive
A *clause* that expresses what someone or something is or does. It does not contain a negative word.
see also *negative*

possessive determiner
A word that comes before a *noun* and shows belonging, e.g. **my**, **our**, **his**.

possessive pronoun
A word that replaces a *noun* and shows belonging, e.g. **mine**, **ours**, **his**.

prefix
Letters at the beginning of a word that change its meaning, e.g. "re-" in **replace**.
see also *suffix*

preposition
A short word that links two *nouns* or *pronouns* to show a relationship, e.g. **to**, **at**, **with**, **from**.

prepositional phrase
A phrase that starts with a *preposition*, e.g. **on the bus**, **at five o'clock**.

present continuous
A *tense* that is formed with the present of **be** and the *present participle*, e.g. **is doing**. It expresses an ongoing action in the present.

present participle
The *participle* form of a *verb* that is used to make *continuous tenses*, e.g. **walking**, **doing**.

present perfect
A *tense* that is formed with the present of **have** and the *past participle*, e.g. **have done**. It expresses an action that started in the past and is still continuing or that happened in the past but has a result in the present.

present perfect continuous
A *tense* that is formed with **has / have been** and the *present participle*, e.g. **has / have been doing**. It expresses an ongoing action that started in the past and is still continuing.

present simple
A *tense* that consists only of the present form of a *verb*, e.g. **walk**, **say**, **eat**. It expresses a general truth about the present.

pronoun
A word that replaces a *noun*, when the noun has already been mentioned, e.g. **it**, **that**.

proper noun
A noun that is the name of a person, place, day, etc., e.g. **Maria**, **France**, **Sunday**.

quantifier
A word that usually comes before a *noun* and expresses a quantity or amount, e.g. **several**, **many**, **much**.

question
A *sentence* that asks for something, usually information. The *verb* usually comes before the *subject*.

question word
A word is used to start *open questions*, e.g. **What**, **Which**, **Who**, **Why**, **How**.

question tag
A short phrase that makes a *statement* into a *question*, e.g. "isn't it" in **It's hot today, isn't it?**

reflexive pronoun
A word that refers to the *subject* of the *clause*, when the subject and *object* are the same, e.g. **myself**.

regular
A word that behaves in the same way as most words like it, e.g. **books** is a regular *plural noun* and **waited** is a regular *past simple* form.
see also *irregular*

relative clause
A clause that gives information about the *subject* or *object* of the *main clause*.

relative pronoun
A word that introduces a *relative clause*, e.g. **who**, **that**, **which**.

reported question
A question that is repeated after it was actually asked, often by another person, e.g. **She asked if the bus was full.**

reported speech
Statements and *questions* that are repeated after they were actually said, often by another person, e.g. **He said the bus was full.**

reporting verb
A verb that introduces *reported speech*, e.g. **say**, **tell**.

root
The part of a word to which a suffix or prefix is added, e.g. "employ" is the root of **employable**.

second conditional
A sentence with "if" that describes an imaginary future situation, or an impossible present situation, e.g. **If I were you, I'd take an umbrella.**

sentence
A group of one or more *clauses*.

separable phrasal verb
A *phrasal verb* that can be used with the *particle* after a noun or pronoun, e.g. **bring the subject up / bring it up**.
see also *inseparable phrasal verb*

short answer
An answer to a closed *question* that only uses the *subject* and *auxiliary verb*, e.g. **Yes, I do.**

short question
A question with just an *auxiliary verb* and *subject*, which is used to show interest in a conversation, e.g. **Is it?**

simple
Simple *tenses* are formed with a *main verb* only; they don't need an *auxiliary verb* in their *positive* forms.

singular
The form of a word that is used to refer to just one person or thing, e.g. **book**.
see also *plural*

stalling
Using words or short phrases in conversation to give yourself time to think about what to say, e.g. **Let's see...**

state verb (stative verb)
A type of verb that describes situations, thoughts, or feelings, e.g. **seem**, **think**, **like**.
see also *action verb*

statement
A *sentence* that offers information, i.e. not a *question* or an *imperative*.

stress
Saying one *syllable* in a word, or one word in a *sentence*, more strongly than the others.
see also *emphasis*

subject
The person / thing / place, etc. that usually comes before the *verb* in a *clause*.

subject pronoun
A word that replaces a *noun* as the subject of a *clause*, e.g. **I**, **she**, **they**.

subject question
A question where the question word is the *subject*, e.g. "Who" in **Who invited you?**
see also *object question*

subordinate clause
A *clause* which is dependent on the *main clause*, usually introduced by a *subordinating conjunction*.

subordinating conjunction
A word that links two *clauses* that are not of equal importance, i.e. a *subordinate clause* to a *main clause*, e.g. **because**, **if**.
see also *coordinating conjunction*

substitution
The use of a word to replace another, e.g. "He" in **He's in the kitchen.**

suffix
Letters at the end of a word that change its meaning, e.g. "-able" in **enjoyable**.
see also *prefix*

superlative adjective
An adjective that indicates the most extreme of a group of things, e.g. **best**.
see also *comparative adjective*

syllable
Every word is made up of a number of syllables, each of which contain a *vowel* sound, e.g. **teach** (one syllable), **teacher** (two syllables).

tense
The form of a *verb* that shows the time of the action, e.g. *present simple*, *past simple*.

third conditional
A sentence with "if" that describes an impossible past situation and its impossible result, e.g. **If I had studied harder, I would have passed the exam.**

time marker
A word or phrase that indicates a time, e.g. **now**, **at the moment**, **tomorrow**.

transitive verb
A verb that takes a *direct object*.
see also *intransitive verb*

uncountable
A *noun* that cannot be counted, e.g. **water**, **money**.
see also *countable*

verb
A word that refers to a situation or an action, e.g. **stay**, **write**.

vowel
The English letters **a**, **e**, **i**, **o**, **u**.
see also *consonant*

word class
Shows the function of a word in a sentence, e.g. *noun*, *verb*, *adjective* are all word classes.

word order
The position that different words have in a *clause*, e.g. the *subject* usually comes before the *verb*, and *adjectives of opinion* come before *adjectives of fact*.

zero article
When there is no article before *plural* or *uncountable nouns*.

zero conditional
A *sentence* with "if" or "when" that describes a present situation or a regular action, e.g. **If it rains, the roads flood.**

Index

All locators refer to unit numbers. Numbers in **bold** indicate the main entry for the subject. Locators with the prefix R, for example "**R1**," refer to information in the reference section.

Acknowledgments

The publisher would like to thank:
Carrie Lewis for proofreading; Elizabeth Wise for indexing; Lili Bryant and
Laura Sandford for editorial assistance; Tim Bowen for language advice;
Chrissy Barnard, Amy Child, Alex Lloyd, and Michelle Staples for design
assistance; Gus Scott for additional illustration.

All images are copyright DK. For more information, please visit
www.dkimages.com.